CULTURE, IDEOLOGY AND SOCIALISM

For my parents, Dennis and June.

This book is to be returned on
or before the date stamped below

UNIVERSITY OF PLYMOUTH

PLYMOUTH LIBRARY
Tel: (01752) 232323
This book is subject to recall if required by another reader
Books may be renewed by phone
CHARGES WILL BE MADE FOR OVERDUE BOOKS

Culture, Ideology and Socialism

Raymond Williams and E.P. Thompson

NICK STEVENSON
Department of Sociological Studies
University of Sheffield

Avebury

Aldershot • Brookfield USA • Hong Kong • Singapore • Sydney

© N. Stevenson 1995

Published by
Avebury
Ashgate Publishing Limited
Gower House
Croft Road
Aldershot
Hants GU11 3HR
England

Ashgate Publishing Company
Old Post Road
Brookfield
Vermont 05036
USA

British Library Cataloguing in Publication Data

Stevenson, Nick
    Culture, Ideology and Socialism
    I. Title
    320.531

    ISBN 1 85972 174 5

Reprinted 1997

Library of Congress Catalog Card Number: 95-77346

Printed in Great Britain by Antony Rowe Ltd,
Chippenham, Wiltshire

Contents

Acknowledgements

The first person I would like to thank is my supervisor Anthony Giddens. His advice and criticisms gave me the courage I needed to finish my PhD. I would also like to thank Anthony Elliott, Paul Ransome and Eilish English who all made their special contributions to the words enclosed in this book. Also much is owed to Donna Luff whose encouragement, love and conversations did much to push me on to finish the final draft. I also remain indebted to Gill Brown, Marg Walker and Amy Jaram for their expertise in helping produce the manuscript. Finally I would like to thank my parents; Dennis and June Stevenson to whom this book is dedicated; and my sister and brother in law, Jane and Steve who are more significant than they think.

Preface

This book originally began as a PhD thesis, finally submitted in 1992. Since that date the kind of socialism represented by Williams and Thompson seems even more unlikely to materialise than it did three years ago. Yet, perhaps paradoxically, if I were to begin the study now I think I would have written it more sympathetically. There are many reasons for this. I am even more convinced than I was that humanist versions of socialism will continue to have a distinctive role to play in the future. We may wish to distance ourselves from many of the specific positions adopted by Williams and Thompson- yet there is no denying their commitment to values such as truth, beauty, solidarityand social justice. These values, as they both recognised, are likely to struggle for survival in a world ruled by economic forms of reason. In this respect, their assembled reflections provide a guiding light connecting future, past and present. That they still have much to contribute to ecological questions, notions of human-nature, as well as, ideological and cultural critique should keep their writing alive for future generations. That their specific remedies to these problems have occasionally been overtaken by the passage of time should not blunt the importance of the questions they asked. Finally, the period that I have been working on the manuscript has witnessed the deaths of both Williams and Thompson. Perhaps it is for this reason that I have felt unwilling to let the text go ? It may sound 'unprofessional', but I hesitate before criticising those who contributed so much and who can not answer back. Even now I feel that I have not done them justice. Yet, despite many of my own reservations concerning the words carried within this book, I hope that others will read it, and also see the value of reading Williams and Thompson for themselves.

Introduction

The writing of Raymond Williams and E.P.Thompson has, since the late fifties, been the subject of a number of theoretical and political debates. Although they remain largely unknown outside of Britain, they have had a marked impact on the development of contemporary perspectives on culture and ideology, while making a more public contribution to the development of political movements both new and old. In confronting the work of Raymond Williams and E.P.Thompson, I have offered a sympathetic critique that seeks to revise and reconstruct their approach, rather than simply reaffirm their intellectual dominance against revisionists. This dialectical approach posits an acceptance of the fact that Williams and Thompson exhibit critical insight into a range of disputes in social theory, and an acknowledgement that, in certain respects, their adopted positions are in need of further development. Here, I shall argue that, while their writing does retain a certain unity around a form of cultural Marxism, they neither occupy perfectly interchangeable positions, nor always exhibit similar thematic concerns. In developing their respective responses, therefore, I have shown a respectful concern to locate their texts in the appropriate discursive field, while relating their writing to the wider concerns of culture, ideology and politics. Once this task has been completed, through recourse to other thinkers and theoretical traditions, the aim of the book is to provide a critical reappraisal of the issues addressed by Williams and Thompson, rather than a detailed intellectual biography.

Raymond Williams and E.P.Thompson were probably the most prominent members of the British post-war New Left. In their effort to subordinate economically determinist forms of thinking that dominated the traditional Left, both were concerned to broaden their analysis to incorporate cultural institutions, processes and dispositions. Williams's *Culture and Society* (1961) and E.P.Thompson's *The Making of the English Working Class* (1980a) were two of the founding texts of British cultural studies. These two seminal works developed previously held definitions of culture, and went some way towards calling into question established disciplinary boundaries.

The origin of the term culture comes from 'cultivation'(Williams 1981:10). This term was first used in conjuncture with land and animals, before it was connected to the development of human minds. Thereafter'culture'took upon a variety of meanings. Many of the current disputes can be related to an earlier usage that emerged in the eighteenth century connecting culture to the process of progressive civilisation. Indeed it is historically significant, as Williams reminds us, that just at the point when capitalism had reduced the work of art to a commodity, the Romantics began to claim that it had a transcendental status. The work of art comes to have a utopian significance in that it offers a critique of the present, with a suggestion as to how human beings might grow and develop. Despite post-modern celebrations of pluralism, Williams argues, culture remains related to questions of value. However, as Williams points out in *Keywords* (1976), there was a distinctive change of emphasis in terms of the word culture elsewhere in the eighteenth century. Herder criticised the idea that culture should be used to signify 'the historical development of humanity'(Williams 1976:79). This construction was informed by a narrative account based upon the superiority of European forms of life. Herder wanted to use culture in connection with specific histories, nations and social and economic groups. Slightly later there emerged in the nineteenth century a third definition of culture which spoke of the distinctive activity of intellectuals and artists. Here culture became a descriptive category that was held to signify the actual practices of those involved in so called creative processes.

Social theorists have historically sought to defend at least three approaches to culture. These bear a resemblance to the historical account offered above. The first approach, traditionally found within literary analysis, emphasises culture as something special that has strong aesthetic and moral qualities. Here culture is thought to be contained within high art that has a definite civilising mission. This idea of culture can be found in a diverse range of social critics from the early Frankfurt school to the English literary critic F.R.Leavis. Here an 'elite' or 'high' culture is juxtaposed against mass cultural forms. Popular culture is assumed, in comparison, to be aesthetically shallow and intellectually impoverished. Much current literary analysis is sceptical of this account, uncovering some of the elitist propositions that arguably lie behind such terminology (Said 1992).

Next, especially within the Marxist tradition, culture is theorised in terms of an ideology that seeks to legitimise the domination of certain ruling groups. These accounts have sought to emphasise that the ruling class not only own and control the means of material production, but also the means of mental production. This argument points to the global dominance of international conglomerates in the production of cultural forms, and the marginalisation of critical perspectives from the public sphere. Yet this definition has also had its critics. This account is unable to separate 'culture' from a more restricted use of the term ideology.

Finally culture is also used in a more neutral sense, as in early anthropological accounts. This approach portrays human culture as being made up of shared cultural meanings. These meanings are utilised reflexively in everyday contexts enabling agents to make sense of the world. Here the criticism is that by supposedly abandoning a notion of culture as 'special' everything becomes cultural. That is we are unable to distinguish culture from other domains such as economics and politics. This theoretical tendency produces an overly voluntaristic account of the social world. Also, in recent years, anthropological definitions of culture have been largely displaced by more symbolic conceptions. A symbolic approach to culture emphasises that when we investigate a 'culture'- we are making an interpretation of certain symbolic forms that already have meaning for the agents the sociologist is seeking to understand. A symbolic account, seeks to make as clear as possible, the meaning that cultural forms and social expressions have for the lay actors themselves. The importance of an interpretative dimension is largely absent from more 'culturally stable' anthropological studies.

My particular argumentative strategy is to suggest that each of these definitions of culture has something to contribute towards a sociology of culture. Indeed they are variously incorporated by Williams and Thompson. Although having said this, all of these approaches are in need of revision and reformation. Thus I would argue that none of these three cultural paradigms allows us to

3

effectively appreciate the institutional relations that are involved in the production of culture; how culture is semiotically structured and coded, and the ways in which culture is actively interpreted by agents in asymmetrical relations of power. That Williams and Thompson are instructive in this respect will be explored within this book.

In chapter one, I aim to show how Williams, by radicalising the writing of Leavis, merged a romantic conception of culture with an anthropological definition. In Williams's first major work *Culture and Society* (1961) he couples a sociological concern for shared meanings and values, with a commitment to the'perfection'of individuals through a literary culture. In his next work, *The Long Revolution* (1965), Williams gives his previously developed definition of culture a more institutional grounding. He does this through a discussion of the impact of capitalism and mass democracy upon the production of culture. This more sociological concern is later developed through his proposals for a pluralist media in *Communications* (1962). This is related to the idea, evident in most of his writing, that through artistic practice, cultural production could produce a common communicative culture. The aim to produce such a culture was not an argument for a unified homogeneous common culture, but one where the channels of communication encouraged the presentation of a wide range of concerns and experiences. This more democratic culture would not entail the repression of cultural diversity or difference, but hold out the possibility of bringing otherwise fragmented world views together in a democratically formed community.

While Williams's writing maintains a contemporary relevance, especially through his desire to take cultural institutions seriously, his arguments need to be substantially reconstructed. Here, I shall argue that Williams, in this initial period of his writing, remains entrapped within cultural idealism. Cultural idealism is the assumption that an elite literary culture has a universal validity and appeal for all forms of life across complex social and historical relations. Such a disposition, on the part of the theorist, not only neglects to analyse how certain literary traditions have been maintained within institutional relations, but also how certain texts have come to be differentially interpreted in distanciated social contexts. Also Williams displays a moralistic attitude towards commercial forms of culture. In this sense, Williams remains intellectually connected to Leavis through a shared desire to preserve a more civilised and ethically based culture against Americanised forms of commercialism. I will argue that this not only misrepresents modern global cultural processes of fragmentation and unification, but that it is also evidence of Williams's distance from the reception contexts of ordinary people.

In chapter two, I seek to emphasise the communicative nature of Williams's writing by outlining his response to post-structuralism, Western Marxism and similar criticisms to those made above. In *Marxism and Literature* (1977) and *Culture* (1981) Williams develops his theory of cultural materialism. Here he abandons the'transcendental'component of cultural idealism to adopt a more sociological definition of culture. Culture is now analysed by Williams in terms of specific social practices that are both material and symbolic in form. In modern society, according to Williams, cultural practices are organised into hegemonic relations, which serve through traditions, institutions and artistic formations to endorse some practices while excluding others. Certain social and historically selected versions of society's culture can be said to be either residual, dominant or emergent, while other experiences continue to exist outside of dominant institutions. *Television,Technology and Cultural Form* (1974) and The *Country and the City* (1973) produce more specifically historical and social accounts of culture, while opening up issues related to cultural domination. Despite the considerable theoretical advance made by Williams's theory of cultural materialism it is evident that he has made his account overly material. By making culture'ordinary', Williams is no longer able to defend the privileged status that literary practices have in his writing. On this count, Williams's attempts to bring sociology and literature into a closer dialogue remain flawed. He consistently privileges the role that artistic practices play in the formation of a culture in common.

For E.P.Thompson the notion of culture never occupies the foreground in quite this way. In chapters three and four, I argue, that Thompson's early historical writing offers a view of cultural processes that is the result of the dialectic between social being and social consciousness. In The *Making of the English Working-Class* (1980a) Thompson shows how the active agency of working people helped to culturally shape themselves as a class. Here Thompson has been rightly criticised by Perry Anderson (1980) and others for the voluntaristic conception of agency that is implicit in this argument. I would, on the other hand, suggest more sympathetically, that his work should be read less as a history of the working-class, and more as an interpretation of the birth of a radical collective culture. In this revised reading, Thompson is arguably tracing through a cultural tradition centred around'the free born Englishman'. This culminates

5

in the independently robust politics of the early labour movement. Thompson's project is the resurrection of lost voices from the past that are usually marginalised in more traditional historical writing. His writing contrasts past and present by bringing the critical perspectives of an older radical culture to bear on the modern world. Thompson provides a voice for the early proletarian movement within the academy, while connecting these perspectives to an ethical consideration of the good life.

At this early stage, Williams and Thompson are in general agreement that culture is the site of connection, belonging and community. But Thompson wants to argue that culture is also a point of conflict. For Thompson (1961), Williams neglects this aspect of culture, as he mistakenly focuses on the abstract evolutionary changes of institutions to explain the future possibility of a democratic culture. Also Thompson suggests, as I argued earlier, that culture has to be related to social practices or what he calls social being. Thompson is more concerned than Williams to connect the way agents interpret culture to their position in the social structure. In Thompson's later writing, however, he becomes increasingly disenchanted as the Left seem to have turned their backs on the spirit of the'free born Englishman'. This pessimism is also projected onto his attempt to theoretically understand the Cold War or Exterminism, which he argued, was representative of a culturally deformed logic (Thompson 1980b).

One of his main themes throughout the eighties was that the peace movement should occupy a'third space'between the two superpowers. The peace movement had to strategically ensure that it did not lend credibility to attempts by the two Cold warriors to discursively align it's protests with the other side. This new form of politics from below, for Thompson, represented the possibility of a non repressive dialogue with others who shared the same continent and a similar commitment to democracy and ecological security. Thus the peace movement emerges as holding out the utopian prospect of more democratically sustainable forms of life, in a world which is dominated by destructive forms of rationality. Despite Thompson's pessimism, it is the utopian and ethical components within culture, that he first discovered in his biography of William Morris (1955), which reaffirms his sense of hope through out the eighties.

While there remains much that is suggestive in Thompson's writing on culture, his account remains open to criticism. Firstly, Thompson is guilty of uncritically celebrating the masculinist culture of the early labour movement. This is particularly marked in his historiography

6

and some of his political writing. Secondly, despite the cr'
comparisons between past and present that are opened ꜟ
Thompson, he produces a certain nostalgic connection to idealisℓ.
family relationships and to preindustrial forms of labour. As with his
intellectual distance from contemporary feminism, the root of
Thompson's nostalgic leanings can be traced through William
Morris's romantic socialism. Thirdly, as much of ·chapter three
demonstrates, Thompson's (1978) overly polemical and exaggerated
response to Althusser prevents him from responding as reflexively as
he might to some of the contemporary debates within modern social
theory. Had Thompson replied less aggressively this might have led
to a more constructive theoretical dialogue. In this respect, Thompson
remains blind to the implications strands of social theory, such as
hermeneutics, post-structuralism and psychoanalysis, have for his
theory of the subject and philosophy of history.

Ideology and hegemony

There can be few more contested concepts within the social sciences
than that of ideology. The work of Raymond Williams and
E.P.Thompson, comparable with their writing on culture, attempts to
rethink notions of ideology in terms of their role as public
intellectuals responding to ongoing academic debates. Here, I will
argue, in accordance with Williams and Thompson, that a theory of
ideology is essential for social theory, and that it should be
thematically distinguishable from culture.

   The term ideology was first coined by the French ideologue Destutt
de Tracy at the end of the eighteenth century (Larrain 1979). Ideology
is related to the notion that our beliefs about the world should be
based upon science, justification and progress. A just and happy
society in revolutionary France was to be grounded upon reason. The
notion that ideology can be based upon value free observation and
scientific critique is usually called a positive conception of ideology.
Such a definition of ideology is currently difficult to defend due to
the cultural presuppositions that inevitably inform any attempt to
construct a scientific critique. Napoleon used a negative version of
ideology to describe the doctrinaire activities of intellectuals like
Destutt de Tracy. Napoleon argued that writers like Destutt de Tracy
had become overly dogmatic. Their obsession with rationality and
justification had distanced them from practical reality. A negative
view of ideology is often held to signify a rigid unyielding
commitment to a specific set of ideas. While this form of ideology is

common in everyday talk, I want to argue against such a construction in favour of a critical conception of ideology, that retains a connection with unequal relations of power.

For Marx and Engels, the problem with writers like Destutt de Tracy, was not so much their rationalism as their idealism. In other words, our consciousness, for Marx and Engels, has to be related to material conditions. But, as Raymond Williams, in *Marxism and Literature* (1977) argues, Marx and Engels make the mistake of suggesting that consciousness becomes completely determined by material conditions. The mechanical materialism of Marx and Engels, according to Williams, holds that the'brute facts'of our existence become imprinted on our consciousness. This, as Williams suggests, was perhaps an overly polemical response to idealism, but also an important step forward for a theory of ideology. Both Marx and Engels grasped that'ideas'have to be related to specific social practices and social institutions. In this sense, the Marxist tradition has sought to defend a critical conception of ideology. J.B.Thompson (1984) has argued, in this context, that we may define a critical conception of ideology; as the ways in which meaning is mobilised in order to sustain relations of domination. One should, therefore, abandon the attempt to argue that meaning merely reflects social relations of domination, and instead seek to uncover the numerous ways in which the operation of ideology sustains relations of power. According to Jorge Larrain (1979), the writing of Marx and Engels, despite the problems of mechanical materialism, provides us with a number of critical insights into the workings of ideology. For Marx and Engels the main function of ideology was to obscure forms of contradiction that were manifested within class division. In other words, it was in the interests of the ruling-class that workers would see themselves as sharing common goals with the bourgeoisie, instead of alternatively seeking to create the conditions for a more emancipated society. However while there remains much that is suggestive in the writing of Marx and Engels - their concept of ideology needs to be considerably reconstructed in the light of more recent contributions in social theory.

Finally our fourth version of ideology is related to the structural and contextual production of ideas and beliefs. This is a view of ideology that relates the social production of certain world views to their location within the class structure. This account is closely connected with what has been called a neutral conception of ideology. Here ideology is defined as a distinctive set of ideas. For example, in accordance with this approach, one can talk of the ideology of the working-class or the ideology of the Labour Party.

But again, I would argue, such a perspective severs the link between ideology and domination.

Williams and Thompson take up different positions in the ideology debate. The term for Williams is usually held to signify a distinct set of ideas and beliefs that are internally held and produced by a particular class or social group. Hence ideology is separable from culture. The cultural retains a socially transcendental function and a connection to an aesthetic dimension. Later, in his revised theory of cultural materialism, Williams explicitly argues, that the ideology of a social group concerns its actually held beliefs, while the category of culture includes material as well as signifying practices. Alternatively, while Thompson would certainly accept that structural positions presupposes agents towards certain cultural dispositions, he usually employs a notion of ideology in terms of what I have called a critical approach. In the following chapters, my own strategy, is to develop a pejorative or critical account of ideology, that fulfils some of the criteria suggested by Williams and Thompson. Such an account of ideology would aim to be distinct from culture, while avoiding some of the problems encountered by writers like Althusser on issues of truth and justification.

One of the problems with Williams's and Thompson's writing on ideology is that they often use it interchangeably with a discussion of hegemony. Here I want to both demonstrate the usefulness of some of the critical insights the concept of hegemony can offer, but again argue, as with culture, that it should be thematically separate from a concern over ideology. The writing of Antonio Gramsci (1982) is perhaps the best place to start any discussion of hegemony. The term hegemony can be taken to mean the way in which patterns of domination are secured through processes of force and consent. A ruling alliance may hegemonically seek to maintain its position through economic, political or ideological means. Hence hegemony is made up of three components, and should not be conceptually reduced to the narrower concerns of ideology.

A ruling group can be said to be hegemonic if it transcends its more limited economic concerns, and provides the people with moral and intellectual leadership. In contemporary class society only the working-class and the dominant capitalist class are capable of becoming hegemonic. A hegemonic project that was transformist would seek to gradually'neutralise'the interests of other social groups, preventing the emergence of counter-hegemonic strategies. An expansive hegemonic project, on the other hand, occurs when the hegemonic class attempts to engage genuinely with other social groups symbolically creating a national-popular will. Notably it was only the working-class who would be able to engage in the expansionist mode of hegemony, as the ruling-class would be prevented from doing so by their structural position. Hegemony, in Gramsci's writing, is best thought of as a continuous battle ground, where the two'essential'classes attempt to construct alliances with other social groups in order to mobilise them for change. Gramsci's concept of ideology is interesting in this sense. Ideology is represented as the justification of relations of domination (critical), internally produced world views (neutral), and as the social'cement'that binds together differing hegemonic projects. The way we should judge ideology, according to Gramsci, is as to whether or not it is 'effective' in the process of political mobilisation. In order to do this hegemonic strategies would have to connect with the contradictory zone of experience Gramsci called the 'common sense' of the masses.

One of the problems that theories of hegemony have traditionally encountered has been their tendency to rely upon what I will call the 'incorporation' thesis. This is a social process whereby oppositional voices are institutionally dealt with through the management of criticism and resistance. While such strategies are essential to a theory of hegemony, in certain versions of the concept, there has been a tendency to overstate the degree of social consensus that exists in modern societies. This is certainly true, I would argue, of Williams's writing, even before he adopted the term hegemony, and of Thompson's later writing on the Cold War. An alternative, and in my terms more plausible, definition of the concept is suggested by some of the early historiography of E.P.Thompson. Here the term hegemony is linked to a historical process that is continually remaking and reshaping cultural relations of domination, which is challenged from below.

In this context, Thompson also stresses both the critical importance of the utopian imagination, and the rebirth of the peace movement which were marginalised both politically and within the media of mass communication. Williams, on the other hand, argues that the emergence of more critical perspectives are dependent upon a democratic reformation of dominant institutions . This would radically democratise the practice of ideology critique thereby undermining some of the elitist presuppositions of writers like Althusser. In short, and despite some of the limitations of the perspectives of Williams and Thompson, I aim to show how a consideration of their writing could make a more substantial contribution to a critical theory of ideology and hegemony.

Politics and socialism

The New Left was born in post-war Britain out of a dissatisfaction with state socialism and social democracy. They can be formally associated with the setting up of the journals New Reasoner and Universities and Left Review. These journals ran between 1956 and 1962, at which point they were replaced by New Left Review. The intellectual tone of these publications substantially differed before and after 1962. Before this date, the two journals concentrated on a much wider range of issues that included radical theatre, cinema, new youth cultures, the meaning of work, Eastern European socialism and the threat of the Cold War. After the merger of the two journals, the New Left Review became far more self consciously theoretical, and was principally aimed at a more'intellectual audience'. This change in orientation probably found its sternest critic in E.P.Thompson. Thompson criticised the elitism of the theoretical positions upheld by members of the early Frankfurt school and Althusser. Williams, who was never as closely associated with the journal as Thompson, adopted a more accommodating stance towards the continental strains of social theory that were finding a wider British audience. However,Williams and Thompson, and various others, were still intellectually close enough to contribute towards the writing of The May Day Manifesto (Hall 1968). The aim here was to combine more traditional class centred issues such as poverty with the new emerging agenda around culture, peace and race. But the grouping around the manifesto were caught between the undisciplined organisation of students and the more bureaucratically formed political parties. As with Williams's attempt to open up a public debate in *Communications* (1962) the collaborative manifesto largely failed to reach its target audience in the broader political community.

As is widely appreciated, the New Left, after the eclipse of the radical sixties, became marginalised as post-war social democracy came under increasing attack from the New Right (Rustin 1985). The end of the historic compromise between capital and labour opened the way for the New Right to articulate an aggressively neo-liberal strategy. In this period the Left were reduced to a number of isolated splinter groups, while the Labour Party, dogged by internal division, failed to respond adequately to the offensive from the Right. The New Left were critical of the particular form of socialism that had taken root in the East. But they also remained attached to some of socialism's more traditional aims such as the socialisation of the means of production. In this respect, neither Williams nor Thompson, adequately considered the reasons for the extreme unpopularity of'actually existed socialism'. While Thompson developed an ethical critique of Stalinism, Williams, influenced by Bahro, sought to argue for an ecologically sustainable self-managed socialism. Here, I would argue, that while the socialist tradition maintains a valuable point of critique, it has to be considerably reformulated in light of the political and theoretical challenges posed by modern social theory and contemporary social conditions.

The collective attempt by the New Left to articulate a so called'third way'between Labourism and communism, had a number of distinctive features. Firstly, while the category of class remained important, there was a concern to widen the base for socialism by constructing alliances with newly emerging communities of interest. The New Left had its critics in this respect. They were either accused of abandoning a strictly defined class politics, or of not going far enough in the process of accommodating the positions of the new social movements. Both Raymond Williams and E.P.Thompson occupied distinct if not opposed strategies in this respect. For Williams, the labour movement was the natural home of radical politics, although he maintained it had much to learn from the new social movements. While the working-class remained the main agency of change, he argued, in his later writing, that to construct a notion of the common good it should articulate its programme around human needs. Such a programme would break with an emergent structure of feeling of 'militant particularism'(Williams 1985). This would be achieved by placing individuals and groups in discussion around mutually held objectives. But, as we shall see, Williams often assumes that social movements like feminism and the labour movement share common interests in the defeat of capitalism. Here, I will argue, this assumption does not bear the weight of critical scrutiny. The labour movement, while remaining important, can no longer be presumed to have the'leading role'in the construction of a radical politics.

E.P.Thompson, on the other hand, abandoned the presupposition that the working-class would always be the principal agency of change. This became obvious to Thompson through the peace movement's desire to end the Cold War (Thompson 1981). Thompson was only able to reconnect the aims of the peace movement to class politics, through the argument that a de-militarised Europe would considerably strengthen the opportunities for more independent forms of socialism. What Thompson did not appreciate was that this process could also lead to the end of socialism as a progressive political project.

The importance of the category of culture had a defining quality for the New Left. Both Williams and Thompson, through a notion of culture, sought to criticise the economic reductionism of productivist Marxism, and investigate the emergent cultural identities and institutions within social democracy. While both writers position themselves within the Marxist tradition, neither accept some of the intellectual positions usually associated with these perspectives, such as the base and superstructure metaphor. For Williams and Thompson, base and superstructure represents a reified theoretical construction, that omits a notion of historical process, does not adequately address the cultural complexity of society, and subordinates needs to economic concerns. A cultural dimension is important because it opens an investigation into questions of identity and mass forms of culture. Further, one of the defining qualities of Williams's and Thompson's socialism is that the economy should become subordinated to the collective needs of society. The value Williams and Thompson place upon community, democracy, ecology and aesthetics enable them to question destructive forms of rationality. In this sense, as we shall see, their shared cultural Marxism owes a great deal to the critique of capitalism developed by the Romantic movement.

Finally, Williams and Thompson can be usefully placed within a tradition of socialist humanism or ethical socialism. This tradition can be understood in a British context developing through the writing of Orwell and Tawney, or as related to more European writers associated with existentialism or the Budapest school. Although, I should make clear at this point, Williams and Thompson remain isolated from the main currents of European philosophy and politics. E.P.Thompson's humanism, in this respect, was developed in opposition to the ethically asphyxiating practices developed by state socialism. His critique of Stalinism, which largely mirrors much of his later polemic against Althusser, is based upon the democratic insistence that the state and civil society should be separate (Thompson 1978a). Thompson's argument is not merely for the restoration of a negative form of liberty, rather he insists that freedom and autonomy can only be realised in a collective context. Human nature, for Thompson, is both the product of specific historical and social processes, as well as the reflexive ethical agency employed by individual subjects.

Williams also considers ethical questions, especially in relation to personal and political commitment. In this respect, Williams's early writing discusses a view of human nature. For Williams humans are communicating and learning beings. This provides the theoretical underpinning for the long revolution. However Williams links a view of how humans might grow to the politically dubious idea of the pursuit of perfectibility. This aside, Williams's and Thompson's humanism, in this and other contexts, has a definite radical purchase opening up concerns related to needs and values. Normative questions remain, I would argue, central problems for social theory, and should not as a consequence be left to other related disciplines such as literature and philosophy.

Williams's and Thompson's political writing remains instructive. However, I would argue, that a working-class socialist project based upon a national self-managed society only has a limited value. In the final concluding section, I will consider whether the Left should become reoriented around a commitment to socialism. Here I shall consider a number of perspectives including; classical socialism, radical nationalism, market socialism, post-Marxism and post-industrial socialism. Despite some of the claims currently being made concerning the triumph of liberal democracy, I shall argue that a form of socialist humanism should remain an important resource for those involved in emancipatory political movements. Raymond Williams's and E.P.Thompson's concern to replace damaging types of instrumental reason with more sustainable democratic forms of life remains as important today as it was when they were alive. This said a revitalised radical politics would have to revise its relation to democracy and citizenship. This is particularly true in the light of the revolutions of 1989 and the contradictions of social democracy. By focusing on contemporary debates concerned with the reconstruction of economic, political and cultural relations within late capitalism - the book will attempt to point to how a progressive politics could be recast in contemporary conditions. I will tentatively suggest that the Left, picking up on the thought of Williams and Thompson, should adhere to the values of democracy and community. In addition, I shall also claim, that unless the Left becomes a European Left, maintaining a critique of global, national and local institutions, it will become increasingly irrelevant in the modern world.

1 The long revolution

Raymond Williams was born in the Welsh working-class village of Pandy, the only son of his parents Henry and Esther. His family's activity in the Labour party had an early impact on Williams; by the age of fifteen he was working for Michael Foot, the Labour candidate in the 1935 General Election. In 1939, when he entered Trinity College Cambridge, Williams crossed the cultural divide that was to preoccupy him for the rest of his life. Williams's journey from Pandy to Cambridge, as has been well documented, was a move from a popular Welsh radical culture to the culture of an English educated ruling elite. Williams's movement between social locations, however, can not be thought of as a simple cause determining his subsequent development as a thinker, instead it forms the submerged context of most of his writing. This is particularly evident in his novels. Williams's novels deal extensively with the way the crossing of cultural borders shapes identity, throws individuals into crisis and informs moral dilemmas.

In 1941, Williams was forced to leave Cambridge to fight in the Second World War, before returning in October 1945. At the beginning of *Politics and Letters* (1979a) Williams discusses with the New Left Review collective how, on returning to Cambridge, the thriving socialist culture he had participated in as an undergraduate had almost disappeared. The young Williams, who had been previously preoccupied with Left political activity and modernist cinema, became on his return a follower of the literary critic F.R.Leavis.

The period leading up to the publication of *Drama from Ibsen to Eliot* (1952) finds the influence of Leavis at its most intense. Leavis argued that in all historical periods it was left to a minority to maintain, criticise and contribute to the 'great tradition' or culture. With the arrival of industrial society, Leavis argued, the elite literary culture, essentially the carrier of universal moral values, was put under threat by a debased machine civilisation. For Leavis, new technology, such as the family car, could not be seen in traditional liberal terms as increasing freedom and mobility. Instead the motor car fragmented communities and provided a source of cheap distraction (Johnson 1979).The insolubility of societies malaise in Leavis's criticism reveals his conservative cast of mind. The role of the critic, for Leavis, was to draw attention to the subsequent decline that mass industrialism had inflicted upon society and to build a literate community amongst like-minded scholars. Leavis attempted to forge such a community of sensibility around his teaching at Cambridge University, and through the literary journal Scrutiny. He became the main spokesperson for what has been called 'practical criticism' .If one applied practical criticism to a text, the critic, was obliged to sever the text from its historical context, and to attend closely to the experience of the writer. The finely tuned analysis of practical criticism claimed to be able to put the reader into an immediate relationship with a writer of a different historical period. The problem with this mode of interpretation was that an increasingly small number of readers were capable of undertaking the role of the active reader.

Much of Williams's early writing is best seen as a struggle with the elitist aspects of Leavis's criticism. That Williams never completely reworks Leavis's cultural conservatism seems to validate Gadamer's (1975) argument - that once the critic calls into question certain aspects of tradition, other areas fall into darkness. One can see the beginning of a more critical reception of Leavis with the publication of Williams's first major work *Drama from Ibsen to Eliot.* (1952). Here a community of sensibility, which once existed between the author and the audience in Elizabethan theatre, had been fractured by an industrial civilisation. The decline of a community of feeling had meant that:

> The pressure of a mechanical environment has dictated mechanical ways of thought, feeling and conjunction, which artists, and a few of like minded temper, reject only by conscious resistance and great labour (Williams 1952,p. 27).

Despite Leavis's influence on Williams, there is an important distinction to be drawn between the two. In this respect, Alan O'Connor (1989: 80) has argued, that even at this early stage, Williams consistently represented cultural forms in a more sharply distinct historical fashion than Leavis.

Culture and society

In *Culture and Society* (1961), Williams reassesses Leavis's cultural theory in order to develop a more democratic conception of culture. Here Williams discusses a range of mainly English writers from Burke to Orwell, with Marx being the major exception. In this respect Williams reinterprets the significance of the Romantic tradition. Romantic writers, in Williams's writing, embody a radical critique of society that is always more than an inward retreat from industrial society. This tradition, according to Williams, provides the moral basis for a democratic socialist society through the term 'culture' . Beginning with the Romantics, culture was held to signify a 'whole way of life' that could not be reduced to a separate private sphere. Culture was a critical concept in that it preserved an idea of human perfection. This provided a 'court of appeal' continually bringing into focus contemporary society. These two meanings of culture first come together in the writing of Coleridge. Coleridge employed the related term 'cultivation' to contrast the destructive values of industrial society with those of a creative imagination, the latter being linked to the pursuit of perfection. Human beings, however, could only be perfected if society provided the collective basis for their improvement. For Coleridge this process would be overseen by a national church . Cultural values were not the preserve of an atomised private sphere, but could provide new forms of enabling community.

Williams argues that the organic romantic mode of thinking became deeply compromised by the contributions of Leavis and T.S.Eliot. Neither Eliot, nor Leavis, offered a critique of the very economic system which had produced the fragmented, isolated and alienated culture they both intellectually opposed. Eliot and Leavis both failed to successfully connect the romantically inspired notion of an organic culture, with radical demands for the democratisation of society. For Williams the coming together of romanticism and socialism, in writers such as William Morris, offers a more persuasive version if the Romantic tradition. Abandoning Leavis's argument that traditional culture required an elite to guard it against mass society;

our cultural heritage should be collectively owned by everyone. Thus the widening of access to cultural institutions, or 'left Leavisism' (Eagleton 1976), is not to be feared due to the responsible nature of the labour movement. Williams wrote that the labour movement:

> has never sought to destroy the institutions of this kind of culture; it has on the contrary, pressed for their extension, for their wider social recognition, and, in our own time, for the application of a larger part of our material resources to their maintenance and development. (Williams 1961,p.314)

Williams argues that the self-activity of ordinary working people was being held in check by their exclusion from Britain's dominant institutions. Artists and workers are united by common interests in the reform of society. However it was the guiding light offered by the exceptional artist which predominated in the forming of their commonality. The artist as an especially privileged figure is reflected in Williams's discussion of common culture. This is suggested when Williams writes:

> A culture has two aspects: the known meanings and directions, which its members are trained to; the new observations and meanings, which are offered and tested. These are the ordinary processes of human societies and human minds, and we see through them the nature of a culture: that is always both traditional and creative; that it is both the most ordinary common meanings and the finest individual meanings. We use the word culture in these two senses: to mean a whole way of life - the common meanings; to mean the arts and learning - the special process of discovery and creative effort. (Williams 1958,p.4)

The idea of a common culture first appears in *Drama from Ibsen to Eliot* (1952) under the guise of a community of sensibility. As a Leavisite concept the community of sensibility has a nostalgic quality, linked to the idealisation of a peaceful organic past that existed prior to the industrial revolution. Later, in *Culture and Society* (1961), the formation of a common culture is still seen as desirable, but is more closely associated with the 'forward march' of the labour movement. The achievement of a common culture would not mean that all British people would come to share the same cultural experience.

18

Instead Williams sought to widen the opportunity to interpret and criticise a shared literary and artistic culture. A truly common culture would be based less on shared values and beliefs, and more on the chance to contribute to a shared store of social experiences. But it remained the informed disposition of the artist that was of greatest significance in the process of continual critique. It would be a difficult argument for Williams to maintain that society is solely dependent upon the artistic community for insightful observation and the creation of new meanings. The only way this position is sustainable is if Williams believes the artist to be an exceptional person - in keeping with Coleridge, Leavis and Eliot. This would certainly seem to be what he would try to defend, without ever explaining what constitutes the artist's specialness. On the other hand, he does argue, against Coleridge, that the artist is not so privileged that he can afford to be continually defying artistic convention. The artist is ethically, and for the sake of the quality of his or her own work, required to conform with what Williams calls a recognisable structure of feeling. The artist that failed to do so would not only fail to communicate his or her experience's to others, but would not enrich the common culture. However, working-class creativity could only be trusted if it did not challenge the legitimacy of the dominant culture, and the moral guidance of its defenders.

The long revolution

Williams's next book, *The Long Revolution* (1965), develops many of the themes that had preoccupied him in previous works. The long revolution refers to the slow historical unfolding of three inter-related transformations: the democratic, the industrial, and the cultural that had been taking place since the eighteenth century. In the book's middle section he discusses the development of Britain's cultural institutions and popular cultural practices. The gradual broadening of access to the education system, along with the growth of the reading public, popular press, and the use of 'standard English' , provides the backcloth of the long revolution. The aim of this revolution being the formation of an educated, participatory democracy. Despite the potential for radical change provided by Britain's cultural institutions this goal remained a distant one. The labour movement, who were to provide the necessary political agency, were becoming increasingly integrated into the social structure. Hence the socialist project, according to Williams, needed to be renewed along humanist lines. The political necessity of the long revolution was secured by a particular view of human nature. Williams writes:

> If man is essentially a learning, creating and communicating being, the only social organisation adequate to his nature is a participatory democracy, in which all of us, as unique individuals, learn, communicate and control. Any lesser, restrictive system is simply a waste of our true resources (Williams 1965,p118)

In his novel *Second Generation* (1964), Williams infers that the nature of human beings should be democratically connected to what he repeatedly calls 'certain rhythms of growth' . The car factory, used to symbolise contemporary capitalism, has a jarring, alienating rhythm, outside the control of the men who labour on the production line. This is a rhythm of discontinuity, isolation and despair which often leads those who attempt to fight it feeling tired and hollow at the end of the day. The rhythm of democracy, autonomy and humanity is in distinction a steadier more organic process. When he describes the timbre of community and democracy he uses terms such as 'growth' , 'connectedness' and 'care' . These words are used in conjunction with moments of authenticity, harmonious family life and remembered lived connections with a previous life in rural Wales. This is favourably compared with the rhythm of domination characterised by the factory. The more integrative tempo, arguably based on an idealisation of rural Wales, offers a more communal way of life than that of the city. The roots of this juxtaposition can be found in an attachment to Leavis and his own family. Once people come to realise this rhythm of cultural growth, as an alternative to industrialism, it gives them a radical populist feeling to unite and struggle around. Kate, the central character of the novel, comes to realise this after a period of self-delusion. By regaining contact with her essential nature, and the desire for radical change, she is able see through the ideology of a capitalist system. She says to her son Peter:

> Can't you at least try to recognise it ? Can't you reach this moment of feeling, beyond yourself, and the power of others to change you ? The real power, don't you see, when you are bound up with others, involved with them? When at last you can know people and trust them (Williams,1964,p.197)

It is noticeable that the characters in Williams's (1960,1964) first two novels are only able to encounter the feeling of connection during personal moments of existential crisis. Later with the publication of *The Fight for Manod* (1979), the final novel in the 'Welsh trilogy' , the necessary connections are made out of intellectual effort and political feelings of commitment.

The idea of the long revolution, I would argue, sets up a dualism between the progressive forces of change such as human nature and socialism, and the reactionary orientation of those who would maintain capitalism. The problem was how would the labour movement carry through the long revolution ? This question became increasingly pertinent for Williams. The labour movement had become incorporated into the system it had originally set out to change. This was a comparatively more pessimistic conclusion than the one he had outlined previously in *Culture and Society* (1961). It is also worthy of note that Williams adopts the term 'capitalism' as opposed to 'industrial society' during this period. This would seem to signify his deeper involvement in New Left circles. The decisive break in Williams's thinking came in 1966 after the election of a Labour government. As Williams comments, he :

> decided to leave the Labour Party and write some sort of a manifesto, stating very clearly that the Labour Party was no longer just an inadequate agency for socialism, it was now an active collaborator in the process of reproducing capitalist society. (Williams 1979,p.373)

Structures of feeling

In 1954, Williams produced a largely forgotten work with his friend Michael Orrom called *Preface to Film*. This book is of interest, providing one of the first discussions of structures of feeling. As in his earlier writing, the text defines the primary task of the artist as the ability to communicate an experience to others by working within specifically defined conventions. Artistic conventions are imaginatively drawn upon to achieve what Williams calls total expression Total expression is achieved in dramatic production where the author has control over speech, movement and design. For this to be achieved certain conditions need to be satisfied; firstly, the dramatic scenario should be performed, as far as is possible, in line with the intentionality of the author. The other precondition being that the audience should leave a performance, or put down a novel, with an idea of what the author was 'really trying to say'. The author and the audience are able to achieve such a harmonious understanding by sharing the same structure of feeling. In other words, by connecting artistic conventions to a recognisable structure of feeling, the artist is able to be both of her age, and to help constitute it. Thus the structure of feeling is a dialectical generational construct that helps form, and is formed by, those cultural workers who are doing new or important work.

Williams develops the idea of structure of feeling later in *The Long Revolution* (1965). Here he writes:

> In one sense, this structure of feeling is the culture of the period: it is the particular living result of all the elements in the general organisation. And it is in this respect that the arts of a period, taking these to include characteristic approaches and tones in argument, are of major importance. (Williams 1965,p64-65)

The structure of feeling is constructed by the artistic conventions that best express the consciousness of an age, and what he calls the predominant social characters. Social characters are internally and structurally produced class ideologies or world views. For example, in Williams's analysis of the industrial novels of the 1840's, he discusses three social characters; the aristocratic, working-class and the middle-class. These class ideologies exist in constant tension and mediation with one another. The specific historical relations between them, coupled with the dominant artistic conventions, informing the structure of feeling.

The knowable community

A related concern to that of structures of feeling is knowable community. Williams discusses the connection between the novel and the knowable community in *The English Novel from Dickens to Lawrence* (1985). Here Williams argues that the Victorian novelists were facing a crisis of an unknowable community, as social life after the industrial revolution became increasingly diverse and complex. The organic Leavisite community had been shattered by an industrial division of labour and the accelerated growth of modern towns and cities. The fragmentation of social life posed the Victorian novelists recognisable social and existential problems of belonging. These difficulties were particularly evident for writers who attempted to represent the experience of those who were not directly present in everyday encounters, and who did not share the social language of the novelist. This is not just a historical problem for Williams, but one that is keenly felt in his own fiction. He illustrates this in *Politics and Letters* (1979). Here he defends his characterisation of university dons as the 'class enemy' , rather than the owners of the car plant, in his novel *Second Generation* (1964). He says:

> I still mainly know the actual ruling class only by reading about it. But it's incredibly difficult to create characters who you don't feel in the gut; at some level if you don't know who they are you perhaps don't have sufficient energy to project them(Williams, 1979,p.289).

Sentences like the preceding one are often interpreted as evidence of Williams's latent empiricism (Hall,1989). What is usually meant by this charge is that Williams's use of 'experience' tends to ignore the way in which the subject has been de-centred by determining linguistic and social practices. However, I would want to argue that this is as inadequate expression of the relation between subjects and structures as Williams's own, and further, that such a criticism does not grasp the complexity of his writing. The desire to create, for Williams, should always be linked to the need for the artist to communicate with the audience and community. As Michael Merrill (1978-9) has suggested, on this count, for Williams no cultural unit or individual could be understood other than in connection with other individuals and cultural units. Creativity then is intrinsically related to an intersubjective dimension, presupposing the existence of culturally connected others. The subject in Williams's writing is continually searching for experiential contact with others, and is always as much formed by being with others, as through actual conscious choices. For example, Matthew Price, in the partially autobiographical *Border Country* (1960), is struck by a strong sense of belonging when leaving the bedroom of his dying father. Williams wrote :

> Matthew stood for a moment with his eyes closed, then walked out of the bedroom. As he walked downstairs to the kitchen, he felt the past moving with him: this life, this house, the trains through the valley (Williams 1960, p.24).

The sense of being socially and biologically bound up with others is often something we attempt to deny, before we can come to realise feelings of obligation and connection which sustain the self.

Cultural idealism

Williams's early writing works within a paradigm that I shall call 'cultural idealism' . He conceives of the informing spirit of culture to be the embodiment of absolute human values, that have at their core the potentiality to make human beings perfectible. Secondly, despite Williams's attempt to reconnect artistic production to socio-historical contexts, that follows the writing of *The Long Revolution* (1965), the artist is consistently privileged in Williams's writing. In accordance with the Leavisite tradition, it is exceptional artists with special insight who are the main carriers of society's moral values. It is significant however that as Williams takes questions of cultural domination increasingly seriously, he adopts a more obviously materialist stance in his writing.

Cultural domination and romantic culture

Leavis's influence on *Culture and Society* (1961) is profound. Williams follows Leavis in representing artists as passing on to succeeding generations absolute human values. While this was noticed by a number of Williams's critics at the time - it was not specifically connected with Leavis's influence. V.G.Kiernon (1959) in a review of *Culture and Society* makes a related point. He argues that by not historically locating the writers under review in terms of their class position, we are left with the procession of the idea of culture coming down to us through the ages. Williams, in other words, by not contextualising the writers in *Culture and Society* (1961) may have reinforced certain patterns of cultural domination.

Marcuse (1972) argues that the bourgeoisie have traditionally made a number of related claims for their own symbolic and cultural representations. Firstly, these forms were considered to have a universal validity. Hence the meanings and values expressed in exceptional works transcend the status position of the audience. Secondly, the bourgeoisie also claim that its own cultural productions are continuous with the symbolic forms preserved from past civilisations. The claim to universality, Marcuse argues, is deeply ideological as it obscures forms of symbolic domination that are prevalent in the modern world. Initially, in *Culture and Society* (1961), Williams presents culture in a similarly universalistic fashion to how Marcuse describes the bourgeoisie. For Williams culture as a 'court of appeal' exists as the embodiment of ultimate values, which are not historically and contextually produced by social groups in specific social relationships. Instead, Williams argues, that culture's 'ideal' component is both universally valid and transcends the context of its production and reception.

In addition to his exposition of a universal culture, Williams also blandly describes culture as being a 'whole way of life' E.P.Thompson (1961) argues that to simply state that culture forms a way of living is to obscure the complexity of cultural relations past and present. Thompson criticises Williams for failing to recognise the conflicts and divisions which any analysis of culture as a form of domination must encompass. Culture, for Thompson, is the reflexive result of historical agents who articulate cultural practices both for and against something in unequal relations of power. Williams, by failing to connect culture to a social structure:

> never really considers how far a dominant structure of feeling plus the direct intervention of power plus market forces and systems of promotion and reward plus institutions make and constitute together a system of ideas and beliefs, a constellation of received ideas and orthodox attitudes, a 'false consciousness' or a class ideology which is more than the sum of it's parts and which has a logic of its own. (Thompson,1961,p.37)

The structural organisation of *Culture and Society* (1961) reaffirms the influence of practical criticism. Williams presents the reader with lengthy quotations from the work of the writers under inspection. This is intended to provoke the close inspection that should reveal their inherent meaning. The meaning of the texts under discussion, Williams assumes, have an obvious self-presence to the reader that does not have to be fleshed out by the critic. To fail to develop an adequate theory of interpretation should not be conceptualised as an isolated academic problem, but as reinforcing certain forms of cultural domination. Williams, in other words, did not reveal the extent to which the Romantic tradition had been selected and maintained in relations of power.

Williams's adherence to practical criticism blinded him to two theoretical problems a theory of interpretation should address. The first task would be, as far as possible, to restore the text to its original context. In these terms, Quentin Skinner (1988) has argued, that the intellectual historian seeking to uncover the meaning of the text should take account of authorial intentionality, and situate the text in its original linguistic and ideological context. This should reveal the historical and political questions the text was trying to debate, and those it either repressed or considered unimportant. The need to adequately contextualise the text was absent from Williams's early writing. Although he addressed this issue in *The Long Revolution* (1965), culture remains linked to the pursuit of perfection and transcendent social values. The second task in seeking to historicise the text is to be aware that the interpreter's horizon has a historical distance from the text. John Keane (1988) has used this argument, inspired by Gadamer, against Skinner, in a way that could be equally applied to Williams. Keane argues that Skinner assumes that one can historically recover meaning without involving, at least at some level, the subjective prejudices of the observer. Similarly Williams, when he does begin to take historical contexts seriously in his theory of structures of feeling, does not recognise his own horizon as playing a role in the interpretative process. Thus Williams's theory of structures of feeling attempts to locate the text in specific historical formations, while the impact of his own reading of the text is 'scientifically' obscured from view. Williams assumes that the essential meaning of the text, and this is a point I shall be returning to, can be uncovered once we have accurately located the text in the appropriate structure of feeling. In opposition to Williams, I shall argue, that once the text has been historicised, one can then proceed to uncover how a particular text has been interpreted in a plurality of social and historical contexts. This relationship is often an ambiguous one as texts do not have intrinsic hegemonic or counter-hegemonic qualities that exist independently of the way they are interpreted. The same text could be a means of legitimising domination in one context, and of calling the dominant social relations into question within others. Thus Williams's theory of structure of feeling radically underestimates the extent to which texts become detached from their original site of production. Paul Ricoeur (1981) has called the process of the decontextualisation of symbolic forms distanciation. According to Ricoeur, the text has:

> threefold autonomy; with respect to the intention of the author; with respect to the cultural situation and the sociological conditions of the production of the text; and finally, with respect to the original addressee (Ricoeur 1981, p.91).

For example, Trotsky in *The Revolution Betrayed* (1973), written after his expulsion from the Soviet Union in January 1929, could be said to be attempting to construct a counter-hegemonic alliance in opposition to Stalin. Here Trotsky challenged the dominant interpretation of Marx sanctioned by the Stalinist regime. He did this by arguing that the revolution needed to be renewed along classical Marxist lines. The original works of Marx, being reformulated by Trotsky, were the same texts that were being mobilised to ideologically legitimate the dictatorship of the party. The *Revolution Betrayed* (1973) was interpreted by the ruling Communist party as a counter-revolutionary text, and was subsequently banned from publication in the Soviet Union. Yet Trotsky's famous work has another history. The text can also be read as a specific interpretation of the failure of socialism in the East, that has been subsequently debated by interested parties. In this context, Trotsky's text has inspired revolutionary movements in the West, acted as a focus of hatred for Stalinist regimes in the East, and has been variously considered by academics seeking to understand Soviet history. By no means exceptional, *The Revolution Betrayed* (1973) serves to illustrate that texts can have very complex histories, and can not be categorised as essentially hegemonic or counter-hegemonic.

Problems in culture and ideology

From The Long Revolution (1965) onwards, Williams wrote about the English novel as embodying an aesthetic dimension and as being historically produced in definite social relations. However the presence of Leavis is still discernible in his writing. The notion of a structure of feeling is not intended to be a philosophy of language or of consciousness. Williams intended the idea of a structure of feeling to provide a critique of Leavis and vulgar Marxism. In distinction to Leavis, Williams argued, that feeling should not be conceived as a merely personal disposition achieving its fullest intensity in the developed sensibility of an elite. Feelings are alternatively, as indicated by the word structure, individually and collectively produced. Further certain Marxist approaches that identify within the text either a bourgeois or revolutionary ideology are criticised for repressing the internal complexity of great works of art. If the literary work, as Williams argues, is informed by artistic conventions and competing world views, then the text is likely to contain a number of fragmentary perspectives. Why then does Williams discuss feeling rather than consciousness? Firstly, Williams's romanticism makes him suspicious of theoretical forms of abstraction. Hence concepts like consciousness represses the full experience of human beings. Communicative beings are not only capable of thoughts and ideas, but of feeling and emotion. Thus, consciousness, as a theoretical construct, suggests an overly instrumental account of human nature. The dominant structure of feeling of capitalism being one of economic rationality, where emotional and intellectual needs are denied validity in the public sphere, and are maintained within a private realm. Similarly, Agnes Heller (1979) has identified in the nineteenth century bourgeoisie's relationship to feeling two ideal types. The first set of feelings, which Heller calls the cult of the moment, sought to stimulate the senses in such a way as to bring about emotional reactions of suffering or delight. The other range of feelings, that she labels emotional construction, bears a stronger relationship to Leavis's aesthetic theory. This particular sensibility rested upon the cultivation of human values in the private sphere away from the impersonal forms of competition manifest in the public sphere. Heller argues that the Victorian public sphere was so dominated by the bourgeoisie's desire for money and power, that all other heterogeneous feelings were subordinated to this end. This left little space for the public development of feeling and connection. Both Heller and Williams argue that this distinct tendency within capitalist society is contradicted by other feelings that exist within rural communities, artistic formations and the labour movement. Willimas's radicalism, on this issue, lies in his break with the distinction between public and private and his ethical critique of capitalism. However, I now want to address, the theoretical difficulties that remain connected to this venture, with reference to the notion of structures of feeling.

The text, in Leavis's writing, was a repository of human values that were revealed through close analysis by a well developed sensibility. Similarly, for Williams, one gets in touch with these values through feeling rather than through thought (Williams 1979,p.159). The literary text has an aesthetic dimension that Williams associates with feeling. Unfortunately, within Williams's early work, he often presents the aesthetic dimension as having an absolute autonomy from the social. This is apparent in his discussion of the Bronte sisters. Williams writes:

> Indeed, to give that kind of value to human longing and need, to that absolute emphasis on commitment to another, the absolute love of the being of another, is to clash sharply with the emerging system, the emerging

priorities, as in any assault on material poverty (Williams,1985,p.61).

This quotation reveals a certain affinity to Marcuse's essay *The Aesthetic Dimension* (1979). Marcuse comments:

> the radical qualities of art, that is to say, its indictment of the established reality and its invocation of the beautiful image of liberation are grounded precisely in the dimensions where art transcends its social determination and emancipates itself from a given universe of discourse and behaviour while preserving its overwhelming presence. (Marcuse,1979,p.24)

Contrary to Williams and Marcuse, Janet Wolff (1983) argues that the relationship between aesthetics and politics is best conceptualised as related but irreducible spheres. She correctly, in my view, emphasises that aesthetics have a relative rather than an absolute autonomy from the social. Thus political values can intrude into aesthetic values. This can come about by bringing political concerns into the assessment of a text, and by either supporting or undermining vested interests in the persistence and dominance of particular art forms. Williams's own understanding of an aesthetic dimension is closely related with what I have called ideal culture. Williams describes ideal culture as 'a state or process of human perfection, in terms of certain absolute or universal values' (Williams,1965,p.57).To represent the aesthetic as transcendental is to argue that it has an absolute autonomy from the social. This is curious, as one of the theoretical possibilities opened by the concept structures of feeling, leaving to one side criticisms of its precise formulation, was to bring a social consideration into the assessment of art. However what becomes apparent in Williams's later more materialist writing is an increasing scepticism concerning the privileged role of art.

Alan O'Connor makes two important criticisms of the structure of feeling when he writes:

> Each 'structure of feeling' is loosely associated with a generation of writers or artists: the Romantics, the Victorian novel, Expressionism, and so forth. This notion has been criticised because it seems to lack any sense of conflict within a single generation. As well as this there

are often practical problems in identifying such generations (O'Connor,1989,p.84).

While I would agree with O'Connor, his argument does not go far enough. Before following this up, I want to link the idea of a recognisable structure of feeling to the related concept knowable community. The artist is both constrained and formed by her experience of the knowable community. The tradition of literature from Dickens to Lawrence shares with Williams(1985) the need to write about an experiential community that is directly known. The writer, in this perspective, can neither escape the complex relational web of the community, nor can she gain complete knowledge of it. The experience of the knowable community, despite being contradictory and uncertain, is contained within the ideological limits that have been set by the writer's position in the social structure. Without denying Williams's respect for the creativity of individual writers - there does seem to be a homologous relationship between the knowable community and the world view offered in the text. Hence the sociological content of the text is determined by the structural position of the writer, while the aesthetic dimension is transcendent of the social altogether. Similarly Williams(1965) describes a reflective relationship between the class position of the writer and her social characteristics in his discussion of structures of feeling. Here classes or social characters produce their own sets of ideological beliefs for internal consumption only.This particular view of ideology is often linked with discussions of Lukacs and Goldmann, with whom Williams is often compared (O'Connor 1989). Here, I would argue, that Williams's notion of ideology could have been improved through a closer engagement with ideas of hegemony. Nicos Poulantzas (1983) in a consideration of Lukac's theory of ideology argues that theorists should conceive of the relation between class and ideology dialectically. Poulantzas argues that to tie class consciousness to a particular world view denies the ideological instance even a relative autonomy. According to Williams, the social experience of the writer takes place within the confines of a knowable community and a particular structure of feeling. But, as Poulantzas argues, world views of social classes are not hermetically sealed off from one another. Williams, it should be noted, partially recognises this point, as social characters, within the structure of feeling, have some mediating effect upon one another. But in the prior formation of social character, as well as within the knowable community, ideas do seem to have a certain class belonging. If this were true, one could not convincingly argue for a definition of ideology as a means of class

30

domination. For Gramsci, one of the defining features of a set of social forces that has achieved hegemony is its ability to take on the concerns of other subordinate groups. Thus, following Poulantzas, ideological representations do not automatically reflect class positions. While Poulantzas has a point to make against Williams, others such as Laclau (1977) have suggested that there is no connection between class and ideology. Laclau defines ideological perspectives as being contingent on their social and historical context. Thus there is no necessary relation between the working-class and socialist perspectives. Yet, this view, obscures the relatively durable conventions and practices that have sought to symbolically and materially represent such a relationship. This is an abandonment of dialectical thinking. Where as Poulantzas would give cultural prejudices a relative autonomy from social class - Laclau would sever the connection altogether. In this respect, Williams and Laclau are guilty, from opposing view points, of abandoning a rich dialectic between the world and the text.

The long revolution: hegemony and culture

The long revolution was in danger of entering into a political impasse in the late sixties.The labour movement, who were the main agents for change in *Culture and Society* (1961), had by the end of the sixties become incorporated into the dominant ideology. The incorporation thesis, as it became manifested in Williams's writing, was namely the idea that the labour or socialist movements were no longer capable of radically transforming society. This conception would seem to have three main sources; (1) Williams's closer engagement with politics;(2) the arrival of Gramsci in left critique; and (3) his continued attachment to Leavis.

Williams (1961) was not directly involved in political activity when he argued that the labour movement were the collective embodiment of the creativity of the working-class. His more sharpened interest in politics in the sixties coincided with a period of right-wing leadership in the Labour Party. This undoubtedly, along with the rest of the New Left, led Williams to underestimate the resilience and achievements of social democracy. Secondly, Gramsci's travelling theory finally reaches the shores of Britain in 1957 (Forgacs 1989). The Gramscian concept of hegemony would at a slightly later date reach a wider New Left audience through the so called Nairn-Anderson theses. Later I shall discuss this controversy and its impact upon the writing of E.P.Thompson. Our concern for the present is to locate the way in which Gramsci's theory of hegemony has been interpreted in British social theory. While I can not be sure that Williams had read Gramsci by the time he came to write *The Long Revolution* (1965) - what I can be more certain of is that his interpretation of hegemony in his later writing is consistent with the incorporation thesis. The idea of a dominant culture acting as a homogeneous conservative force blunting more radical impulses is a powerful one in his writing. Williams writes in a 1975 article:

> the essential dominance of a particular class in society is maintained not only, although if necessary, by power, and not only, although always, by property. It is maintained also and inevitably by a lived culture: that saturation of habit, of experience, of outlook, from a very early age and continually renewed at so many stages of life, under definite pressures and within definite limits, so that what people come to think and feel is in large measure a reproduction of the deeply based social order which they may even in some respects think they oppose and indeed actually oppose. (Williams,1975,p.74)

The third reason for Williams's attachment to the incorporation thesis came through his intellectual connection to Leavis. Leavis and Williams, as we saw earlier, believed that high forms of culture were in danger of being swamped by a commodified culture. For Williams this exchange culture threatened to engulf the oppositional practices of the labour movement. While the working-class were disproportionately excluded from higher education they were denied access to a rich literary tradition. This left them susceptible to the cheap pleasures offered by a commercial culture. I want to argue here that Williams consistently overstates the incorporating effect of the dominant culture. Further, I should like to make a nimber of related criticisms of Williams's conception of the long revolution.

Italian social theorist Norberto Bobbio (1987b) argues that the European Marxist tradition has been overly dominated by debates concerning the mobilisation of social forces. While these discussions obviously have their place; over emphasis on these issues has led to an absence of critical thinking in relation to a socialist theory of the state. According to Bobbio, the proliferation of Marxist tracts on strategic thinking is connected to Marx's original belief that the state would eventually 'wither away' . Similarly, Williams did not develop either a theory of the capitalist state or a model of what a future socialist state might be like. That he does not completely ignore this issue will become obvious in my discussion of democratic realism. But, for the present, this leaves the sympathetic critic with a contradictory set of problems. Williams evidently wants to preserve the connection between socialism and pluralism, but without directly addressing European state dominated socialism, or what he was later to call 'actually existing socialism' (Williams 1980a). Williams is not necessarily wrong to argue that socialism and cultural diversity go hand in hand, but what he neglects to address is how this relationship could be theoretically demonstrated. This is particularly marked in view of the historic relationship between socialism and Eastern European societies. Further the argument in *The Long Revolution* (1965) concerning the state appears to be contradictory. Firstly, Williams embraces the idea predominant in liberal theories that the state acts as a neutral arbiter of different interest groups. One of the core assumptions of the long revolution is that the state can just as easily act on behalf of a left progressive programme, as it can for rightist political projects. This belief seems to underscore Williams's contention that once the working-class are brought into cultural institutions in greater numbers, they would automatically transform existing social practices by their very presence. Alternatively, Williams is more in tune with Marxist approaches to the state through the theorisation of the incorporation thesis. Marxist approaches usually emphasise the state's ability to manage internal voices of opposition and dissent. While one might charitably argue that his ambivalence is indicative of a certain need to express his dissatisfaction with both Marxist and liberal approaches, he fails to discuss these problems in any theoretical depth.

Williams bases his socialist humanism on a specific view of human nature. Hence the long revolution rests on a view of men and women as being essentially communicating beings. The basic need for communication with others could not be satisfied as long as citizens were excluded from the dominant cultural institutions, or indeed incorporated into a dominant ideology. Once the self-activity of ordinary people had become democratically integrated into the means of communication, this would inevitably lead to the reorganisation of internal institutional structures in line with the underlying nature of men and women.

The socialist humanist tradition, that can be traced back to Marx's early Hegelian writing, has historically relied on a notion of human potentiality that in itself presupposes a view of human nature. In the Marxist and socialist traditions a conception of human potentiality has a critical function in that it can point to the denial of human expression and creativity evident in the dominant social structures.

For Williams human nature depends on the historical development of cultural institutions for its realisation. Thus Williams argues that the working-class remain the main agency for change as long as their essential communicative nature is not allowed full expression. But, I would argue, that the human need for communication gives the historical trajectory of the long revolution a teleological shape. Williams replaces Marx's emphasis on the need to expand economic production, with a view of history that is determined by the separation of artists and the working-class from the means of communication.

This aside, I would agree with Williams, that without an idea of human potential it becomes difficult to argue for freedom from certain forms of oppression. For example, feminists have argued, that women should not be solely responsible for the raising of children and household labour. One of the reasons that this argument is convincing is that the burden placed upon women in the domestic sphere denies them the opportunity of playing a full role as social citizens. The sexual division of labour also denies men the opportunity of being actively involved in the rearing of children. In other words, human beings have the potentiality to be creative in the public sphere, while acting in a responsible and caring fashion in the household. Thus unless contemporary subjects are deemed by social theory to have the capacity to be creative, caring and responsible, there would seem little point in objecting to the unequal division of labour between the sexes. But, in Williams's writing, despite the historical context offered by the long revolution, he retains a tendency to represent human nature as historically fixed, rather than socially mediated.It is not that Williams is wrong in his argument that human's are essentially material beings who also use language in acts of creative expression. The trap that he arguably fall's into is that he expects social institutions to become oriented around this nature. This presupposes a Left will become generated around these ideals and that institutions are infinitely plastic. In a globalised economy where the mechanisms of control have been removed from the national level and where the cultural left have embraced a form of identity politics, these views seem somewhat dated.

Charles Taylor (1985d) and Agnes Heller (1990) have argued that a theory of human nature should emphasise the common capacity to be relatively self-determining. Men and women, according to this view, have the potential to realise themselves given a shared cultural context that no longer emphasises a premodern sense of predestination.In Taylor's terms Williams has a concept of human potential that avoids an atomistic morality. One of the central themes of Williams's later novels (1979b,1985b) is that one has to live in an uncertain world which poses a series of ethical and political problems, without supplying very many easy answers. These questions are mainly centred around issues related to commitment, belonging and solidarity that critically intersect public and private relationships. The way in which a particular dilemma is resolved does not simply have an effect upon the agent in question, but often restructures the lives of intersubjectively connected others. Thereby Williams manages to link a view of men and women as only being self-determining within a supportive cultural context. Alternatively, an atomistic conception of human nature would tend to see men and women as isolated bearers of rights. This perspective, Taylor (1985) argues, tends to ignore the view that rights are dependent upon specific views of human potential.

However Williams would not completely satisfy Taylor's critique. For Taylor conceptions of human potentiality should recognise that human beings are not perfectible. A politics that does not recognise certain human limitations can quite quickly convert itself into a contempt for those members of society who do not seem to be quite as perfectible as others. Williams conflates a discourse of human growth with one of perfectibility, when following Taylor they should be seen as distinct. Historically the inability of the socialist tradition to make this separation has produced disastrous consequences, such as Stalinism. The Bolshevik party, after the civil war, consistently substituted their own will for those of the proletariat. The disintegration of Soviet civil society meant that the Bolsheviks tended to identify themselves as the keepers of the revolutionary spirit and the true consciousness of the working-class (Polan 1984).Thus social forces, such as the kulaks, that existed outside of the party were not to be negotiated with as they stood in the way of the future harmonious society. In this context, the belief in the perfectibility of individuals was coupled with a utopian desire for the end of all social conflict. The eventual, although not inevitable, outcome of this process being the Gulag. This is not to offer the absurd suggestion that Williams was a Stalinist, as this would not only misrepresent him, but the New Left in general. It is to argue, however, that he did not think through some of the historical problems raised by the socialist movement.

Williams's incorporation thesis combines what Giroux and Simon (1988) describe as the two essentialist traps of cultural studies. The first perspective views high culture as a transcendental sphere free from the barbarism of popular culture. The function of high culture, as it exists outside of relations of domination, is to construct a critique of popular culture. Writers who hold to this paradigm are often theorists of a mass society. They retain a tendency to over emphasise the homogeneity of institutions and cultural practices. This category includes writing as politically diverse as Leavis, and certain works by the early Frankfurt school (Adorno 1973). Other social theorists radically opposed to the idea of a mass society have embraced a different form of essentialism. Here the notion of an authentic culture, that could have its basis in sex, race or class is projected as a romanticised expression of resistance. Theorists in this category fail to discuss the very real divisions that exist within the social group, upon whose agency the possibilities of social change are often dependent. In keeping with this approach, the theorist, usually without consulting the group in question, is able to ascertain the essentialised groups 'true interests' , which are assumed to be historically and socially fixed.

If one contrasts the two paradigms outlined above with Williams's writing up until *The Long Revolution* (1965) he could not be comfortably equated with either category, while simultaneously being unable to intellectually transcend both set of limitations. The first essentialistic trap of cultural studies, as we saw, encapsulates the writing of Williams's mentor Leavis. While Williams retains some of Leavis's prejudices, his work on popular culture does not assume, as does Leavis's, that all popular forms are intrinsically debased. For Williams film and television were capable of being either the cultural forms of reformed democratic communities, or the cynical expression of domination. As we shall see more clearly later, Williams's writing on synthetic commercial forms of culture is the source of his cultural conservatism.

Further the early Williams often counterpoises a potentially vibrant working-class self-activity to a repressive social system. Here the problem was that the labour movement were failing to be directed by authentic working-class resistance. This allowed the economic system to overly determine the dominant cultural institutions. In other words, in Williams's early writing, the working-class are seen as having historically defined objective interests in line with the long revolution. These interests can be referred to as essential as they are related to Williams's teleological projections on the basis of human nature. But Williams's own paternalistic leanings means that he often romanticises the extent to which the working-class are yearning to express themselves through the dominant culture. Yet his own immersion in educated culture ensures he never celebrates working-class agency for its own sake. Williams is only willing to recognise working-class resistance the extent to which it acts responsibly, and does not challenge the cultural hegemony of the 'great tradition'. If the labour movement collectively decided that their need for cultural institutions was of marginal significance, and what was of overriding importance was a better material standard of living - Williams would have sympathetically disassociated himself from such a productivist project. Again we can see how Williams remained related to essentialist modes of thinking, without ever adopting the compromised stance of other writers.

Hegemony, as a theoretical concept, has on the other hand, the potentiality to theoretically escape the essentialist traps I traced out above. Hegemony demonstrates that 'consent' is structured through a series of social relations, marked by an on going political struggle over competing impressions and views of the world. Gramsci (1982) argues that a ruling bloc can engage in a political and pedagogical struggle for the consent of subordinate groups only if it is willing to articulate some of the values and interests of those groups. Thus a theory of hegemony necessitates at least some form of cultural and ideological incorporation. A ruling hegemonic bloc that could not convince at least some sections of subordinate social groups of its legitimacy would not last very long. Here, I shall argue, that one needs a weak rather than a strong conception of hegemony. Such a definition would explain the mobilisation of consent as always a partial, fractured and contradictory process. There are a number of sociological perspectives that warn against overestimating the degree of consensus that exists in modern social life (Abercrombie,1980; Mann,1970). The notion of a dominant ideology, that is given coherence through a collection of core values, would seem to be a totally discredited concept in modern social theory. But there seems nothing immediately contradictory about agreeing with anti-consensus thinkers, while developing a theory of hegemony.

Following on, ideology shall be discussed as a symbolic process that seeks to justify relations of domination (J.B.Thompson,1984). Williams remains sceptical of a critical notion of ideology, preferring, as we saw in my analysis of structures of feeling, to discuss the term in relation to specific world-views. The reason for Williams's resistance to a critical theory of ideology seems to be connected with his rejection of 'false consciousness' (Williams,1977,p.69). Here, I would argue, instead of a dominant ideology engendering a false as opposed to a true consciousness, ideology should be conceptualised as a process of signification that serves to secure relations of domination. Relations of domination are, according to this view, sustained through discourses which seek to justify rather than criticise asymmetrical social relations. In this respect, ideological forms may foster what Michael Mann (1970) has called pragmatic or normative acceptance, within subordinate social groups. Thus pragmatic acceptance is the ideological closing down of realistic alternatives to existing social relations, where as normative acceptance implies that 'consent' has been mobilised by the ruling hegemonic bloc. Such a definition would not by necessity commit one to a view of ideology that rests on an absolute view of truth. Instead a critical theory of ideology would specifically aim to critique 'false beliefs' , while more generally relating symbolic conceptions of the social to unequal relations of power. Following the writing of Stuart Hall (1988) and Laclau and Mouffc (1985), without committing myself to some of their theoretical assumptions, I shall develop a non-essentialist conception of ideology. This will promote an analysis of domination that takes account of a plurality of forms of domination such as racism, militarism and sexism. But, while Hall, Laclau and Mouffe disconnect hegemony from class essentialism, they fail to separate the terms ideology and culture. By retaining distinctive usages for both terms, I aim to argue that the writing of both Williams and Thompson remains instructive, without being entirely free from error and evasion.

Finally it would seem appropriate to address the nature of the dominant culture into which the labour movement were being incorporated. Williams tends to assume, especially in his writing on culture in the sixties, that the dominant culture of capitalism is both synthetic and homogeneous. These twin assumptions are best brought out by the character Peter in Williams's novel *Second Generation* (1964). Peter reflects on the constraining cultural of capitalism:

> That was the trouble, really, with fashion. This air of fantasy now - in the hairstyles, in the gay dresses, in the glass and bright plastic colours - imposed too single a style. He watched the girls in the street, hurrying to the buses from offices and shops. The elaborate hair, the brightly painted eyes, the short flaring skirts, the patterned emphasis of the tightly enclosed breasts and legs. But if the girls could choose, there'd presumably be every kind of variation. Skirt lengths would go up and down, with each individual, to every conceivable level (Williams,1964,p.148).

The overall impression given by this paragraph (other than voyeurism) is of a constraining cultural sphere, which acts as a rigid regime disciplining docile bodies. Williams uses the terms 'imposed' and 'enclosed' to create the impression of a mass culture that has been forced on the people from the outside - disconnecting the populace from their inner democratic nature. Imposed cultural sameness also has certain implications for the values that lie behind these symbolic forms. Williams describes the popular culture of the sixties as an:

> anti - culture, which is alien to almost everybody, persistently hostile to art and intellectual activity, which it spends most of its time in misrepresenting, and given over to exploiting indifference, lack of feeling, frustration, and hatred (Williams,1962,p.115).

What was initially the creative activity of ordinary people attempting to gain access to dominant institutions, had become mass conformity within an increasingly uniform culture. To talk, as Williams does repeatedly, of a morally debased synthetic culture, fails to address the way social actors interpret culture at the point of reception. Williams took this issue more seriously when he argued for a culture based upon what I shall call democratic realism.

His discussion of popular culture as a 'low' form of cultural practice, also colludes with what Williams describes as massified ways of thinking (Williams,1976).According to Williams, the expression 'the masses' has been coined by intellectuals of the political Right and Left as a means of crudely classifying together diverse social groups. The masses do not exist empirically instead there only exists ways of thinking about people that represents them as such. The use of the term 'the masses' reveals for Williams something about the values of the writer. Not only is the writer repressing the plurality of cultural differences that exist in contemporary society, but is simultaneously demonstrating a lack of concern for lived experiences. Thus Williams is falling into an intellectual trap of his own making. Instead of addressing the way social agents actively make sense of a commodified culture, in specific power relations, under certain historical conditions - he prefers to contrast a rich literary culture with a superficial popular culture.

The argument that the long revolution was becoming engulfed in a uniform market culture, misrepresents the forms of political and cultural domination that exist within British society. It would seem reasonable to suggest that just the opposite of what Williams is arguing is true. Post-war society has not seen the growth of a more homogeneous culture, but the explosion of cultural distinctions that are the worked upon response of social groups divided and unified around class, age, sex and ethnicity. The problem for exponents of radical change is not that oppressed groups are integrated into a dominant hegemonic culture, rather that these groups are culturally divided. In short, dominated groups have been unable to achieve the symbolic unity necessary for a counter-hegemonic strategy. As Laclau and Mouffe(1985) have argued at length; if the working-class can not be thought of as a culturally unified hermetically sealed unit, which it can not, then this must have a profound effect on how you seek to mobilise them for change.

Democratic realism

The long revolution advocates a structure of feeling based on democratic realism; this is articulated against the synthetic cultural forms I discussed above. In keeping with this project, the democratisation of the means of communication would allow for the expression of authentic points of view, less subservient to the demands of dominant institutions. This remains a radical project in a society where the state has encroached upon the media's independence and certain dominant interests control the political economy of the mass media. But, as we shall see later in E.P.Thompson's writing on the Cold War, such a perspective does not address how the media construct and contextualise marginal voices. It is not just, as Williams assumes, that representatives of alternative perspectives are not heard. More to the point is the way in which forms of mass communication culturally frame the debate, and how these messages are interpreted by the audience.

While many critics would support, in sentiment at least, Williams's desire to democratise the means of communication; his commitment to artistic forms of realism is more difficult to defend. Williams's discussion of realism bears a close connection to the early Lukacs. Williams (1979) shares Lukacs's concern that realism should portray the individual as being in a dialectical relationship with society. An artist commitment to realism should avoid portraying individuals as isolated from society - as did much Expressionist drama (Williams 1968) - without representing the same individuals as being crushed under the dominant symbolic order. Realist forms of art are characterised by what Williams calls an 'attitude to reality' (Williams 1989). This is offered, by Williams, in preference to more traditional conceptions of realism that tend to connect the term to a certain

40

naiveté in relation to issues of representation. For the artist to call himself a realist, in Williams's terms, she has to take two problems seriously. The first is, as with Lukacs, to make the radical move of going beneath 'outward appearances' to what the artist believes is 'really going on' . Edward Said(1983) characterises the realism of Lukacs:

> the very act of looking for process behind what appears to be eternally given and objectified, makes it possible for the mind to know itself as subject and not as a lifeless object, then to go beyond empirical reality into a putative realm of possibility (Said,1983,p.232).

The second problem is one of reception; the artist should try to secure, as far as possible, that she is reaching the target audience and that the work is being understood in line with her intentions. One of the reasons why realism remains a progressive force is that it embodies the structure of feeling of working-class writers (Williams 1984). The British working-class, according to Williams, were initially sceptical of the novel as a genre and took to an autobiographical form of expression, which formed a more obvious relationship with 'lived experience' .

So far I have presented the discussion as if there is a broad consensus between Lukacs and Williams on the subject of realism. However Lukacs argues that realist cultural practices directly represent social and economic reality as if it were a reflection in a mirror (Rose 1978). Williams would surely disagree. Writing, for Williams, as with other cultural practices, does not reflect reality but actively produces it in symbolic forms. The writer as an active creative agent is a common theme in Williams's work. He carries this theme through his early cultural romanticism, to his later more sophisticated theory of cultural materialism. Williams writes on the English novel:

> It was a creative working, a discovery, often alone at the table; a transformation and innovation which composed a generation out of what seemed a separate work and experience. It brought in new feelings, people, relationships; rhythms newly known, discovered, articulated; defining the society, rather than merely reflecting it ; defining it in novels, which had each its own significant and particular life (Williams,1985a,p.11).

41

The difficulty Williams has, however, is in squaring the creativity of the writer with what I described earlier as his tendency to set up homologous relationships in structures of feeling. Yet Williams must, on at least some level, believe that agents are to a large extent capable of choosing and forming themselves; otherwise there would be little sense in attempting to persuade artists to adopt a realist mode of representation.

The broader issue still remains; whether or not realism in an age which is suffering from a crisis of representation in both an artistic and political sense is an adequate genre for a radical politics. Roland Barthes (1974) has made two related criticisms concerning realism's adequacy for this task. Firstly, realist fiction treats language as being identical to the real world and structures the various discourses it employs to produce this effect. Secondly, the realist text also produces a unified subject position from which the unfolding of the narrative can be read. The dominant reading position represses the way in which the text is produced not by an isolated creative genius, but out of an intertextuality of writing and discourse. For Barthes the idea of a radical realist text is a contradiction in terms; the text is being asked by the writer to address contradiction and struggle on the level of the information conveyed to the reader, while simultaneously repressing it from the narrative. Alternately the radical readable text should produce a certain noise made up of 'connotations and not superimpositions' (Barthes 1974,p.122) This breaks with the naturalness of bourgeois ideology by not reproducing it within the texts internal organisation.

Williams answers these criticisms, without ever directly addressing Barthes himself. Williams does not examine language as a theoretical problem until the development of cultural materialism in *Marxism and Literature* (1977). But he consistently recognises that language is always something more than the reflection of external reality. As Williams argues:

> The real communicative 'products ' which are usable signs are, on the contrary, living evidence of a continuing social process, into which individuals are born and within which they are shaped, but to which they then also actively contribute, in a continuing process. (Williams 1977,p.37)

For Williams (1984a) the very act of transforming ideas and experiences into writing; changes the way the author himself perceives the initial impetus. Experience can never be directly transported onto the blank page. Writing is always an act of interpretation. Thus Williams clearly believes along with Barthes that there is a division between language and the real. Where as Barthes may have a point to make against Lukacsian realism - Williams develops a more sophisticated position. Further Williams's (1968) writing on drama amply demonstrates that he had always maintained a sharp distinction between realism as a form of representation, and a realist aesthetic on the part of the artist. Realism, which historically developed out of a theatrical naturalism, is portrayed by Williams, as a dramatic illusion rather than the direct unmediated representation of reality.

Barthes's second criticism concerning realism's acclaimed tendency to construct dominant reading positions is also considered by Williams. Many of the texts, according to Williams, that are usually referred to as realist do not provide a unified position from which the text can be read. More often the case, the text, or horizon of the text in question, is internally contradictory resisting a so called dominant reading. Williams (1984b) makes this clear in an essay on Dickens's novel Hard Times . The internal construction of the novel is drawn from two contradictory perspectives. For Williams, Dickens argues, that the environment absolutely determines character and that certain subjects can change the environment.

If we follow Williams, and characterise realism as a specific attitude to reality, instead of an outmoded theory of representation, then this seems to question Barthes's theoretical characterisation of the genre. This allows one to be a realist, and take a more sophisticated stance on language and representation than Lukacs. Disturbingly, Barthes does not seem to address the question as to which social groups are going to interpret the sort of cultural forms he is advocating. In stark contrast, Williams (1989a) contends that the realist aesthetic must firmly connect with the structure of feeling of the audience, and that its ability to perform this function is decisive in assessing the politics of a text or performance. While Williams overestimates the extent to which authors can influence how their texts are interpreted; if one's intention is to stimulate public debate through artistic and cultural practices, then one can not help but ask questions as to how one's contributions are likely to be received.

What I have termed democratic realism is democratic to the extent to which it widens the number of perspectives and social groups that have access to the media, and realist in that it symbolically captures 'what is really going on' . This form of practice is in opposition to Williams's description of a synthetic mass culture; the product of the economic systems dominance over the cultural. The long revolution seeks to redress this balance by opening up channels of communication to create a culture in common. This process is guided by the responsible nature of the labour movement and a new generation of cultural contributors. Later we shall see later that while Williams's commitment to a communicative culture is preferable to the revival of a modernist avant guard - his ideas have to be considerably revised to take account of contemporary cultural processes.

2 Cultural materialism, ideology and socialism

In the preceding chapter we saw how Williams's writing retained an affinity with that of Leavis. Here, I will argue, that Williams adopted an increasingly materialist account of culture, which further distanced him from cultural idealism and sharpened his theoretical commitment to the sociology of culture. Approaching a fully worked out account of 'cultural materialism', Williams's writing moved through a transitional stage with the production of *The Country and the City* (1973) and *Television, Technology and Cultural Form* (1974).

The Country and the City (1973) is an analysis of the shifting representations of urban and rural life that can be found in literary and poetic writing. The work of art was no longer perceived by Williams to be the mediated reworking of a 'knowable community'. Instead the text was more specifically conceived of as an interpretation formed within historically determined literary conventions that did not reflect a particular class ideology. Here Williams attempts to clearly establish a theoretical separation that he had not previously achieved. His revised account of culture enabled him to draw a distinction between a historical period as such, and those representations that were of 'value' in the received literary traditions. Thus Williams had both theoretically revised his tendency to construct homologous relations between the text and the class position of the writer, and, quite notably, abandoned his notion of an ideal culture. The more materialist account of cultural processes offered in *The Country and the City* (1973) is captured through his discussion of pastoral poetry. The origins of pastoral poetry can be traced back to before the birth of Christ, and give expression to two

45

historically related experiences of the landed labourer. The first was a popular form of protest against 'a reduction of most men to working animals, tied by forced tribute, forced labour, or bought and sold like beasts' (Williams, 1985). The other interconnected tradition was one that celebrated and glorified the physical beauty of nature. But the critical and penetrative aspect of pastoral poetry became repressed when the cultural form fell under the hegemony of the aristocracy. By focusing on the aesthetic content of nature this converted the received tradition of the pastoral into an affirmation of the feudal order.

Williams's second book on television, *Television, Technology and Cultural Form* (1974), developed a more substantially materialist approach than he had previously adopted in *Communications*. (1962). His primary concern here is to distance himself from sociological explanations that rest on forms of abstraction such as technological determinism. The attempt to explain a cultural form, such as television, in a narrative of scientific progress does not allow for an adequate account of human intentionality, or for the theoretical realisation of the complex relations between capital and the state that have had a determining impact on the development of the mass media. According to Williams, cultural forms should be analysed from an historical perspective that seek to explain culture through the institutional organisation of the cultural relations of production

Cultural Marxism: considerations in base and superstructure

The theoretical developments around base and superstructure have emerged as one of the central problems of contemporary Marxist theory. A writer who seeks to employ a notion of base and superstructure is normally taken to mean that developments in the economy set limits upon, or have and explanatory priority over, the superstructure. These debates have of course a long and chequered history within the Marxist tradition. The base and superstructure model has been the subject of serious scrutiny in the social sciences, and would now appear to be a largely discredited means of explaining social change (Geras,1987;Giddens,1981,1985; Held,1987,1989; McLennan, 1989). Despite Williams's conversion to a more avowedly Marxist philosophical position, at no point in his intellectual career can he be regarded as a defender of the base/superstructure argument. In *The Long Revolution* (1965) Williams discussed four theoretically separate, but interconnected systems called maintenance, decision, communication and nature. Williams's later theory of cultural materialism similarly distinguishes separable levels of analysis, which following Althusser, were critical of Hegelian forms of totalising thinking that sought to explain the mechanisms of the social structure through the discovery of an uncoverable essence. But, where Althusser was referring to essentialising definitions of human nature, Williams turns the argument back on Althusser's own perspective. Williams, contrary to Althusser, argues that the demand that the base be thought of as determining even in the 'final analysis ' is overly reductive. With this in mind, there would seem to be a number of arguments , scattered through Williams's later writing, as to why social theorists should abandon the base/superstructure metaphor. Let us unpack these items.

Marxist arguments that employ the base/superstructure model often reduce the superstructure to a dependent realm of ideas that reflect a material economic base. This danger inherent in the base/superstructure argument runs counter to Williams's desire to make cultural practices material. The cultural, for Williams, is made up of signifying material practices that combine an idealist and a material component. Williams writes:

> (a) an emphasis on the 'informing spirit' of a whole way of life, which is manifest over the whole range of social activities but is most evident in 'specifically cultural' activities - a language, styles of art, kinds of intellectual work; and (b) an emphasis on a 'whole social order' within a specifiable culture, in styles of art and kinds of intellectual work, is seen as direct or indirect, product of an order primarily constituted by other social activities (Williams,1981,p.p.11-12).

By focusing on actual cultural practices, Williams would argue, he is able to respect their material and significatory specificity within a social order, in a way that is absent in the the Marxist tradition. In *The Grundrisse* (1973), Marx argued that a crafts person who constructed a piano out of raw materials was involved in a productive activity, where as the pianist who plays the piano was not. This was because, for Marx, the maker of the piano was directly involved in a set of social relations that reproduce capital, which was not true of the person playing the piano. Williams, contrary to Marx, insists that the material practice of playing the piano cannot be reduced to an idealist moment in the superstructure. Instead the pianist and the piano maker are both involved in a productive activity that was simultaneously material and symbolic. Previously, as we have seen,

Williams represented culture as a 'whole way of life', that received its most original contributions in literary and artistic movements. Culture, in theory at least, was now made up of material signifying practices that are no longer blandly assumed to be part of a 'whole way of life', but structured into hegemonic traditions, institutions and formations. Later, through a comparison between cultural materialism and the writing of Pierre Bourdieu, I shall demonstrate that Williams had a distinct tendency to privilege material over symbolic definitions of cultural forms, in such a way that displaces the symbolic production of meaning. Also, and connected with this argument, Williams remained committed to forms of 'high' culture that precluded a detailed investigation of more popular forms. One major source for Williams's (1980b) emphasis upon culture as a material rather than a symbolic process comes from his reading of Timpanaro. Timpanaro argues, in *On Materialism* (1976), that human beings are more significantly formed through their common biological structures than they are through economic and cultural practices. Men and women have what Timpanaro describes as a 'passive relationship' to nature, rather than the active transformative role ascribed to them by Marx. To talk, as Marx does, of men and women coming to historically dominate nature, obscures the more powerful relation that nature has over human beings. While Williams wants to disassociate himself from Timpanaro's biological determinism, cultural materialism was also an attempt to express the relationship between the biological and the social. Thus the reproduction of the sound of a human voice, accompanied by musical instruments, involves material and significatory components. The material aspect utilises the expression of certain bodily or biological practices that enables the production of the 'sound', where the signifying element of the music is captured by the lyrical content or the style of the music being played.

The separation of the base from the superstructure produces a reifying abstraction that is characteristic of bourgeois social theory. The material base and the idealist superstructure are thought of as fixed 'essences' that are not informed by historical processes. In other words, in discussing the base as separate from the superstructure, one could easily fall into the trap of viewing the base as a fixed technological abstraction, rather than the result of human agency. Williams makes a related criticism of the linguistic theory of Saussure in *Marxism and Literature* (1977). Saussure is shown to be guilty of what Williams describes as 'objective materialism'. Saussure's error lies in his famous theoretical separation between langue and parole, which prioritises the structure of language, over language as a form of human praxis performed in social contexts. Here Williams writes:

> Language came to be seen as a fixed, objective, and in these senses 'given' system, which had theoretical and practical priority over what were described as 'utterances' (later as 'performance'). Thus the living speech of human beings in their specific human relationships in the world was theoretically reduced to instances and examples of a system which lay beyond them(Williams,1977,p.27).

Williams's criticisms could also be aimed at structuralist and post-structuralist writers who have utilised Saussure. Foucault and Althusser, for example, can be said to have subsumed a notion of agency to structure, similar to the way Marxist theory has focused on the base to explain the development of modern society. On the other hand, Williams's argument that the reproduction of structures like language can only be understood through the intersection of agency and structure, should not be construed as an endorsement of certain naïve humanist versions of the subject. In the writing of Sartre (1966), for example, language has a natural exteriority that left the existential subject unchallenged. The writer has the task of coming to subordinate language to his or her will in order to communicate with others. Williams, unlike Sartre, does not conceive of language as a passive tool to be manipulated by an external agent, instead language is conceptualised as a constitutive process. Individuals are born into a pre-existing structure of language that, 'is at once their socialisation and their individuation' (Williams,1977,p.37). The materiality of language, therefore, allows social agents to be creative through their use of language in everyday contexts. But, despite my endorsement of the general drift of Williams's argument, he does not ever provide an adequate discussion of questions of structure and agency.

To accept that the economic base has a priority over cultural institutions and expression, according to Williams, unintentionally conforms to a debate that has been framed by the supporters of capitalism. Apologists for capitalism have traditionally argued that industrial productivity has precedence over artistic and cultural production, while Marxists have similarly sought to defend the dominance of the base through a discussion of 'primary production'. Primary production, Marxists assume, can be credited with a certain precedence as it aims to satisfy basic material needs, such as physical requirements for food and shelter. But, Williams argues, human needs cannot be politically confined to the need for food and shelter.

There are needs that can only be satisfied by human forms of community. Human beings have a basic need for connection and belonging with others that can only be realised through democratically organised institutions and shared social practices. This need is most often satisfied in the act of communication through literature, political commitment and in our everyday social relations. The others who one needs to communicate with are often not immediately present in face to face encounters, but have to be recovered from the past or brought into more direct forms of dialogue through the democratisation of cultural institutions. Williams's emphasis upon a richer and more diverse combination of human needs forms the basis of his critique of impoverished economistic thinking that is prevalent in both conservative and radical modes of thought.

To theoretically privilege the base over the superstructure has led to an isolation of cultural questions from issues related to economic organisation. Williams (1980a) shared with other cultural Marxists, such as Barho, the conviction that economic rationality should be subordinated to social and cultural goals. The problem being, for Williams, that in contemporary capitalist and socialist societies economic production is valued over other cultural activity. The concept of the long revolution was fashioned as a theoretical critique of traditional Labourist and Marxist-Leninist emphasis upon problems of political economy, that were often considered in isolation from cultural questions. Williams, for his part, insists that the economic realm should be readjusted from the vantage point of the cultural sphere, in such a way as to promote human growth and enlightenment.

Marxists as a consequence of these four arguments need to redefine what they mean by 'forces of production'. The forces of production, in the cultural materialist argument, cannot be restricted to the means by which a society creates an economic surplus. The forces of production are instead a whole set of material cultural practices, including economic practices, that help to define the basic character of a social order. These practices are embedded in institutional structures, such as the media, publishing companies, the education system, and multinational manufacturing concerns, and are simultaneously in relations of variable autonomy. While the historical materialist is concerned with the objective laws of historical development, the cultural materialist should, according to Williams, keep a firm grip on social totality, while tracing out the actual relations of a variety of economic, political and cultural institutions and practices.

Arguments in agency and structure

Williams intellectually shifted his ground between his first explicit formulation of agency and structure in *Modern Tragedy* (1966), and the later *Marxism and Literature* (1977). The discussion in *Modern Tragedy* (1966) seems to have been influenced by his reading of Brecht, who is a key figure in Williams's (1968) later books on drama. Williams writes:

> we both create and transcend our limits, and that we are good and evil in particular ways and in particular situations, defined by pressures we at once receive and can alter and can create again (Williams,1966,p.213).

In his writing on Brecht, Williams represents what is normally referred to as the dialectical conception of agency and structure. This view has a tendency, while recognising social subjects as capable of agency, to overestimate the extent to which human agents are faced with an ultimately manipulable social reality. The dialectical view, in the writing of Williams and Brecht, loses sight of the degree to which society is a precondition of human activity, rather than being the direct product of it. Williams, as we have seen, revises this approach in *Marxism and Literature.* (1977). Here, through the writing of Volosinov, Williams was able to theoretically question the Durkenheimian opposition between the individual and society. Williams represents the subject as always amounting to more than the product of objective structural categories; being capable of intentionality and moral reflexivity. But, despite Williams's considerable efforts in this direction, his intellectual connection to Timpanaro often led him to theoretically reproduce a notion of the individual that was formed not only materially, but also socially through an underlying biological structure. Further, Williams's account of institutional processes often seemed to oppose, in a way that was not true of his discussion of language, determining social structures and the intentionality of cultural producers.

Hegemony

His first explicit discussion of hegemony was written in a 1973 *New Left Review* article called *Base and Superstructure in Marxist Cultural Theory* (Williams, 1980c). Hegemony is defined, consistently with the incorporation thesis, as a core set of values that are transmitted by dominant cultural institutions. There is again a certain vagueness that pervades Williams's writing; he does not explore what these core values are, or how they are connected to the reproduction of dominant social relationships. Later, however, in *Marxism and Literature* (1977), Williams revises his concept of hegemony in an attempt to overcome a number of related difficulties which he associates with the concept of ideology. They can be conveyed in three basic points, outlined below.

The Marxist tradition has tended to reduce ideological representations to a reflective relationship with the material base. In *German Ideology* (1963), Marx, through the use of his famous camera obscura metaphor provides the most obvious basis to this tradition of thinking. This approach, for Williams, is guilty of a dualism which he calls 'mechanical materialism'. The 'brute facts' of material existence would, if Marx were correct, imprint themselves on the consciousness of men and women. Here Williams proposes that culture should be analysed neither as ultimately separable from economic or institutional relations, nor as reducible to them. Instead culture is produced through material social practices that are institutionally separate but related to the economic system. Williams writes:

> the idealist separation of 'ideas' and 'material reality' have been repeated, but with its priorities reversed. The emphasis on consciousness as inseparable from conscious existence, and then on conscious existence as inseparable from material social processes, is in effect lost in the use of this deliberately degrading vocabulary' (Williams,1977, p. 59).

Williams (1977) argues theories of ideology often lapse into an elitist discourse. The detached social theorist places him or her self into a complex intellectual tradition, that is radically separate from the lives of the masses who are represented as slaves to an ideology. The focus of Williams's attack here would seem to be those social theorists, whom following Althusser (1984), made a neat conceptual split between science and ideology. Althusser, and others, assume that Marxist social theorists are able to objectively attribute certain interests to agents independently of the way they actually make sense of the world. While Williams also assumed that there was a close link between the working-class and socialism, that, as we saw contained certain reductive assumptions, he did however, always attempt to connect the long revolution to the aspirations of ordinary people. Here, as we will see later, he is making a similar argument against

Althusser, to that of E.P. Thompson in *The Poverty of Theory* (1978a). To radically oppose a revolutionary science, practised by party intellectuals, to a mass ideology, is to obscure how men and women have historically formed 'lived' connections with a radical tradition. This is always, for both Williams and Thompson, an uncertain historical process of discovering cultural connections with others in communities and political movements. In addition, the science/ideology distinction, is not able to adequately account for forms of practical consciousness that provide the basis of everyday interactions. For Williams and Thompson in Althusser's reading everything outside of the Marxist academy thereby becomes a sphere exclusively dominated by scientifically refutable false beliefs. Instead a notion of practical consciousness would argue that there are spheres of activity, such as brewing beer or baking bread, which it would seem absurd to argue form part of a dominant ideology.

The way that some social theorists have employed the term ideology effectively reduces the cultural to the ideological. I can think of a number of social theorists, following Althusser (1984), who have made this move (Laclau and Mouffe 1985, Hall 1988). In *Culture* (1981), Williams suggests, that one should maintain a specific usage for the term ideology, otherwise the concept would seem to lose its critical purchase. In this context, consistently with his concept of structures of feeling, Williams uses the term ideology to signify a distinct set of ideas and beliefs that are internally held and produced by a particular class or social group. Here a concept of hegemony was particularly useful for Williams as it enabled him to argue that cultural practices are hegemonically organised through dominant social institutions.

The manner in which Williams deployed the term hegemony is never, in keeping with his emphasis on historical process, static or systematic in its formation. Hegemony is always characterised as a fluid process, which is produced out of internal contradictions, and competing counter-hegemonic positions. The hegemonic, in Williams' analysis, is a combination of three cultural processes, these are; traditions, institutions and formations.The hegemonic culture is constantly being invented and reinvented, while being presented as fixed, final and neutral. What a nation-state defines as traditional has always already assimilated dissenting voices into its midst. The establishment of a hegemonic version of tradition is dependent on a collection of state and private institutions, that materially produce and reproduce particular selected versions of the past and present. For Williams the most important of these institutions are the mass media and the education system, which never neatly reproduce a dominant ideology, but are the sight of a contested cultural politics. If Williams, for example, had argued that the literary traditions that have been institutionalised in University curriculums unambiguously secured the structural dominance of the ruling class, this would undoubtedly have cast a heavy shadow over any political project that sought to broaden access to the existing cultural institutions. Within any dominant institution, there are always sites of contestation and dispute, even if on the whole they will be internal to the historically defined dominant hegemony. Finally, within Williams's concept of hegemony, formations are conscious movements and tendencies like literary movements that often see themselves in direct opposition to the values upheld by modern institutions. But, in Williams's writing, literary formations often misrecognise their distance from the central value system of the hegemonic bloc. Williams challenged the predominant self-image of literary formations when he wrote:

> it can be persuasively argued that all or nearly all initiatives and contributors, even when they take on alternative or oppositional forms, are in practice tied to the hegemonic: that the dominant culture, so to say, at once produces and limits its own forms of counter-culture (Williams, 1977,p.114).

In Williams's posthumously published *The Politics of Modernism* (1989c), he argues that the early twentieth century modernist movement held no overt political affiliations other than being anti-bourgeois. The deep political ambiguity of the modernist movement is characterised by Williams through the political biography of August Strindberg. In January 1921, Strindberg participated in a procession of revolutionary Stockholm workers, having previously allied himself to a Rightist denunciation of democracy. This can not be explained simply in terms of a change of mind by Strindberg, but for Williams, goes right to the heart of the politics of modernism. The claims to liberation made by the avant-garde against the bourgeoisie, whom the artist must shock and deride, is informed by a structure of feeling of robust individualism that denies all connection with others. Williams identifies this strand of thinking as lying behind Nietzsche's and Strindberg's anti-feminism and aggressive masculinity. In more contemporary times the modernist stress on the 'sovereign individual' can be found historically informing the discourse of the contemporary New Right.

As the relationship between tradition, institutions and formations are historically variable the cultural sociologist should also consider what Williams calls the dominant, the residual and the emergent. The residual and the emergent are an association of cultural practices that are contained within the dominant hegemony. The residual operates as a cultural 'overhang' from previous dominant cultures that still has an active purchase on the experience of the present. Williams' treatment of the pastoral in *The Country and the City* (1973) i s representative of what he meant by the residual. Although pastoral poetry had been largely assimilated by the dominant meanings and values of the aristocracy it also contained a structure of feeling that remained critical of contemporary societal relationships. On the other hand, the emergent culture is continually articulating new ways of thinking and feeling. A culture that was emergent would ultimately contain fragments of the dominant culture, along with certain cultural 'penetrations' that sought to undermine dominant hegemonic values. Moreover, the recognition that the emergent, the residual and the dominant are all hegemonic should not blind the cultural theorist to the argument that:

> no mode of production and therefore no dominant social order and therefore no dominant culture in reality includes or, exhausts all human practice, human energy, and human intention, on the contrary it is a fact about the modes of domination, that they select from and consequently exclude the full range of human practice (Williams,1977,p. 125.).

But, despite this final remark, Williams consistent with my earlier comments, considerably overestimates the cohesive power of hegemonic practices.

Towards 2000

The struggle for a democratic socialist society, in terms of the long revolution, remains central to a critical appreciation of Williams's writing. His most consistent attempt to revise this commitment can be found in *Towards 2000* (1983). Since his earlier formulation of these issues in *The Long Revolution* (1965) there have been four major social changes that led him to reconsider his initial arguments. These four interrelated societal shifts were the emergence of the new social movements, the threat to peace and security posed by the Cold War, the increasing globalisation of capital and the rise of the New Right.

As before the labour movement remained the central agency for change, despite its inability to mobilise the population around the objectives of the long revolution. The organised working-class had been unable to counter a double sided process that both normatively integrated subjects into capitalism, while fragmenting interest groups who articulated differing perspectives in the public sphere. Processes of cultural fragmentation meant that the labour movement could no longer be equated with the socialist movement. Instead the dominant structure of feeling of the late twentieth century was such that it became increasingly difficult for one to construct a notion of a general interest, in opposition to those who sought to celebrate difference, or those who pragmatically accepted the dominance of a competitive market.

The division between the long and short term goals of the working-class acted as a barrier to the achievement of a socialist society. For Williams, the labour movement and the new social movements both shared a common enemy and set of objectives in transcending capitalist society. These common interests, however, could not be politically articulated while the relevant political groupings failed to come into dialogue with one another. Williams calls the dominant disposition militant particularism.

The socialist movement in order to counter the tendency towards fragmentation had to be reformulated to politically secure the satisfaction of primary needs. Primary human needs are loosely defined by Williams in this context as the need for 'peace, security, a caring society and a careful economy' (Williams, 1983). These needs could not be met by the capitalist market economy, which was inherently undemocratic, profit oriented and ecologically dangerous. Williams's (1988a) essay *Towards Many Socialism's* argues for a socialist politics that rejected centralised state planning by embracing the idea of complex planning. Complex planning, he argues, involves a number of decentralised planning initiatives that aimed to maximise the number of institutions based upon self-management. Such a socialist programme should thereby be able to meet primary needs, while acting in the general interest.

Capitalism ensured the dominance of a certain form of rationality that Williams described as Plan X. Plan X, as a form of instrumental reason, has systematically failed, by focusing upon short term gains, to raise issues related to the ultimate ends of political agency. The dominance of Plan X has led to an attitude of pragmatic adoption to the existing agenda. This colludes with the hegemonically secured disposition of atomised individuals pragmatically pursuing short

56

term goals. The dominance of a specifically capitalist rationality ensured:

> a totalitarian and triumphalist practice in which, to the extent it succeeds, there is nothing but raw material: in the earth, in other people, and finally in the self (Williams, 1983,p.262).

Hence, similar to his critique of modernism, the greatest task facing political theory was no longer to connect the working-class with a humanising literary sensibility, but to combat the destruction of the ethic of community and economic reason.

History, domination and discontinuity

In the preceding chapter, part of the criticism that was levelled at Williams was that he did not have an adequate theory of historical interpretation. This was due to the intellectual dominance exercised by Leavis and practical criticism over Williams's thought. Williams' s attachment to practical criticism meant that he failed to account for his own historicity and immersion in culture and ideology. He tended to assume that the meaning of texts could simply be 'read off' without the need of an interpretative framework.

Williams came to recognise the importance of some of these problems particularly with the writing of *The Country and the City*. (1973). The writing of history, for Williams, as it was for E.P. Thompson, inevitable involved the choosing of sides. Thus the recovery of the critical element within the pastoral was a political attempt to reconnect a rural working-class with their own history. Williams defended this move on both ethical grounds and in terms of his own personally felt connectedness with the rural Welsh working-class of his childhood. Williams had become aware that the cultural historian was always writing within a tradition that is in alignment with certain historical communities and political-moral positions. Williams's deeper awareness of his own historicity, that probably came through his relationship with E.P. Thompson, is more precisely alluded to in his article *Art: Freedom as Duty* (1988b). Williams presents us with an argument which was as applicable to himself, as it was to other cultural producers. He writes:

> We should be trying to understand alignments not just as conscious choice or commitment or bias, although these

things happen at certain important stages of life, but also in terms of those things which are, so to say in-built, which are the ground of our real connections with our own people and our own time (Williams, 1988b,p.p.94-95).

The task of the radical critic was no longer the preservation of a set of absolute human values contained in the great work of art. Instead Williams was writing to produce a notion of historical process for the oppressed, and particularly for the working-class. Dai Smith, in this respect, argues, that Williams's novels have consistently attempted to redefine his own sense of national identity. Williams decisively distanced himself from the romantic mythology of a rural Wales that is often contained within Welsh folk museums. *The People of the Black Mountains* (1989b) along with his other novels, particularly *Loyalties* (1985b), offer historical accounts of the formation of current communities. But, as Terry Eagleton (1984) has remarked, the central tragedy of Williams's intellectual contribution was that he consistently failed to reach the broader left-working class audience that he sought. This opened up perhaps an inescapable paradox for Williams. It was through the 'success' of the long revolution that working-class people would encounter the writing of Raymond Williams, but while the political agenda of the late seventies and eighties remained dominated by the New Right, Williams would find himself becoming an increasingly isolated voice.

While Williams had certainly revised his earlier connection to a Leavisite cultural conservatism some of his critics maintain that his presence can still be discerned in his mature writing. Tony Bennett, for example, contends that Williams and Lukacs have:

> concentrated either on constructing a radical and progressive past popular tradition in order that the 'people' might learn from and take heart from the struggles of their forbears, or on constructing 'the people' as the support of 'great culture' so that they might eventually be led to appropriate that culture as their own. Either way, a similar orientation is produced. The struggle for 'the popular' is conceived as one of seeking to displace the current and actual forms of 'the people's' culture so as to replace it with another(Bennett,1986,p.15).

Bennett's proposition would be sound if one focuses, as I have done previously, on Williams's attitude towards popular culture and his

58

continued connection to Leavis. This said, Williams's account is substantially more complex than Bennett suggests. Williams in *The Country and the City* (1973) formally broke with Leavis's nostalgic attachment to feudal organic communities. Williams describes preindustrial societies as reducing people to working animals. If Williams does maintain a nostalgic attachment to the past it is to the Welsh rural working-class community of his boyhood. Williams demonstrates an acute self-awareness of his continued connection to a Leavisite organic community that can still be found in rural Wales, rather than in preindustrial society. It is true that Williams is rarely critical of the kind of rural working-class community into which he was born. In fact he often posits their 'natural' decency against corrupt outsiders. Yet, in opposition to many in the Marxist tradition, he does not treat them as being epistemologically privileged.

In *The Fight for Manod* (1979b) connections have to be made out of political necessity in order to uncover the wider political and social manipulation of multinational capital. These connections intersect the local, the national and the global, and could not be comprehended if one were confined to a Foucauldian local politics. More critically, for Williams, this process involves challenging how things 'appear to be' at the local level in order to form an understanding of larger determining social forces.

Similarly, *Loyalties* (1985b) questions the sense made of collective forms of struggle by the working-class. What is needed, Williams tentatively suggests, is a more complex account that neither treats those persons as sovereign subjects, but also avails the pretence of a divine spectator. Williams (1984c) criticised Orwell on precisely this point; Orwell, for Williams, too often took up the role of the objective commentator that ignored his own cultural prejudices through a certain naïve realism. Williams wrote on this theme in *Loyalties* (1985b), capturing a conversation between university educated Gwyn and his working-class mother Nesta. The dialogue concerns Gwyn's father and Nesta's husband Bert.

> 'I live in the wrong place, Mam. I was smiling to think of him in London: as one of those aggressive militants, those subversive and greedy communist workers.'
> 'They don't know Bert up there. I don't know what you mean?'
> 'That's because you live in the right place.'
> 'Here?' Nesta said, pushing her hand towards the valley, which was now darkening rapidly, with lights springing along it.

'Among people,' Gwyn said, 'who don't need it explained.'
'Well that's where you are wrong, Gwyn. You give us too much credit. We don't hardly understand one thing that's happening to us, and them that make out they do are just in for themselves ' (Williams,1985b, p.105).

While Williams was slow to criticise the social relations in his own community - this would seem particularly evident in the relations between men and women - he is more insistent in undermining their general perception of events in his later novels. But, it is also Williams's often nostalgic attachment to the rural Welsh working-class, that provides him with a critical insight into the destructive rationality of capitalism. This dominant rationality could be critically opposed to an ethic of care that is grounded in traditional practices evident in rural Wales. The act of mending a stone wall, or planting and growing crops, presupposed for Williams, a notion of connectedness with the environment and with other people, that is often denied expression by economic forms of rationality. To refer back to the earlier discussion, while Bennett is justified in his critique of Williams's rather reactionary stance on popular culture, he represses a more critical dialectic that emerges through Williams's writing. Williams's attachments to rural Wales, therefore, not only distanced him from popular culture, but shed light upon many of the destructive practices of the modern world, of which Green movements have made us only too aware. His continued and intensely felt connection to 'his own people' also brought to the fore a critical dialogue in his writing. This critical interchange, despite Bennett's claims to the contrary, never became subsumed with the desire to completely displace people as they actually are.

A matter, however, not subjected to dialectical treatment by Williams is his involvement in working-class family patterns where women remained subordinate to men. Jardine and Swindells (1989) argue that Williams, in the tradition of other left literary figures such as Orwell, is playing on a distinct tradition of the 'comely' family that can be associated with the nineteenth century novel. Williams's more mature thought was at pains to admit that he often neglected feminist analysis. But it remains the case that issues related to masculinity never made a significant impression upon his work. The reasons for this are partly generational, but are also distinct from those of his colleague E.P. Thompson. As we shall see, Thompson often seemed to celebrate a form of masculine agency that did not have the same resonance for Williams. On the other hand, Williams's uncritical relationship with his own family origins disables him from opening up of questions related to power and sexuality. This is particularly marked in relation to Williams's character Kate in *Second Generation* (1964). Kate has an affair with a University professor and is represented as being guilty of a form of class betrayal. She had previously felt trapped into a life of class struggle, often subordinating her own needs to those of her family and her husband's trade union. That this conflict is eventually resolved by Kate re-entering the family with the realisation that she was connecting herself with her people, begs certain questions concerning male domination over women. Another reason that Williams may have had difficulty in developing a theoretical critique of the family was his understanding of the work of Timpanaro. Williams's writing, from *Marxism and Literature* (1977) onwards, wanted to abolish the notion of a private individual formed outside the public categories of language and culture. But, in an essay I want to return to later, called *Problems of Materialism* (1980b), he reasserts this very position. Williams writes:

> It is also when sexual love, the love of children, the pleasures of the physical world are immediately and very powerfully present. To attempt to deny the reality of the kinds of fulfilment that are possible in these ways, even under repressive social orders, to say nothing of social systems which have cleared significant space for them, comes in the end to appear a desperate dogmatism (Williams,1980b,p.13).

The theoretical division between public and private realms is not only a theoretical error, but remains politically conservative because of the extent to which it is uncritical of familial relationships. As these are issues I shall return to, they will not be pursued here, suffice to say, in summary, that Williams's attachment to certain forms of male domination and Leavisite communalism compromised his representations of historical processes.

The sociology of culture; Raymond Williams and Pierre Bourdieu

The writing of Raymond Williams has through its many transitions contributed substantially to the sociology of culture. Williams's arguments can be compared with the equally important contribution made by Pierre Bourdieu, who similarly wants to offer a sociological account of the reproduction of cultural institutions. In what follows, I shall offer a brief synopsis of Bourdieu's writing on culture before moving on to make a critical comparison.

Williams, as we have seen, came to write about the sociology of culture as a means of resolving his interest in Leavisite aesthetics, Western Marxism and post-structuralism. Bourdieu's intellectual lineage is rather different. Like many French post-war intellectuals his writing bears the stamp of structuralism and post-structuralism. However Bourdieu has become progressively critical of this particular theoretical approach. It remains outside the bounds of this book to give the detailed analysis that Bourdieu's writing undoubtedly deserves, instead I shall concentrate on three works that best bring out the comparison between himself and Williams. They are; *Reproduction in Education, Society and Culture* (1977), *Distinction* (1984), and *Homo Academicus* (1988).

Bourdieu's (1977) work on the education system, compiled with his colleague Jean-Claude Passeron, was a sociological investigation in to the symbolic transmission of the dominant culture. The dominant culture of the bourgeoisie secure the material and symbolic interests of the dominant class. Bourdieu and Passeron refer to the dominant culture as 'arbitrary' as its legitimacy is ensured through a cultural process they call symbolic violence. Symbolic violence is the complex process that involves the differential allocation of material and symbolic goods by virtue of social agents positions in institutional structures. The education system, for example, aimed to reproduce the life style of the dominant class through the recognised superiority of the dominant cultural arbitrary. It is ' arbitrary ' in the sense that it is not naturally or biologically pregiven. This can only be imposed by cultural strategies that are misrecognised by social agents as being culturally disinterested.

Bourdieu is not as interested in the specific content of the curriculum as he is in the 'hidden curriculum'. The ideological act of misrecognition is essential to this process; the education system presupposes that each person has the same relationship to language acquisition and has similar cultural dispositions, while assuming what Bourdieu calls the habitus of the dominant class. The habitus is a class specific set of dispositions whose content is determined by the dominant class relationships, in the social field. Hence the habitus of a social class contributes to a particular style of life. This is capable of generating other social practices and being transformed by social institutions. The education system, therefore can be said to have two symbolic functions. They are to secure the institutional conditions for the dominant habitus, and to ensure the systematic misrecognition of these very conditions. The impact of the dominant habitus does not serve to socialise subjects into the cultural patterns required by the economic system, but results in the exclusion of the working-class from the educational system. Through a process of symbolic violence members of the working-class deny themselves further advancement in higher education by recognising that the dominant habitus is superior to their own.

In *Distinction* (1984), Bourdieu further develops his study of the specific class nature of the habitus and cultural forms of domination. The habitus of the dominant class can be discerned through the ideology of natural charisma, or the idea of 'taste' being a gift from nature. In a study mainly based upon information gained from survey material, Bourdieu argues, that the social field contains two basic aesthetic dispositions to the cultural field, they are; the disposition of the bourgeoisie and the popular aesthetic of the working-class. The dominant aesthetic is upheld by those who were socialised into the dominant habitus and those who have accumulated educational capital. Further, it also emphasises the primacy of detachment and contemplation over active forms of involvement. For Bourdieu the dominant life-style is historically born out of the bourgeoisie's separation from material necessity. While there is a distinction to be made within the dominant class between those concerned with material production in the economic sphere, and those concerned with the 'disinterested' production of symbolic capital in cultural institutions, both groups define themselves in opposition to the working-class. The social position of the working-class produces a disposition towards a desire for participation and immediate gratification rather than the contemplative practices of the bourgeoisie. To give an obvious example; the popularity of soccer as a spectator sport amongst working-class males (given the opportunities for participation through fashion, chanting and singing as opposed to the more 'constrained' and the less spontaneous atmosphere one might encounter at a Checkov play) might be explained with reference to the habitus. It is through these two distinct social fields, Bourdieu argues, that social agents interpret modern cultural forms.

Again, as in Bourdieu's earlier study on the education system, it is the ideology of misrecognition that ensures the symbolic dominance of the bourgeoisie. Working-class life styles, on this reading, are culturally dominated and are evaluated from the perspective of the dominant cultural arbitrary. This is true even of those who uphold a life-style in keeping with the popular aesthetic. But, perhaps more importantly, the cultural strategies of the bourgeoisie are commonly perceived to be disinterested. According to Bourdieu:

> culture is the site, par excellence, of misrecognition, because, in generating strategies objectively adopted to the chances of profit of which it is the product, the sense of investment secures profits which do not need to be pursued as profits; and so it brings to those who have legitimate culture as a second nature the supplementary profit of being seen (and seeing themselves) as perfectly disinterested, unblemished by any cynical or mercenary use of culture (Bourdieu,1989,p.86).

Finally, in this introductory section, Bourdieu's study of the academic field *Homo Academicus* (1988) is worthy of consideration. One of Bourdieu's many themes is that academics, akin to others involved in cultural production, exercise strategies of disinterestedness which enable them to conceal from themselves and others the structural relations that make up the field. Hence sociologist's should treat the University as one would any other field concentrating on the relations and strategies which seek to maintain or transform the existing objective relationships. As academic power, according to Bourdieu, can only be accrued through a heavy expenditure of time in various committees, this reduces the overall time available for actual research. In contrast, lecturers in more peripheral academic institutions spend less time in administration and have more academic autonomy, while being well represented in the new disciplines. Bourdieu's intention is not to structure the field in terms of progress and reaction, but to aid the 'scientific' understanding of the way the academic field is constructed. Thus Bourdieu aims to give an objective account of the cultural relations that are evident in the fields of education, taste and the academy. Now that I have introduced the writing of Pierre Bourdieu into the discussion, I shall concentrate upon five areas of convergence between Bourdieu and Williams. Each of the five sections that follow are not only important for an understanding of the writing of Bourdieu and Williams, but are central questions for the sociology of culture generally.

A political economy of culture

Of fundamental importance for Williams' theory of cultural materialism is his break with the base and superstructure model of the Marxist tradition. Williams, I would argue, wanted to retain a certain theoretical openness to historical process without reducing the material operation of cultural institutions to an economic base. In *Television, Technology and Cultural Form* (1974), Williams's analysis of the historical development of television demonstrates that the evolution of cultural forms could not be theoretically understood by marginalising the role played by the modern state. Thus the institutional structure of the state should not be thought of as somehow less 'real' than the economic structure. Instead, Williams offers the reader, an intellectually compelling account concerning the relation of money and power in producing the cultural form we know as television. Williams, probably influenced by E.P. Thompson, seems acutely aware that most Marxist writing on the state has tended to overly concentrate upon its role in reproducing the economic structure. He offers an analysis that is historically specific in its stress upon of the cultural and institutional differences between Britain and the USA, and does not ritualistically presuppose the economic to be determinant, even in the final analysis.

In opposition to Williams, Terry Eagleton (1989) has argued that historical materialism cannot rest on the materiality of social practices, but must address the problem of institutional determination. Eagleton implies that if one does not hold that some practices are more determinant than others - that is economic practices - then the centre would seem to fall out of Marxism. Eagleton makes the point that Williams's attachment to the Marxist tradition seems puzzling if we accept his critique of the base/superstructure model. But, as we shall see later, Williams maintains his connection to Marxism through his writing on political mobilisation. In addition, Eagleton is surely wrong to argue that if one gives up on economic determinism this ultimately means one must defend a form of pluralism, where the theorist blandly describes a proliferation of causes. Returning to Williams's writing in *Television, Technology and Cultural Form* (1974); the material structures of the economic and political system are consistently weighted against forms of technological determinism. Williams is arguing that the economic system and the political system had a determining role to play in the process of television's development. Eagleton's argument, on the other hand, is a form of economic essentialism. This is where the economic is consistently privileged over other practices, even if it is only in that final determining moment that never seems to arrive.

Bourdieu similarly does not adopt the base and superstructure model in seeking to explain the functioning of cultural institutions. Through notions of field and habitus, Bourdieu argues that the education system has its own distinctive set of structural arrangements. The educational field, therefore, should not be thought of as a reflection of the class habitus of the bourgeoisie, as the field, in theory at least, is capable of transforming the habitus itself. A field is constructed through structural distinctions and oppositions that assign positions and attributes as either high or low. Yet Bourdieu, despite his claims to the contrary, seems to be lapsing into a form of economic reductionism. While this is less evident in *Homo Academicus* (1989), as the field does not seem to be structured through the opposition of the two 'essential' classes, it is certainly apparent in the two other works under discussion. As Bourdieu has a distinct tendency to attribute the operation of a field to the relationship between class forces, to what extent, one could object, is it meaningful to argue that a field is autonomous from the economic structure? In *Distinction* (1984), Bourdieu cautiously separates the political and economic fields, but the life-styles of agents is the direct result of class relations and class practices. Bourdieu demonstrates his residual economism when he writes that the working-class habitus generates cultural strategies that:

> rule out all alternatives as mere daydreams and leave no choice but the taste for the necessary (Bourdieu,1984, p.34).

To conceive of the relation between class and culture in such a reductive fashion would not theoretically capture a number of life-style choices, that while remaining related to class, are not directly determined by class positions. In other words, just as Williams created reflective relationships between class and the knowable community, so Bourdieu's (1990) analysis slips into a similar form of reductionism.

Williams and Nicholas Garnham (1986) make a related point when writing on Bourdieu; they argue that while Bourdieu interestingly divides the bourgeoisie into cultural producers and economic producers he underestimates the extent to which this division could be the source of class conflict. Bourdieu's analysis represents the two fractions of the bourgeoisie as occupying a form of symbolic unity around their common class habitus and opposition to the popular

66

aesthetic. Instead Williams, as we saw in his earlier work *The Long Revolution* (1986), argues that the working-class and cultural producers have common interests opposed to the economic power of the bourgeoisie. There is for Williams a conflict of interests between those that are involved in cultural production and those involved in economic production. The conflicts that arise from this opposition, Williams justifiably argues, are not always the result of processes of misrecognition, but are matters of political priority. While Williams is not exempt, as we will see later, from forms of economic reduction, he seems to recognise in his later writing, more concretely than Bourdieu, the need to be aware of reducing cultural expression to class position. Further, his reflections also contain a critique of the colonising power of economic rationality that is abscent in Bourdieu. Bourdieu's intellectual distance from questions of political economy means that he fails to address commodification processes that invade the life-worlds of the working-class and cultural producers. Hence Williams, along with other branches of critical theory, is able to draw attention to the way cultural forms of reciprocity are pulverised by economic reason.Bourdieu's reductive focus on class life-styles seems to bracket off this crucial level of analysis.

Culture and aesthetics

One of the central arguments of *The Long Revolution* (1965) was that there existed an 'ideal' culture that every citizen should have the opportunity to comment upon and criticise. But as Williams develops his theory of cultural materialism he rejects the idea that artistic practices inhabit a separate aesthetic dimension. This is a serious theoretical strategy undertaken by Williams to intellectually reformulate some of the problems I outlined earlier with respect to Leavis's aesthetic theory. Art, in Williams's more material analysis, no longer performs a transcendental function operating as a guide towards human perfectibility. In Williams's revised theory art has become a material practice like any other. This is, on the face of it, a considerable advance given his earlier intellectual attachments, and an important contribution towards the sociology of art. Janet Woolf (1990), recognising Williams's contribution in this area, argues that cultural materialism has been able to combine a specific concern with the social structures and institutions within which art is produced, along with a sociological reading of the text, that grasps literary representations as being social and ideological. This is a break with Williams's earlier defined tendency to treat artistic forms as being both socially produced and as the carriers of absolute moral values. The capacity of cultural materialism to relate artistic production to questions of representation and social relations of production, also acts as a corrective to certain strains in contemporary literary theory.

Much literary theory that has been influenced by writers like Barthes and Derrida has failed to adequately contextualise the institutional production of the text, and is often theoretically hostile to such a move. Further, I would add, that Williams's materialism retains a critique of those theorists who overstate the importance of language. One of the writers who can be perceived as having an important influence on Williams's development of materialist aesthetics is Timpanaro. Williams wrote on Timpanaro:

> he usefully reminds us that certain works of art expressing feelings of sexual love, of fear of death, of grief and loss of the death of others, while undoubtedly varied by particular forms, retain elements of common content which enable them to communicate, actively and not only as, documents beyond and across historical periods (Williams,1980b,p.113).

Kate Soper (1979) has written in defence of Williams's theorisation of Timpanaro that the social and the biological should be seen as interrelated spheres constantly mediating one another. This relationship entails that one can not have an expression of the biological or the cultural in a pure state; instead human beings share a common biological structure which endows them with certain instincts. How these instincts are satisfied, and the value placed on certain physical characteristics, cannot be understood apart from cultural classifications. In common with other Marxist art critics like Peter Fuller (1988), Williams argues that certain biological expressions have an almost timeless significance once they become encaptured in the work of art. This enables the spectator, across dimensions of time and space, to form a culturally mediated understanding of certain works of art that capture human emotions such as love and bodily suffering But, if one reads Williams's later writing on culture as an attempt to bring sociology and literary theory into a closer relationship, then his work still leaves us with a number of unresolved dilemmas.

In *Culture* (1981), Williams was aware of the problem that if artistic practices were merely material signifying practices, then how could one theoretically distinguish between art and non-art? After considering a number of ways of resolving this problem, he decides the issue in favour of what could be called an institutional definition of art. As the relationship between art and non-art is a continually shifting one this makes it difficult to say in any absolute sense what art is, although one way of resolving this problem is to argue that art is whatever becomes presented as art. Hence spectators come to realise that they are viewing a work of art through the operation of significatory signals that 'cue in' the audience, making them aware that they are in the cinema, or at the theatre.

This definition of art would seem difficult to reconcile with the way in which Williams initially constructed the long revolution The 'great tradition' the long revolution was seeking to democratise and bring to the attention of the masses seems to have lost any intrinsic notion of aesthetic value or worth. The aesthetic of the text would therefore seem to be dependent on the creative practice of the artist, and the relationship between form, institution and representation of the social. Despite the intellectual complexity of this theory, William's writing retains a certain amount of confusion over the category of the aesthetic. He expresses this in *Politics and Letters* (1979a), when he replies to a question on the distinctiveness of an aesthetic dimension, he comments:

> I am absolutely unwilling to concede to any predetermined class of objects an unworked priority or to take all the signals as equally valid. We need a very complex typology of occasions and cues, which I think is quite practicable, although it will inevitable be partial (Williams,1979a,p.348).

Williams's dilema is that his new theory of cultural materialism allows him to situate artistic practice socially and historically, without being able to account for the 'specialness' of art. While Williams would certainly want to insist that art and literature remain worthy of study, he recognisably can no longer prioritise the study of art over related critical disciplines such as history, politics and sociology. Although this tension remains unresolved in Williams's writing, he does, at least partially, reformulates the significance of art and literature for the long revolution. It is noticeable that his later writing on the long revolution has very little to say about the working-class engaging critically with the 'great tradition'. In this respect, his attention shifts towards the future realisation of democratic communities. Art and literature remain worthy of intellectual consideration as 'good' art places one in a dialogue with an other. This artistic practices continue to have distinctive and important things to say about the world in which we live.

The need to provide the political and institutional means of communication became a major theme building on what I described earlier as democratic realism. Williams (1989a) stresses the political need to break with the dominant structure of feeling of late capitalism. This expresses feelings of isolation and the difficulties encountered in actual attempts to communicate. In terms of the long revolution, therefore, art is no longer valued explicitly because of its connection to an aesthetic dimension, but because it has historically been a medium through which people have traditionally chosen to communicate their experiences to others. The long revolution is an essential requirement for the promotion of democratic forms of life. This historical process enables communication in an increasingly socially fractured world. But again Williams's social distance from popular cultural analysis means that he is never able to question whether or not the so called dominant structure of feeling is as representative of ordinary people, as it is of artistic movements and formations.

Much of Williams's later writing is not so much concerned with how people interpret the culture of the mass media, fashion, or life-style, as it is to locate artistic movements historically into hegemonic formations. Williams's expressed concern to merge an anthropological definition of culture and a more restricted artistic definition of culture is always weighted in favour of artistic practices. Even after Williams had broken with cultural 'idealism', he never approaches Bourdieu's concern with the cultural practices of everyday life. Bourdieu (1990a), has usefully described the position of the critic, like Williams, who assumes that everyday agents make sense of popular cultural forms in the same way as people in academic communities, as the scholastic fallacy.

In Paul Willis's *Common Culture* (1990), a study of the way young-working class people actively make sense of popular forms, Williams's cultural conservatism is further exposed. Without waiting for the cultural benefits of the long revolution young people are seeking pleasure, autonomy and a sense of self through a commercial culture. Willis would accept Williams's arguments that culture is necessary as human beings are essentially communicating beings, with the self being realised through the recognition of others. However, Willis insists, somewhat contrary to Williams, that it is not only artists and critics who are capable of self-realisation. The symbolic creativity of young people in everyday activity is also dependent upon this process. If anything traditional artistic practices disempower cultural forms of solidarity, because as Williams himself was aware, access to an educated culture is dependent upon the amount of cultural capital one can command. In contrast to educated culture, Willis argues, commercial culture is more democratic in that it is potentially open to everyone. This is not to argue that access to commercial culture is not heavily structurated by social division. However Williams's neglect of issues related to reception means that he is unable to appreciate some of the pleasures and freedoms commercial cultures undoubtedly offer.

Cultural forms, in opposition to some of Williams's writing on popular culture, are incapable, as Willis's research shows, of imprinting the values realised in their production on their consumption. For Willis, writers like Williams, who do not clearly distinguish between the production and the reception of modern cultural forms, are usually unable to account for the possible liberating consequences of much of modern culture. Two examples will suffice to bring out Willis's argument with more clarity. The first is Willis's own. Many young working-class people, if they are able to find paid work, are often employed in occupations that disable the worker from demonstrating very high levels of skill and autonomy. In contrast, their leisure time often involves complex mediations with a diverse number of cultural forms. As Willis writes:

> work relations and the drive for efficiency now hinge upon the suppression of informal symbolic work in most workers, the logic of the cultural and leisure industries hinges on the opposite tendency: a form of their enablement and release. Whereas the ideal model for the worker is the good time kept, the disciplined and empty head, the model for the good consumer is the converse - a head full of unbounded appetites for symbolic things (Willis 1990,p.19).

The other example stems from Paul Gilroy's book *There Ain't No Black In The Union Jack* (1987). In this account, Gilroy convincingly demonstrates that black British popular culture is continually attempting to construct and reformulate traditions in black music that protest against racism. For Gilroy these popular cultural forms represent a utopian yearning for a world where one's race is no longer the subject of the domination of one group by another. Gilroy's and Willis's arguments,taken together, amply demonstrate that those social groups, who were meant to benefit from the long revolution, are already forming attachments to, and seek meaning from, popular forms. Williams's isolation from popular cultural analysis meant that he was unlikely to understand if culturally marginalised social groups express indifference, or even hostility, towards educated culture. Put differently; while Williams was attempting to provide a sense of political process for working-class people, without an understanding of the creative and often political processes that are involved in the reception of popular culture, his hope of connecting with the experiences of ordinary people was unlikely to be realised.

What Bourdieu is able to offer a sociology of culture is a more specific concern to relate culture to socially structured contexts. Bourdieu has an awareness, that is absent in Williams, that symbolic forms are not only produced through asymmetrical relations of power, but the way in which these forms are made sense of is dependent upon a network of ideological and structural relations. While Williams's theory of cultural materialism wants to emphasise the importance of social institutions in cultural production and reproduction, social contexts as we have seen, seem to be absent when one comes to ask how people interpret cultural forms. But however commendable Bourdieu's work might be in appreciating social contexts of reception, the way in which such processes come to be represented in his writing remains open to criticism.

At this point in the analysis, I want to concentrate on the way that Bourdieu links together class and aesthetics by focusing on what he calls the popular aesthetic. I shall defer a critical discussion of the dominant aesthetic until later. As early as *Culture and Society* (1961), Williams had argued, that while the working-class movement's great achievement was the promotion of a collectivist culture and the formation of democratic institutions, there existed no separable working-class culture. Later in his writing however, Williams does discover connections between radical politics and realism, and working-class expression and realism. Similarly Bourdieu also discovers a connection between the working-class and realism. Yet the relationship Bourdieu uncovers is more straight forward then the one offered by Williams. The habitus of the working-class, in Bourdieu's writing, presupposes that those persons acting within its sphere of influence are symbolically communicating through, banter, rudeness and ribaldry (Bourdieu 1977). In *Distinction* (1984), Bourdieu similarly represents the working-class respondents as favouring a form of direct representation, in opposition to cultural products where form has precedence over content. The predisposed desire for more active forms of involvement through actual participation, would seem, from my perspective, to obscure perhaps

72

more feminine aspects of cultural agency. Bourdieu is viewing working-class creativity through similar presuppositions to those often made by the Marxist tradition. Both have an attachment to an active, virile, masculine subject. Terry Eagleton aware of the limitations of such an approach suggests:

> Such an ethical outlook would seem to leave little space for the values of stillness and receptivity, of being creatively acted upon, of wise passiveness and all the more positive aspects of the condition which Heidegger will later term Gelassenheit. There is probably in this sense a certain sexism structural to Marxist thought, as there is also in its privileging of that traditional male preserve, the sphere of production (Eagleton,1990, p.221).

Although Bourdieu's writing does not have the same ethical attachment to masculine self-activity one discovers in the Marxist tradition, he often seems to be reproducing similar prejudices.

In her study of young working-class females, Angela McRobbie (1991) discovers that the lives of the girls are structured in relation to their peers, youth leaders and parents. They are also constructed in distinction to the active nature of the boys. The more passive activity of the girls - that is noticeably ignored by Bourdieu - is a sign of boredom and dissatisfaction rather than apathy, and constitutes a policy of quiet non-cooperation. The girls prefer the commercial culture of fashion, beauty and popular music to the officially organised activities of the youth club or the recognised culture of the school. Through processes of subtle subversion the girls play out on a symbolic level their ideas of femininity. These are expressed through cultural strategies of silent refusal. For instance, by bringing fashionable clothing into the school, the girls were gently undermining the institutional distinction between school and leisure. While the girls refusal to participate in anything other than youth club discos was a source of exasperation for youth leaders, this successfully operated as a defensive strategy by the girls to secure their own symbolic space in a male dominated culture. Other youth cultural studies, such as those undertaken by Willis (1980) and Hebdige (1979), by focusing on the active and visibly available working-class male sub-cultures had failed to explore how their cultured agency is constructed by gendered social relations.This cultural bias, that has become presupposed by investigations into youth culture, has systematically obscured the more subtle patterns of resistance offered by young women.

What McRobbie's study emphasises is that through a culturally reflexive relationship with the family and popular culture; the culture of the girls is both pre-structured and actively worked upon in a less confrontational fashion than their male peers. The writing of Bourdieu serves to obscure this relation. In his terms the more understated agency of the girls would have to be the product of cultural forms of domination based upon class, rather than gender. Alternatively what McRobbie's study brings out is not so much the symbolic operation of class domination, as the importance of gendered social relations. Bourdieu's fields, therefore, seem to be constructed primarily through class relations marginalising, although not ignoring, symbolic relations governed by race, age and gender. His writing would equally seem to obscure those patterns of resistance in the working-class that are not dependent upon masculine forms of confrontation, but follow a more elusive cultural logic.

While I cannot explore these relations here one could conclude;Williams's account is compromised by his attitude towards popular culture, where as Bourdieu seems to have constructed the popular aesthetic in overly masculine terms. Willis's study *Common Culture* (1990), on the other hand, combines both a skilful treatment of the symbolic reception of culture, with an analysis of popular forms that focuses on the structured relations of class, gender and race. This aside; Williams, Bourdieu and Willis, all point towards the connection between realist cultural forms and working-class practices. The problem for Williams however remains that while a popular commitment to realist art forms may, as this is by no means certain, enable the production of a democratic community, the absence of a specific aesthetic dimension generally in his writing undermines the privileged position of the work of art.

Hegemony and symbolic violence

Both Williams and Bourdieu have contributed towards our understanding of cultural forms of domination. While Williams concentrated on the interpretation of literary texts, both writers do share a number of theoretical prejudices in common. Both Williams and Bourdieu believe that there is an identifiable dominant culture however differently they represent it in their respective contributions. They also hold that the stability of Western societies can be explained through the operation of such a dominant culture. This is represented as either incorporating marginalised voices into its structure, or as

74

silencing other more originally oppositional cultural dispositions. While both Williams and Bourdieu offer critical insight into the operation of cultural domination, I shall argue here, consistently with the previous chapter, that both writers fail to develop an adequately critical theory of ideology. Both Williams and Bourdieu systematically overestimate the extent to which social reproduction is dependent upon dominant cultural styles, as well shared norms and values. Finally, on the question of ideology, there remain vital differences between the two writers, the most important being Bourdieu's more sophisticated theorisation of language and social context.

Before we can explain how Bourdieu and Williams sought to expose the operation of ideology, we need to form an understanding of their different conceptions of the dominant culture.The dominant culture, in Williams's writing, finds a coherence around a hegemonic set of norms and values. Our own age is dominated by the structure of feeling of capitalism that can be traced back to, and is informed by, the early modernist movement and the intellectual defenders of capital. The dominant feeling of the modern era is the inability to communicate, the fragmentation of cultural communities, and the belief in the sovereign individual. His analysis of Strindberg and Nietzsche argues that the culture of modernism emphasises a form of individual revolt against the bourgeoisie, and that this rupture could equally be translated into a Leftist or a Rightist political programme. Similar to other analyses of modernity, Williams emphasises that the modernist concern with the feelings of alienation, fragmentation, and exile are intertwined with the experience of migration and the rise of modern cities. Williams has also argued that while this has been the experience of those writers and peoples living in the city; these processes are not universal. There exists a more continuous experience of social change formed by those living outside of the modern metropolis.

For Williams (1989c) the political ambiguity of modernism has been settled in favour of the New Right who celebrate the disconnection and fragmentation of the modern world along with the sovereign individuals right to choose in a free-market economy. As in the early Lukacs (1971), Williams argues that the experience of reification and fragmentation denies the subject a sense of historical process. Given a more ideological reading; a reificatory sense of the present represents the status quo as natural and pregiven, rather than the outcome of historically and socially contextualised agency. One of the primary effects of ideology, would in this reading, be to deny one a sense of solidarity with others and a view of the historical process. This

75

remains Williams's major contribution to a theory of ideology. The task of the left literary theorist, therefore, is to symbolically reimagine modern forms of community, while reconnecting their writing to other traditions, such as socialism, that emphasises human forms of belonging.

While Williams's writing on the dominant culture remains suggestive, there do seem to be a number of flaws in the analysis. Although Williams is correct that the atomised 'responsible' individual is an important configuration of the discourse of sections of the New Right, there are other Rightist elements who would also seek to integrate subjects into wider forms of community (Levitas, 1980). Williams seems unaware that a politics of connection and community can easily fall into the ideological trappings of nationhood and ethnic belonging. Further, Williams would still seem to be overestimating the cohesive power of certain cultural norms and values. Williams's literary rather than sociological orientation can again be questioned. He seems to assume that if artistic formations can be demonstrated as upholding certain values such as the sovereign individual, then it can be reasonably assumed that this belief will be reflected in the population generally. This assumption, given the diversity of critical perspectives that exist in modern society, that are informed by structural and cultural divisions, would seem to be highly dubious. The concept of hegemony, as a theoretical construct, should not be assimilated to a discourse of an ideological cement securing the domination of diverse social groups. Instead - as one finds in the historiography of E.P. Thompson - the term hegemony should be reconceived as a project undertaken by dominant social forces seeking to secure consent. This project, as we shall see, more often than not meets with resistance from below.

Bourdieu, on the other hand, represents the dominant culture rather differently to Williams. He does not so much concentrate upon the content of the dominant culture, but on the style of the dominant aesthetic. Through an ideological process I described earlier; cultural domination for Bourdieu depends upon the symbolic violence of the expressive style of the bourgeoisie. J.B. Thompson (1984) has criticised Bourdieu for over emphasising the extent to which cultural domination is dependent upon the style of what is said, rather than on what is actually communicated. Bourdieu argued, in his study of the reproduction of the dominant culture through the education system, that the teacher should not be thought of as a communicator of knowledge, but rather as a pedagogic authority who impresses the symbolic authority of academic language upon the pupil. In contrast, when Williams considers issues related to the reproduction of institutions, he paid little attention to the status certain linguistic markets held over others, instead he emphasised that domination is exercised through the traditions that are allowed entry into the curriculum. However, building on J.B. Thompson's (1984) contribution, one could argue that any sociological investigation of cultural domination would have to include an account of the content of the messages of modern institutions, as well as the competing linguistic styles that are defined as dominant and subordinate.

If Bourdieu has a greater appreciation of symbolic distinctions, he shares with Williams a tendency to overestimate the power of ideology. His analysis does not seem to appreciate the various social contexts where the dominant style is undermined, without the working-class habitus being defensively reaffirmed. Firstly, we saw in the writing of Angela McRobbie(1991), how young working-class girls subtly subverted the dominant culture of the school by preferring a more commercial culture of beauty products, fashion and popular music. Instead of accepting the legitimacy of the dominant style, the girls developed, through their relations in the home and attachment to popular forms, their own cultural hybrid that was based upon passive rather than active resistance. Bourdieu, as we saw earlier, would have difficulty explaining the cultured agency of the girls given the masculine presuppositions that inform the popular aesthetic. Secondly, other youth cultural studies, such as Willis's (1991) own more famous one, have shown that the more assertive masculine agency of working-class boys is not necessarily seen by the agents involved as being part of an illegitimate or subordinate culture. Indeed, Willis argues, that through the act of rebellion in the school, the 'lads' are reaffirming their connection to a broader masculine working-class community that is evident in public and private spheres. As hopefully these two examples demonstrate; to represent cultural forms of domination one must attend more closely to a diversity of cultural practices.

Finally, I want to argue, that Bourdieu's writing has a greater appreciation of the instability of meaning, than is evident in Williams's theorisation of hegemony. Similar to the method adopted in his discussion of structures of feeling, Williams's writing on hegemony is an attempt to historically fix the meaning of a text. His reformulated theory of textual interpretation not only characterises the extent to which Williams believed that meaning was the stable invariant property of the text, but how close he remained to the methods of practical criticism. The central values of the text are 'revealed' by Williams in order that he can position them into hegemonic positions that correspond with what he called the dominant, the emergent and the residual. Williams is still scrutinising texts for their underlying moral values. The difference being that he is now at least partially aware of the role his own political prejudices play in this process. He has, however, discontinued the Leavisite practice of uncovering the central values of the text so that they may be preserved in the face of a 'machine civilisation'.

Williams's inability to treat meaning as a multi-layered and fluctuating phenomena deeply compromises he writing on hegemony. An analysis of his essay on the Bloomsbury group (1980e) should make this point clearer. Here, he argues, the divergent writing produced by the group can be fitted into the 'dominant' hegemonic formation through the central value of the civilised individual. Whether or not Williams is correct in linking the Bloomsbury group together through a central value system is not an issue I want to enter into here. More importantly, Williams underestimates the extent to which the writing of the group has been drawn upon by those in distantciated contexts of reception. This can be illustrated through the work of Virginia Woolf, probably the best know of the group. In more contemporary contexts, Woolf's writing could be criticised for her rather snobbish treatment of working-class characters and in this way legitimating forms of class domination. Alternatively, she has proved to be of enduring value to the women's movement. Her fiction and critical essays have provided a constant source of inspiration for feminist groups seeking to challenge institutionalised male dominance. The critic, one may surmise, should resist the temptation to assign a text or artistic movement to a position in a hegemonic structure, without assessing the various ways that it's meaning has been historically interpreted. Bourdieu's approach to the sociological assessment of symbolic forms would seem to be more satisfactory in this respect. Despite some of the theoretical difficulties encountered by Bourdieu, his concept of the habitus allows him to draw attention to the way in which symbolic forms are interpreted in contexts of reception. As we will see in the following discussion of structure and agency, Bourdieu is able to write a theoretically sophisticated sociological account that pertains to be able to account for the various interpretations of social agents, while relating them to the objective relations of the field.

Humanism and structuralism: debates in agency and structure

Williams's theory of the cultural materialism was not only a reworking of his account of cultural processes, but was also a

78

reshaping of his theory of the subject. Further, in Williams's revised account of subjective processes, human subjects are conceived as capable of making a difference through conscious and intentional forms of agency. Thus Williams remained, as his later novels demonstrate, connected to the humanist tradition whereby the self can be reformulated through a reflexive moral discourse. Here, I want to concentrate, in what follows, on two main threads of argument; the first is that Bourdieu offers a more satisfactory explanation of the relation between structure and agency than that of Williams; the second, that while post-structuralism has sought to undermine the humanist conception of the subject, despite many of the theoretical errors this critique has brought to our attention, there has been, as many authors are now beginning to realise, a neglect of ethical considerations. The theoretical project that is being mapped out here is one where a consideration of agency and structure becomes compatible with the humanist emphasis upon morality and ethics.

Any analysis of culture, argues Walter Benjamin (1977), should seek to understand the material relationships that are entered into in the act of production. Williams, more concretely than Benjamin, has provided the cultural historian with historically variable structural groupings into which artist's can be placed. Williams wants to be able to locate the artist in historically variable associations without reducing the creativity of the artist, as he argued certain structuralist writers had tendency to do, to an effect of their social and historical context. To this end, Williams's analysis seems sound, although there remain problems around his conceptualisation of agency in relation to structure. Williams employs a similarly loose definition of structure through his discussion of determinism. Returning to his writing in *Culture* (1981,p.192), he contrasts the material social practices of a sculptor and an industrial worker. Where as the social practice of the industrial worker is determined by the economic structure, the artistic practice of a sculptor, in Williams's own terms has 'a seemingly absolute autonomy' from the economic base Earlier, I argued, that one of cultural materialism's strengths was its refusal to treat the economic sphere as having a primacy that is denied the political and the cultural. But, through Williams's concentration on the issue of economic determinism, he neglects a range of equally important debates in social theory on the relation between agency and structure. As if one overly concentrates on economic determinism, one could easily conceive of the sculptor, following Williams's description, as existing outside of any recognisable social structure. Further, if one conceived of the sculptor as belonging to an artistic formation, and one wished to discuss notions of intentionality, the connection between the realms of agency and structure are again unclear.

Williams makes the error in his theorisation of determinism that structures are only involved in the setting of limits. Instead, I would argue, they should also be conceived of as rules and resources that both constrain and enable social activity. John Searle (1969) has explored this dimension through his discussion of regulative and constitutive rules. A regulative rule is similar to a commandment; for instance a rule of law that prohibits secondary picketing by trade unions. But not all rules are of this character, as there are human practices that cannot be thought of apart from the rules that constitute them. An example could be the rule in soccer that allows for the team with the most goals at the end of the game to be thought of as the victors. Clearly such a rule could not be adequately conceptualised as restrictive. If soccer did not place a great deal of significance on goal scoring, it would be a very different game. Without this, and other constitutive rules in football, it would undoubtedly throw into question the other rules of the game. There are of course other rules that remain mainly regulative in soccer. These would include restrictions on certain methods of dispossessing the opponents team of the ball. Bourdieu similarly dispenses with the view that structures act as external objective constraints that are theoretically separable from the way social agents make sense of the world. Instead Bourdieu advocates a constructivist structuralism. He is structuralist in that he recognises that social structures are structured like a language through differences and distinctions, but that these objective structures, do not in an Althusserian sense, directly pattern social subjects. By constructivism, on the other hand, Bourdieu means that the way in which agents reflexively monitor their social performance, and interpret the social world, is bound up with their social dispositions and their position in the field. Bourdieu argues that agents internalise their position in the field that is structured through distinctions of high, intermediate and low. While this is not the place for a detailed investigation into Bourdieu's position on agency and structure - I shall make two related criticisms of his writing and that of Raymond Williams. The first is their shared dismissal of a notion of the unconscious; the other is that Bourdieu's work seems to disallow the humanist moment of self-formation through ethical considerations.

Bourdieu's suspicion of dualistic concepts leads him to bypass notions of conscious/unconscious in favour of the habitus. His weakness in this respect is that despite the explanatory weight he

80

gives to the habitus, unlike the psychoanalytic tradition, he only provides the most precursory account of the habitus's role in the formation of the self. More important for our discussion is Williams's attitude towards psychoanalysis. In *Politics and Letters* (1979), Williams replies to his interviewers, that in contrast to other literary theorists, he does not consider Freud to have made a significant contribution to current theoretical debates. It might at first seem surprising that Williams who placed so much emphasis on the complexity of human feelings and emotions in the interpretation of texts, would not be more receptive to psychoanalysis.

Williams's critical suspicion of psychoanalysis seems to have three main sources. In his novels *Second Generation* (1964) and *Loyalties* (1985b), there is an understandable reaction against those who try to explain political commitments solely in terms of the displacement of a deeper and more personal anxiety. But, as Castoriadis (1987) has shown, psychoanalysis could equally be used to explain the motivation and forms of identification of those who seek to dogmatically defend the status quo from criticism. Further Williams's attachment to notions of 'lived experience' and the writing of Timpanaro - who is hostile to Freud - provide the two other main sources of Williams's scepticism. As we saw earlier, Williams's notion of practical consciousness, or the everyday knowledgeability of the subject that allows them to 'go on' in social contexts, lies at bottom of Williams's, and for that matter E.P.Thompson's, critique of Althusser. While Williams, and as we shall see later Thompson, were justified in their repudiation of Althusser's attempt to reduce cultural processes and human subjectivity to ideology, neither of them offer an adequate theory of the subject. Like Thompson, Williams has a tendency to represent human experience as being the product of a rational animal immersed in culture, continually bringing that culture into critique. As will become more apparent later, this remains an important conceptual undertaking against those whose theoretical critique is unable to account for the importance of human reflexivity and an ethical dimension within social theory. While those writers who have represented the subject as being 'written' by discursive strategies, would do well to reflect upon the contribution of some of the writers in the humanist tradition who emphasise this point, what is absent from Williams' work is an adequate account of subjective processes (Elliott, 1992).Williams's subjects appear to be capable of achieving an exaggerated degree of self-understanding through a critical relationship to culture and history. Instead, I would agree with Castoriadis when he writes;

No society will be ever be totally transparent, first because the individuals that make it up will never be transparent to themselves, since there can be no question of eliminating the unconscious. Then, because the social element implies not only individual consciousness, nor even simply their mutual intersubjective inherencies, the relationships between persons, both conscious and unconscious, which could never be given in its entirety as a content to all, unless we were to introduce the double myth of an absolute knowledge possessed equally by all: the social implies that something that can never be given as such (Castoriadis,1987,p.111).

Castoriadis does not suppose that one can never achieve a more informed sense of the self, otherwise it would be difficult to see why people would enter into therapy. Instead, Castoriadis argues, that our theorisation of totality is dependent upon interpretative traditions that are historically and socially mediated, and that while one can gain a better understanding of unconscious processes through psychoanalytic practices, the moment of final interpretative self-understanding, akin to our understanding of other social processes, never arrives.

Yet psychoanalysis, and Williams's emphasis on materialism share a similar account of human nature. Terry Eagleton (1990) has recognised that both traditions of thinking stress a common view of human beings. Materialism and psychoanalysis recognise the universal biological vulnerability of human beings to suffering and death, coupled with the understanding that there is a universal need for love and care especially in the early years of one's life, however this is expressed culturally. These insights could have been developed further had Williams formed a different disposition towards psychoanalysis (Rustin, 1991).

Despite Bourdieu's deeper awareness of the issues related to agency and structure, than is evident in Williams; the second criticism I want to make is explicitly directed at him. Earlier Williams was credited with maintaining specific uses for culture and ideology, but without ever adequately suggesting how this might be achieved. This said, I want to argue, Williams's writing does contain the recognition that culture and ideology are theoretically separable through his representation of human agents as moral agents. Richard Johnson (1979), building on much of the work done by Williams, argues that culture can be separated from ideology in two main ways. Firstly, culture can be thought of as the 'common sense' of a particular group that forms it's ' moral preferences or principles of life' (Johnson, 1979, p. 234). The subject is, therefore, always already embedded in cultural relations providing the ground upon which ideology has to operate. Also Johnson notably wants to maintain the humanist connection between culture and the production of the self. With Althusserian structuralism in mind, he writes;

> to neglect the moment of self-creation, of the affirmation of belief or of the giving of consent would, once more, return us to 'pure mechanicity' (Johnson, 1979, p. 234).

Johnson undoubtedly comes closer than Williams to theorising the distinction between culture and ideology, but his approach is not as clear as it might have been. Following Marx, I have argued for a conception of ideology that is critical in that it enhances relations of domination. Further, I have suggested, that this definition of ideology allows one to distinguish between culture and the symbolic justification of domination. If Johnson is similarly attempting to develop a critical notion of ideology, then it is not easy to see how he theoretically brackets off culture from ideology. Johnson seems to ignore that 'moral principles', and what Williams calls 'lived traditions', can be deeply ideological. Much recent feminist writing, for example, has revealed the extent to which the 'lived traditions' of the labour movement have been built on the traditional family unit and the requirement of a family wage. It could be said that the 'adopted moral principles' of certain trade unions are dependent, on this reading, upon the continued subordination of women. Would this then make the institutional practices in question ideological rather than cultural? Not completely would be the short answer to this question; the traditions of the labour movement could be considered ideological in the sense that they reinforce, or leave unquestioned, relations of domination between men and women. However, these same traditions, despite their many short comings, have grown out of attempts to improve the quality of life for members of trade unions and associated kinship groups.

Despite the limitations of Johnson's perspective he does usefully remind us of the connection between culture and an ethical dimension. Charles Taylor (1985a) has brought out this relationship more centrally in his essay *What is Human Agency?* The primary distinction, for Taylor, between humans and animals is that humans can formulate 'second order desires'. Instead of simply responding to drives, human beings, according to Taylor, have the capacity to evaluate and reflect upon their action in terms of the kind of persons that they wish to be. Agents are able to evaluate 'desires' in terms of criteria that, can be thought of as higher, lower, noble or base. Taylor proceeds by distinguishing his idea of human agency from utilitarianism and Sartre's notion of radical choice. Utilitarianism is discredited for Taylor as human action cannot be simply thought of in terms of pleasures and outcomes. Existential radical choice, on the other hand, considers only extreme situations where there is nothing to choose between two options. Sartre and utilitarianism wrongly assume that past cultural-moral choices would seemingly have no bearing on the decision made by the agent. Both radical choice and utilitarianism fail to treat agents as what Taylor calls 'strong evaluators'. This form of human agency is not practised by 'sovereign subjects', but by human agents informed by cultural contexts. Williams, as I have tried to show, seems to be developing a similar perspective in many of his novels. Williams's own personal border's between England and Wales, Cambridge and Pandy, and the country and the city, were not just a cultural, but were also moral and political. His novels explored contextualised moral problems where cultural decisions in terms of ones life-style and political commitment were always ethical choices that help constitute the self. Bourdieu, similar to Williams and Taylor, also sees human beings as making moral distinctions between what has value, and what has not. For Bourdieu these are not so much ethical borders, as they are the sociological distinctions of an objective field. In Bourdieu's terms one would act ethically to gain what he calls primary profits (success in achieving status) and secondary profits (success in gaining approval of the group in question) (Bourdieu, 1990). Here Bourdieu's writing, I would argue, comes close to what Taylor has described as utilitarianism; where ethical choices are made in view of achieving certain outcomes. The criticism I want to make here is related to an earlier discussion concerning Bourdieu's tendency to concentrate upon the style of what is said, as opposed to what is actually being communicated. While an ethical dilemma may be resolved in terms of our desire, whether conscious or not, to gain primary or secondary profits, it equally may not. My desire to revise the writing of Williams and Thompson could be an attempt to gain status in an academic field, but it could equally be because I find their work has aesthetic, moral and political implications (Soper, 1990). Bourdieu's argument would not explain why I chose this topic as opposed to the many others that are available in my given field. Humanist concerns, on this reading, retain an ethical concern with the self that is lacking in Bourdieu's thinking.

Politics and truth

Bourdieu evidently believes that his writing has broken with the structuralist paradigm, and this would seem to be true if one compared his work with Althusser and Foucault on the nature of the subject. Yet Bourdieu's work retains an unacknowledged affinity with authors like Foucault through notions of truth. As we have already seen, for Bourdieu, claims to truth are only made in relation to one's position in the field, where claims to universality are by definition ideological. Foucault (1976) offers what might be described as a genealogical conception of truth. The act of interpretation, Foucault argues, should not be seen as the uncovering of a hidden meaning as once one moves beneath the 'surface' there are only other interpretations. If this is so, a genealogy should not attempt to discover an essential meaning, but trace out a history of related interpretations. This can be said as there is no guarantee that so called hidden meanings are representative of a 'liberating truth'.

Both Bourdieu and Foucault, I would argue, subscribe to what Peter Dews (1987) has called perspectivism; that is the claim to know better is always tied to particular regimes of power or to positions in the field of play. One could ask, however, how are we to account for their validity as theories if this is the case? For instance, Bourdieu claims to be able to produce an objective account of the academic field. Yet, I would ask, what omits Bourdieu's own cultural productions from a desire to gain status ? Further, such a notion of truth, I would argue, would make a democratic socialist politics redundant, as there would seem to be no way of preferring one perspective over another. The writing of Bourdieu and Foucault would also deny the way in which the term 'truth' is, for example, used in everyday talk. Charles Taylor (1985b) in an essay on Foucault, argues that a claim to truth is always something more than a claim for primary or secondary profits, as such a notion of truth:

> blocks out - the possibility of a change of life-form which can be understood as a move towards a greater acceptance of truth - and hence also, in certain conditions, a move towards greater freedom (Taylor,1985b,p.177).

Williams's commitment to the long revolution would seemingly have been difficult to sustain had he adopted a similar position to that of Bourdieu and Foucault. Williams was not claiming that he had discovered a transcendental position from which he could objectively ascertain the movement of history, but was claiming that a democratic socialist society would promote less destructive and more democratic forms of life. Socialists would, on this reading, have to convince the vast majority of the population that life under a socialist democratic state would be 'better' than it would be if one of their political rivals gained control of the state apparatus. A democratic socialist politics, therefore, must be able to deliver what John Dunn (1984) has called a critique of the present, a version of the good life, and some idea as to how one may move from one to the other. Williams, unlike Bourdieu, links together a critique of cultural domination, an understanding how one may mobilise for political change, and a radical vision of what the good society may be like. For Bourdieu such attempts would always be the expression of interested strategies of those involved in a particular field. The reductive logic of this argument converts ethical and political beliefs into a desire for status. Again, I would argue, this closes down the prospect of a genuinely democratic politics where open discussion could lead to the constitution of universal norms, needs and values to unite and struggle around.

Politics and socialist humanism

Williams's commitment to a socialist humanist politics provides the core of the long revolution. His view of men and women as communicating beings who need to be brought into contact with one another in collective and autonomous institutions, formed the basis of his own political project. The long revolution, however, while deserving serious consideration, has to be radically reworked if it is to remain relevant to the modern world. Here the discussion will concentrate on two main elements of the long revolution, stressing some of its strengths and weaknesses.

Williams's critique of militant particularism is heavily influenced by Lukacs. In Lukacs's classic work *History and Class Consciousness* (1971) it is either the bourgeoisie or the proletariat who are the main proponents of social change. The bourgeoisie are prevented from 'ideologically' grasping the social totality, as they are also the exploiting class, and are capable of recognising themselves as such. The proletariat, on the other hand, have the potentiality to see society as a coherent whole, and as the universal class, they are able to penetrate bourgeois ideology by virtue of their class position. After the revolution, as there will be no exploiting class, the proletariat will be able to govern without reified ideological distortion. The production of revolutionary consciousness is by no means guaranteed by the structural position of the exploited. The consciousness of the proletariat has become fragmented and divided around the objective divisions manifest in the separation of the political from the economic struggle. Thus the consciousness of the proletariat becomes divided between more immediate interests and the long term objectives of bringing about socialism. Political perspectives for Lukacs will either be a step towards the transcendence of capitalism, or will attempt to falsely conceal these interests from the proletariat. Due to the historically privileged position of the working-class, the proletariat always aspires towards 'truth' even in false consciousness. The aspiration towards 'truth' enables the proletariat to develop the knowledge necessary for revolution through conscious self-criticism.

The first issue Lukacs and Williams concur on is the centrality of working-class politics. Any renewal of the socialist project would make little sense unless it gained the support of working-class institutions, such as the trade unions. However Williams's political analysis is highly reductive. He argues that the new social movements have shared common interests with the working-class in defeating capitalism. This is problematic. Firstly, many of the issues raised by the women's movements, ecological movements and peace movement would not necessarily come any closer to resolution by the defeat of capitalism. Although many of these groupings may want to enter into alliances with the labour movement such a strategy could only be secured ethically and symbolically after periods of open discussion. This could not, as Williams occasionally seems to suggest, be an expression of common interests that had been externally imposed by a common enemy, but a series of alliances secured through consensual agreement. The political programme that may become discursively articulated by such an alliance would have to be politically constructed, and could not be thought of as pre-given. Thus Williams does not seem to appreciate that the aims of the new social movements may not be easy to reconcile with certain sections of the labour movement. For instance, trade unions representing workers in the nuclear industry could accept Williams's demand for a recognition of general interests over sectional interests on certain issues, but not others. The labour movement may be able to persuade these workers to accept an erosion of pay differentials to promote greater equality, but these same workers could conceivably see their interests as opposed to those expressed by the ecological, peace and women's movements. Thus Williams's formal rejection of the base/superstructure metaphor does not seem to have penetrated his political writing. This is not to deny that Williams did not offer a direct challenge to forms of economism. But, on the other hand, it is to argue that the influence of Lukacs meant he was not able to theoretically account for relatively autonomous political movements.

This point is related to my second objection; that people's interests can not be 'read off' from their class position. For Williams and Lukacs the working-class are the only structural force capable of challenging capitalism, which is to be overthrown in the name of everyone's long term interests. Yet classes do not have interests that exist independently from their political representation. As Gramsci argued interests have to be politically constructed.

> the dominant group is co-ordinated concretely with the general interests of the subordinate groups, and the life of the State is conceived of as a continuous process of formation and superseding of unstable equilibria (on the judicial plane) between the interests of the fundamental group and those of subordinate groups-equilibria in which the interests of the dominant group prevail, but only up to a certain point, i.e. stopping short of narrowly corporate economic interest (Gramsci,1982,p.182).

If interests are politically constructed, Williams can not be justified in holding that the working-class have an intrinsic interest in socialism. But, one could argue, that there are interests, that through the operation of power and ideology are systematically denied political expression. Steven Lukes (1974) has argued that citizens, to use his example, have an interest in breathing clean air as opposed to polluted air. This interest is held regardless of whether or not the need for an ecologically secure environment becomes articulated politically. But, although Lukes, would seem to have a point in this context, it would be far easier to gain the consent of the population that they had a general interest in clean air, than it would to persuade them that they had the same or similar interests in socialism.

There would seem to be three main problems with Lukes's argument; if applied to working-class politics and socialism. The first being the implicit authoritarianism of this approach. One of the lessons democratic socialist's should surely learn from scientific socialism are the dangers that are implicit in attributing interests to social groups without democratic consultation. Next, to argue that the working-class have an intrinsic interest in socialism is to ignore the social conditions, at the time Williams was writing, of 'actually existed socialism'. Lastly, to dismiss expressed needs and desires, which is effectively what one is doing by attributing interests, would not appear to be politically prudent. Instead the needs and desires of social groups cannot be assumed to correspond to their objective economic position, nor can one expect the way in which their interests are articulated to be unaffected by those same social conditions. The process of linking social groups to movements for political change would therefore have the unenviable task of connecting a general interest to actually articulated interests. Such a process would neither hold particular wants as sovereign, nor assume in advance that they were mistaken. Williams and Lukacs, for me at least, assume that once the working-class movement are able to merge short-term and long term interests then this will automatically lead them to realise a latent interest in socialism. My argument here is that while it is true that historically the industrial working-class has formed a deep connection to socialism, what is needed is an analysis of, in Bobbio's (1987b) phrase, 'which socialism?'. While Williams and Lukacs may be correct that the working-class are the only structural force capable of ending capitalism, what we can not be certain of is that it is in their interests to do so. In other words, while the working-class may not have essential interests in socialism, they continue to have interests, I would argue, in a form of democratic socialism that is based upon a framework of communal provision which allows for the development of difference. Again how a critical theory might undertake this task will be the subject of a later discussion.

Human needs and the limitations of self-management

For Williams the labour movement will capture the general interest by orienting its programme around human needs, rather than class interests. In this sense, Williams remains distinct from Lukacs. Kate Soper (1981) has argued that any consideration of human needs ultimately raises issues concerning values; these come into play as one has to decide which needs are to be met. Williams himself realises this in that he links the socialist idea of a self-managed society to the needs and values connected to notions of sharing (Williams, 1989a). Other writers, like Agnes Heller, have offered more sophisticated arguments for joining ideas of distributive justice and freedom, to socialist notions of economic self-management. Necessarily, for Heller, all radical political philosophy should recognise a hierarchy of values that are both historically dependent and universally valid. Heller attempts to defend the universal validity of values through what she calls 'value ideas'. She states:

> A value idea is a value whose opposite cannot be chosen
> for a value. It is clear that in our times the opposite of
> freedom (unfreedom, slavery) cannot normally be chosen
> as a value (Feher and Heller,1989,p.150).

The value idea of freedom is applicable to arguments for self-management, as all discussions of self-management are an interpretation of the value-idea of freedom. In the modern world, for Heller, one can talk of two kinds of needs; they are formally described as 'wants' and the 'need for self-determination'. The need for self determination or autonomy is given a certain priority over wants. To submit to certain wants that have not been authentically chosen violates the modern quest to be relatively self-determining. The modern self is continually confronted by a number of indeterminate possibilities in it's formation as we actively realise certain possibilities and close down others. In this way we transform contingency into destiny. As Heller puts it;

> the contingent person who is intent on transforming
> his/her contingency into a destiny, not through the
> satisfaction of mere wants, not even by detaching himself
> or herself from a context but by coping with the context
> while giving priority to the satisfaction of the needs of
> self-determination (Feher and Heller,1988, p. 30).

In Heller's discussion our need for economic control is similar to our desire for democracy generally. The self is 'realised ' the extent to which we are able to fulfil our capacity for self-determination. This remains an important argument linking as it does micro inter-personal relations to the more macro political concerns related to democratic forms of representation at the local, the national and the global level. But, while remaining sympathetic to Heller and Williams, in the attempt to provide an ethical basis for politics, they seem oblivious to any consideration that the conditions of late capitalism may impinge on our attempts to control the world in which we live. It surely remains one thing to hold out the ideal of self-determination, but another, to suggest in the wake of 'actually existed socialism', that the economy can be consciously planned. While I will return to these issues later, for the present even those least sceptical of Heller and Williams would surely agree with John Dunn when he writes:

The idea that human social, economic and political relations can be brought into conformity with our moral intuitions and kept in such conformity more or less indefinitely is excessively optimistic as a practical expectation (Dunn, 1984 p. 88).

3. E.P.Thompson and the poverty of theory

E.P. Thompson was one of the most influential figures of the post-war New Left. A member of the British Communist Party during and after the Second World War; he renounced his affiliation with international Communism after the post-war Soviet invasion of Hungary. Like Williams, who never became a member of the Communist Party, Thompson also spent some time outside of official academic institutions in workers education classes. It was during this period that Thompson wrote the two books for which he remains best known: *Williams Morris: Romantic to Revolutionary* (1955) and *The Making of the English Working Class* (1980). Up until the late seventies Thompson was mostly thought of as a socialist historian concerned with eighteenth and nineteenth century British history. But, from this point onwards, he was to temporarily abandon the practice of writing history, and fix his attention on issues of more direct political importance. Along with the rise of the New Right came an increasingly authoritarian state that hegemonically posed a threat to historically won civil and political liberties. Thompson, unlike many of those on the Left, rejects the analytical separation between 'hard' social rights and so called 'bourgeois' political and civil rights. For Thompson the working-class movement has not only benefited from the operation of civil and political freedoms, but has often been at the forefront of their extension. Throughout the sixties and the seventies, Thompson wrote a series of articles that argued these freedoms were being eroded by a bureaucratic nation-state and more global transnational organisations like the North Atlantic Treaty Organisation (NATO). Thompson's concern with civil and political liberties, and his writing on socialist humanism, which was initially developed as an ethical critique of Stalinism, were brought together in his critique of the Cold War. From this point on, Thompson became one of the leading theoreticians of the peace movement until the end of the Cold War following the European revolutions of 1989.

The intellectual sketch offered above only acts as an introduction to the writing of E.P. Thompson; chapter four will deal more extensively with the riddles posed by Thompson's shifting political focus. For the present the discussion will be worked around an extended essay written by Thompson called *The Poverty Theory* (1978a). The primary concern of this essay is an extensive debate of the work of the French post-structuralist and Marxist critic Louis Althusser. There are, however, substantial problems involved in the interpretation of Thompson's writing. His overtly polemical style and his metaphoric use of comic exaggeration as a means to press home his points make it difficult for one to be sure that one has captured his arguments. In this instance, the essay's rambling length and style means that critics should proceed cautiously in any attempt to understand Thompson's simultaneously engaging and exasperating prose. The essay, has however, been widely debated, and remains Thompson's most important theoretical text on the themes of culture, ideology and politics.

E.P.Thompson and the New Left

The formative event in the development of Thompson's political development was the Soviet invasion of Hungary in 1956. Prior to this event, while still a Communist party member, Thompson had exhibited a certain degree of support for the Soviet Union (Thompson,1955). The impact of the Soviet repression of a genuinely popular attempt at socialist renewal in Hungary and Khrushchev's secret speech were such that the British Communist party lost a third of its membership (Soper, 1990b). The attempt to formulate a Left politics that was neither Stalinist nor Labourist gave birth to the twin journals *Universities and Left Review* and *The New Reasoner*. These journals considerably broadened the range of cultural issues that could be discussed by socialists. The arguments, in general, ranged from more traditional concerns with political economy to wider questions of culture and politics.

Due to reasons of economy and organisation it became impossible for both journals to continue as separate forums for discussion. In 1962 a decision was taken to combine them with a new journal called *New Left Review* emerging under the direction of the editor Perry

Anderson. Despite being actively involved in the appointment of Anderson, Thompson found himself in sharp, often violent, disagreement with him over the direction of the journal. The dispute centred around what Thompson perceived to be Anderson's attempt to introduce more continental strains of thinking into British Left social theory. That Thompson found himself out of sympathy with much of the writing of not only Althusser, but also the early Frankfurt school, will become apparent throughout the course of the chapter. Thompson, often striking the pose of what Terry Eagleton (1979:144) called 'the lonely Romantic-individualist dissenter ', took it upon himself to defend a 'peculiarly' English social theory. The writers Thompson sought to associate himself with bore a remarkable similarity with the 'great tradition' discussed by Williams (1961) in *Culture and Society*. That this occasionally plays a similarly dialectical role in Thompson's writing, as it does in Williams's work, will be discussed in the next chapter. For now, it should be emphasised, that Williams exhibits, when compared to Thompson, a comparative intellectual openness to the new ideas offered by structuralist and post-structuralist thinkers. Intellectual generosity on Thompson's part seems to be foreclosed by his overly polemical writing style, and the very personal nature of his dispute with Perry Anderson. Thompson's self confessed involvement in an English cultural tradition, and his refusal to engage with Althusser other than in the most vitriolic terms, has led some critics to accuse him of being xenophobic (Hirst, P.Q. 1985). This charge, while not without substance, has to be seen in the context of the social field that helped form New Left discourse during this period. Also Thompson's idiosyncratic commitment to a specifically national culture does not prevent him from providing powerful correctives to Althusserian social theory.

Althusserian Marxism

By the end of the seventies, Althusser's theoretical leanings to some degree through the journal *New Left Review,* had had a considerable impact on British social theory. Those influenced included not only Raymond Williams and Perry Anderson, but also other writers such as Stuart Hall and Paul Hirst. This is not the place for a detailed investigation of Althusser's writing; this has already been done excellently elsewhere (Elliott, G. 1987; Benton, T. 1984). However, what needs to be undertaken, is a brief theoretical summary of the characteristic features of Althusser's approach. In performing this task I shall concentrate on his critique of humanism and his path breaking writing on the concept of ideology.

For Althusser socialist humanism was the resurrection of a theoretically discredited form of Hegelian-Marxism. The mature contributions of Marx, were conceived by Althusser, to have made a distinctive 'epistemological break' that rid his work of Hegelian and humanist categories. Socialist humanism, along with the writing of the early Marx, was both guilty of essentialism and teleology. All variants of socialist humanism, according to Althusser, represented history as a process with a subject. This view falsely constructs a grand narrative around the emergence of the working-class as a universal class. It was the historically given task of this social subject, through revolutionary action, to realise 'Man's' essential nature. Socialist humanism is 'essentialist' to the extent that it held to an absolute conception of human nature, and epistemologically privileged the working-class. The historicist twist in this Hegelian schema gave history an endpoint in overcoming alienation and the eventual self-realisation of the working-class. In contrast to socialist humanism, Althusser argues, human agents are not constitutive agents who presided over an ultimately manipulable reality. Althusser represents human agents as constituted subjects in history who are allotted places in already existing social structures. Thus it was a fundamental theoretical error to attempt to explain social phenomena with reference to the beliefs and desires of individuals; as individuals themselves are determined by social practices. Althusser, when considering socialist humanism, had in mind the writing of Sartre. This explains why some of his specific objections concerning socialist humanism, when applied to Thompson's writing, seem somewhat wide of the mark.

Althusser's critique of humanism apart it is his writing on ideology that has attracted the attention of social theorists. Althusser's study of the subject of ideology was intended to resolve the problem of how Western capitalist societies reproduce dominant institutional relationships. The requirements of the economic system for labour power are satisfied outside the dominant mode of production, mainly in the education system and the family. For Althusser, therefore, labour power is reproduced under conditions of ideological subjugation. Ideology is not, Althusser insists, as it is for certain variants of Hegelian Marxism, a mirrored inversion of the social relations of production.

> it is not their real conditions of existence, their real world,
> that 'men' 'represent to themselves' in ideology, but above

all it is their relation to those conditions of existence which is represented to them there. It is this relation which is at the centre of every ideological i.e. imaginary, representation of the real world (Althusser,1984,p.30).

Thus both Williams and Althusser reject an approach to ideology found in *the German Ideology* (Marx,1963). Ideology is produced, according to Williams and Althusser, through social practices. The insistence on the materiality of ideology ensures that the argument does not lapse into a form of idealism, or what Williams calls mechanical materialism.

Perhaps Althusser's most famous discussion of the materiality of ideology can be found in his essay *Ideology and Ideological State Apparatuses* (1984). Althusser, principally following Gramsci, makes the distinction between Ideological State Apparatuses (ISA) and Repressive State Apparatuses (RSA). Both the RSA's and the ISA's are grounded in material practices with an ideological function. However, the RSA's operate mainly by force, securing the political conditions for the ISA's. This ensures the ideological domination of the ruling class. These ideological practices are then linked to the formation of the subject. Althusser argues:

> the category of the subject is only constitutive of all ideology insofar as all ideology has the function (which defines it) of 'constituting' concrete individuals as subjects (Althusser,1984,p.48).

Ideology, if Althusser's proposition is followed, converts human-beings into subjects. Ideology lets individuals mistakenly recognise themselves as autonomous self-determining agents, where as in fact, subjects are formed though social and psychic processes. Here the subject thinks of his or her self as a unique individual that is constitutive rather than constituted. Drawing on the writing of Lacan, Althusser argues, the father intrudes into the relation between mother and child by introducing the new human infant into the symbolic order.The child is thus socialised into the structure of language through which it is interpellated as a subject, enabling the subject to recognise itself as a subject, as well as other subjects. A good example of how the subjects formation in and through language can be connected to forms of ideological domination is provided by Nicos Poulantzas (1983). Poulantzas, as the following example bears out, was greatly influenced by the writing of Althusser. The dominant ideology of capitalist society is for Poulantzas the legal system, which 'hails' subjects as individual citizens rather than as members of social classes in relations of domination. Poulantzas calls this function of ideology the 'isolation effect'. Citizens, according to Poulantzas, misrecognise themselves as 'free' individuals entering into a non-coercive relationship with the state through ideological processes.

How then, one might plausibly ask, are subjects going to 'correctly' recognise themselves as members of an oppressed class rather than free individuals? Althusser's answer to this is to insist on a rigorous distinction between 'science' and 'ideology'. Althusser dissects society into four main practices, they are: economic; political; ideological and theoretical. Theoretical practice, as a scientific practice, has three distinguishable levels, including raw material (Generality One), means of production (Generality Two), and the end product (Generality Tree). Just as the worker uses her labour power to transform nature into a product, so the theoretician applies the scientific theory that is available in a mixture of concepts and facts to produce knowledge. But, scientific practice, like historical materialism could not be externally refuted or affirmed by empirical reality, instead the theory has to be internally refined. Hence it is through scientific practice that the interests of the proletariat are philosophically pursued (Althusser,1977).

In what follows I shall draw out the main themes of Thompson's essay *The Poverty of Theory* (1978a), before engaging in a more critical debate. Thompson's essay can be divided into four main themes.

History and theory

One of Thompson's main arguments against Althusser is that he privileges theoretical knowledge over historical knowledge. This, in Thompson's terms, means that Althusser is guilty of idealism. Althusser's particular brand of idealism proposes that the only way one can obtain knowledge about the world is through elaborate theoretical structures. The social 'experience' of ordinary people is inherently ideological. In order to produce knowledge rather than ideology the Althusserian scientist processes the 'raw material' of experience through three stages. In this process, according to Thompson:

> raw material (object of knowledge) is an inert, plaint kind
> of stuff with neither inertia nor energies of its own,

awaiting passively its manufacture into knowledge (Thompson,1978a,p.199).

Thus when the theorist has reached the stage of Generality 3 one can be said to have produced knowledge. This is because, for Althusser, theoretical work is akin to any other material social practice, with the production of theory enjoying a relative autonomy from other social practices. To write theory, therefore, is a distinct social practice that cannot be thought of as simply mirroring an external reality. As one can only gain knowledge thorough theory, social reality cannot be considered determinant. Thompson interprets this argument as breaking the dialectical relationship between theory and historical facts, or what he calls concept and reality. For Thompson this ultimately leads to a form of relativism where theory provides unhistorical self-reproducing categories that have become unhooked from the social world. This renders the practice of the historian, that Thompson describes in a previous work *Whigs and Hunters* (1977), as redundant. Here the historian is engaged in an uncertain process of connecting documentary evidence which is always 'less an experiment in historiography, than a way of muddling through' (Thompson,1977,p.71).

Thompson argues that what historians have to say about the past is not totally dependent on their adopted theoretical position, as he holds, contrary to Althusser, that facts restrain the historian. This certainly does not, in Thompson's view, reduce the historian to a sort of recording machine that represents the past in an objective fashion. In the writing of history, the historian brings into play his or her own intellectual tradition, in this case historical materialism, in order to shape the facts into a narrative. Importantly the facts and the intellectual horizons of the historian form a critical relationship. This relationship escapes the idealism of Althusser, as the theoretical tradition of the historian is continually put into question by the historical facts themselves. Thompson writes that:

> the resulting historical knowledge establishes relations between phenomena which could never be seen, felt or experienced by the actors in these ways at the time, and it organises the findings according to concepts and within categories which were unknown to men and women whose actions make up the object of the study (Thompson,1978a,p.211).

The historian then could be said to have an active interpretative relationship with history, which is always determined within certain limits by a factual dimension. Not of course that Thompson treats the 'facts' themselves with anything other than the most critical scrutiny. He is aware that the facts carry their own ideological load. But, while Thompson's description of the practise of the historian is not without considerable merit, there remain a number of issues that are in need of clarification. Firstly, while Thompson emphasises the intellectual tradition of the historian, his reliance on the determinant quality of facts remains theoretically suspect. This is in part due to the confusion created by Thompson's discussion of the application of theoretical categories, and broader questions on the nature of historical understanding generally.

Agency and structure reconsidered

One of the key components of Thompson's commitment to socialist humanism was the critical importance of issues related to agency and historical process. Althusser, on the other hand, excluded such a discussion by dogmatically concentrating on rigid theoretical categories, which, Thompson felt, represented capitalism as an unchanging monolithic structure. Thompson, despite Althusser's critique, does not represent historical process as inevitably leading to a teleological end point. Such a reading would discount history as an uneven discontinuous formation that is continually producing unintended consequences. Human intentionality informs historical process, whether it is in the form of individuals or groups, in such a way that entails that history is 'not only a moment of being but also a moment of becoming' (Thompson,1978a,p.220). Instead of attributing intentionality to agents, Thompson argues, Althusser mistakenly represents the social system as being in the possession of goals and intentions. Social systems, have in Althusser's terms, to satisfy certain functional prerequisites before they are able to reproduce the dominant institutions. In capitalist society, for example, the state apparatus must secure the reproduction of the material conditions for the abstraction of surplus value. Thompson interprets this as an example of Althusser's latent functionalism. For Thompson it is only human agents, in differing institutional and historical contexts, that can be thought of as having the capacity to formulate competing goals and intentions.

Althusser's deterministic conception of the subject infringes on the capacity of human agents to make moral choices. The ability of social

99

agents to choose to be good or evil, in definite social contexts, being a defining quality for Thompson of being human. In Thompson's writing, however, the necessity of such a choice is often presented as a celebration of the 'heroic virtues' of those who have historically sought to expand and defend social, political and civil liberties. On the erosion of civil liberties, during the sixties and seventies,Thompson depicts himself as the keeper of the flame of 'the free-born Englishman'. This intellectual and spiritual culture is defended against those who have become intellectually incorporated into a conformist bureaucratic system. For now, I would want to stress, that Thompson's connection to 'free-born Englishmen' is not only ideologically suspicious, but can be related to his construction of problems of agency and structure. In Thompson's early historiography, the agency of the labour movement is opposed to the 'limiting' structures of capitalist society. Similarly, his work on the nuclear arms race, as we will see, opposes the agency of the peace movement to the self-reproducing structures of the Cold War. Agency and its association with the moral independence of 'the free-born Englishman', therefore, becomes theoretically separable in Thompson's writing from externally limiting social structures. It is not, as some critics have argued, that Thompson does not attempt to define what he means by structure as opposed to agency. To talk of structures, for Thompson, implies on one level a discussion of 'system', 'organisation', 'laws of supply and demand' and 'institutions' (Thompson,1978a,p.339). He goes on:

> we are talking about structure: and we are likely to be
> talking about the ways in which human behaviour is
> ruled,shaped,ordered,limitedanddetermined
> (Thompson,1978a, p.339).

Yet as with Williams, there is very little attempt to theoretically understand how agency and structure might intersect. This is interesting, as Thompson makes this very same criticism of Althusser. Althusser, for Thompson, conceived of structures as existing as external constraining forces that sought to limit the potentiality of men and women. I shall argue later that both Thompson and Althusser encounter theoretical difficulties with issues of structure and agency.

Marxism, ideology and value

Althusser's treatment of the category of experience as being inherently ideological has elitist connotations for Thompson. Thompson writes of Althusser's conception of ideology:

> people do not only experience their own experience as ideas, within thought and its procedures, or (as some theoretical practitioners suppose) as proletarian instinct, etc. They also experience their own experience as feeling, and they handle their feelings within their culture, as norms, familial and kinship obligations and reciprocities, as values or (through more elaborated forms) within art or religious beliefs. This half of culture (and it is a full one-half) may be described as affective and moral consciousness (Thompson,1978a,p.363).

Thompson argues, if one follows Althusser, this gives ideology such a broadly defined role that it not only reduces forms of practical consciousness to ideology, but theoretically represents moral and affective feelings as a form of false consciousness. In the social sciences, from Durkheim to Althusser, there has been a strong tendency to explain moral norms through processes related to social integration. This precludes the development of substantive forms of evaluation and critique. Thompson, however, sought to develop a specific disposition towards ethical questions that neither adopted a form of atomised moralism, nor assumed that moral agents were the interpolated subjects of Althusserian social theory. In this sense his writing comes close to the kind of communitarian perspective developed by writers like Charles Taylor (1989). Not only are ethical questions related to the good life and collective responsibility, but as the subject for Thompson was always an ethical subject, 'unscripted' moral choices inevitably have to be made in a variety of social contexts. For Thompson one of the major failings of the Marxist tradition has been its inability to tackle ethical problems, which undoubtedly stems from its deep suspicion of bourgeois moralism. Steven Lukes (1985) argues that classical Marxism in this context contains a paradox. Marxism both offers a moral condemnation of the evils of capitalism, while dismissing questions of morality as moralism. Marx and Althusser both argue that Marxism provides a scientific analysis of capitalism, which Lukes suggests should be thought of as a kind of emancipatory morality. The reasons, however, that Marx and Althusser uphold a scientific critique against an ethical one are related but ultimately distinct. For Marx those who concerned themselves with morality supported bourgeois freedoms, defended bourgeois egoism, while holding to the belief that individuals could change themselves without first changing society. Althusser, on the other hand, argues that the idea of being a moral agent acts as a form of ideological misrecognition as it is inevitably linked to humanist versions of the subject. Thompson's humanism, as we shall see, sprang from the need not to reduce persons to theoretical abstractions in such a way that respected their capacity to act as ethical beings. Thompson argued that for the whole of humanity to realise their potential capitalism had to be defeated. Kate Soper (1990) has shown that Thompson was fully aware that his commitment to socialism and respect for the rights of persons could come into conflict. Despite his critique of Stalinism, Thompson never adopted a liberal position; instead there were circumstances when the rights of certain persons should be violated, as it seemed unlikely that one would be able to persuade the ruling class that it had interests in socialism.

Stalinism

Thompson makes the charge against Althusser that he is unintentionally conforming with an intellectual position closely associated with that of Stalin. He was not suggesting that Althusser was an active supporter of Stalin. In the first two issues of *The New Reasoner*, Thompson offers a definition of socialist humanism through which he developed his critique of Stalinism. What is of interest here is the continuity that exists between Thompson's writing at the end of the fifties, and his contribution in *The Poverty of Theory* (1978a) at the end of the seventies. Thompson wrote of Stalinism in 1957, that akin to Althusserianism in 1978:

> instead of commencing with facts, social reality, Stalinist theory starts with the idea, the text, the axiom: facts, institutions, people, must be brought to conform to the idea (Thompson,1957,p.107).

In opposition to Stalinism, and later Althusserianism, socialist humanism was heralded by Thompson as a 'return to man' (Thompson,1957, p.109). Socialist humanism begins with an attempt to locate social agents in their historical and institutional contexts. This should be carried out, he suggests, in an honest spirit that is free from deception and myth. Then the practitioner should pose the more critical question as to whether or not these particular institutional arrangements meet people's immediate needs for shelter, food and clothing, as well as their emotional, moral and intellectual needs. How a critical theory might discover what peoples needs are will be the subject of a later discussion, but suffice to say that both Stalinism and Althusserianism rank as authoritarian social theories for negating the process of critical discovery. The reason that Thompson gives for Althusser's and Stalin's 'retreat from man' is their shared anti-humanism, which Thompson argues:

> If we think about men as the trager of structures - or of their actions as 'unjustified disturbance systems' - then the thought will guide the act. As those lofty theoretical practitioners, the daleks, used to say, when confronted by 'men': 'Exterminate!' (Thompson,1978a,p.333)

Stalinism and Althusserianism, therefore, share a common disposition in terms of the way in which they represent human agents as being ideologically duped, not being in a position to realise, even after contact with a critical theory, what their interests might be. Stalinism sought to stifle the creative moral reflexivity of the people through externally imposed loyalty to an authoritarian state. Althusser similarly represented the people as unquestioningly cemented into certain structural locations within the social structure.

The absence of theory and the presence of history

Thompson's writing, I would argue, displays no consistent disposition towards theoretical categories as a whole. This is of particular interest given that Thompson is often thought of as the sociologist's historian. He has consistently gained the respect of academic sociologists while drawing inspiration, less from sociological literature, than from his interest in romantic poetry and literature. It is through his connection to a romantic culture, that perhaps Thompson's so called resistance to theory is best explained.Thompson wished to emphasise, especially in *The Making of the English Working Class*, (1980a), how a radical literary culture took inspiration from, but also decisively shaped, genuinely popular movements for change. There is, therefore, a deeply held distaste for sociological theory that constructs a narrative around changes in impersonal institutional structures, without investigating how the perceptions of historical agents shape history. Of course, Thompson's writing is littered with references that are derived from a Marxist theoretical tradition. Of particular importance, for Thompson, are references to social being, consciousness, ideology and exploitation. In short, it would seem that it is not theoretical categories themselves that Thompson opposed, but the way in which they were applied.

Here, I would argue, Thompson is making two main points concerning the nature of theory. Firstly, to overly concern oneself with the production of theoretical perspectives is inherently reductive. Such was the factual complexity of history, according to Thompson, one should be more concerned with their interpretation than the development of an elaborate theory. If the historian were to take an overly theory laded approach, she would not be able to provide a sufficiently detailed historical account. This is why Thompson described Marxism, not as an internally consistent theoretical system, but as a set of prejudices and expectations that illuminate the past. Thompson's second point is that theory should not become a set of reificatory concepts that disallow representations of historical processes. The retreat into theory and the development of internally complex theoretical concepts can obscure the distinction between concept and reality. More generally, theoretical practice should be able to 'hook onto' historical and social reality, as theory is only our concern the extent to which it can improve our critical understanding.

Althusser, would agree with Thompson, that theoretical practice should help contribute towards a better understanding of the social world. The difference being, however, that Althusser emphasises that all knowledge is theoretical knowledge. In this instance, Althusser would undoubtedly be deeply critical of Thompson's opposition between concept and reality. Instead, Althusser proposed, that one can only gain knowledge of the 'real' through scientific and theoretical concepts. The status of these concepts is not based upon a Popperian testability, but instead, according to Ted Benton:

> through the technical realisation of scientific concepts nature is made to exhibit phenomena which would not otherwise be available for 'observation' (Benton 1984,p.26).

This entails that Thompson's belief that historical facts can be separable from theory is a romantic illusion. Following in the wake of Saussure, Althusser argues that our knowledge of the 'real' is always linguistically and symbolically formed. Thompson's historical raw material is always already discursively constructed, which makes the distinction between concept and reality meaningless. But, even if one rejects Thompson's arguments concerning concept and reality, this would not necessarily excuse Althusser. What is less acceptable is Althusser's scientism, which is related to the production of 'objective' revolutionary knowledge required by the ideologically subordinate working-class. Why, one might object, should one accept Marxism's claims to be scientific, as against say that of liberalism? What Althusser does not explain is how Marxism can claim the status of a science against other paradigms of political thinking. Althusser attempts to evade this problem through the assertion that Marxism is a revolutionary science, and that philosophy itself should become a site of the class struggle. In this conflict the interests of the proletariat are represented by materialism, and those of the bourgeoisie by idealism. According to Ted Benton (1984), this is an inadequate explanation, as Althusser remains entrapped in a circular argument. The only way that Althusser is able to establish a link between the proletariat and materialism is by using the categories of historical materialism itself. Hence we know that the proletariat has an interest in developing a revolutionary consciousness because of the application of concepts such as 'interests' and 'exploitation'. Here Althusser is asserting what needs to be proven. We have only his word that Marxism is in the interests of the proletariat, and that it provides theoretically superior explannations to its rivals.

To push this argument further, one can perhaps see how Althusser's failure to resolve this dilemma informed the writing of Hindess and Hirst (1977).Thompson wrongly assumes that the position adopted by Hindess and Hirst is interchangeable with that of Althusser. It is Hindess and Hirst, rather than Althusser, who argue that political and scientific practice gain nothing from the study of history. Hindess and Hirst resolve the problem of Althusser's circular thinking by accepting an epistemologicaly relativist position. For Hindess and Hirst, Marxist's have to accept that their reading of history is just another version of the past. One cannot get in touch with the past in the way Thompson argues one can. History is determined by the specific intellectual paradigm one is working within. Thus Thompson, for Hindess and Hirst, is incorrect in his belief that facts are determinant in historical writing.

Before going on to look at Thompson's attempts to resolve this problem, we have to consider what could be called the realist option. This is a position defended by Ted Benton (1984), and Perry Anderson (1980) in his argument with Thompson. Here I want to concentrate on Anderson's (1980) rejection of Thompson's claim that history cannot be a science. According to Thompson, history should not be conceived of in terms of a scientific practice, as the dialectic of concept and reality only produces approximate knowledge. The intellectual cultural assumptions of the historian not only enable him or her to connect with the past, but also prevents the production of a truly objective history. But this does not mean that the historian is at liberty to invent the past to conform to his or her requirements, thereby lapsing into a similar form of relativism to Hindess and Hirst. This is because the writer of history remains constrained by a factual domain, that Thompson conceives of as separate from the cultural context of the historian. To hold to such an argument for Anderson is to suggest that historians could conceivably come into dispute over the date of the October Revolution. That the revolution took place in 1917 is surely beyond historical controversy. For Anderson the task of the historian is through verifiable procedures to extend 'knowledge' building upon the previous contributions of other scholars. But, what Anderson does not seem to appreciate, is that the event itself would still be open to a number of interpretations informed by different value positions. Here Anderson's argument bears a close resemblance to the position of other Marxist realist writers like Alex Callinicos (1983). In their reading all scientific theories have an irrefutable hard core with an auxiliary hypothesis that may be accepted or rejected. The new hypothesis can only be accepted if it can be supported by evidence, and is consistent with the original core area of knowledge. Thompson could respond, that the so called 'realist option', does not take seriously enough the problems of interpretation encountered by those involved in historical research. The narrowness of Anderson's example is illustrative here. Where the date of the October revolution is unlikely to provoke much controversy; the significance of the revolution is surely an open question. The October revolution can be interpreted as; the beginnings of totalitarianism; the birth of a more rational society that failed to fulfil its promise; or as the continuation of autocratic forms of authority from the Tsarist regime. Here the argument is not that historians are unable to enter into discussion on these themes, possibly coming to an agreement, but that it is possible to view the October revolution from differing perspectives. I now want to go on to argue that despite the problems associated with Thompson's distinction between concept and reality, his discussion of the separation between the horizons of the historian and those of the past contain a great deal of theoretical insight overlooked by Althusser, Anderson, as well as Hindess and Hirst. But, before we can proceed, I want to take a slight detour through the writing of Charles Taylor and Gadamer.

The past is best thought of as a foreign country. It could have been this metaphor that Charles Taylor (1985c) had in mind in his essay *Understanding and Ethnocentricity*. Taylor, in this instance, deliberately borrows Gadamer's (1975) writing on historical hermeneutics to ask how one might form a less ethnocentric understanding of other cultures. Taylor rejects what he perceives to be two common approaches to these issues in the social sciences. The first is a model drawn from the natural sciences, this approach bypasses the self-descriptions of agents for a more neutral scientific language. One such example is Althusser's account of ideology. Althusser cannot explain, how in his terms, the dominant ISA the educational system historically took on a particular institutional form. This is because, in Althusser's writing, the education system is functionally required to reproduce the economic structure. He also cannot adequately explain, I would argue, among other things, the differential levels of 'achievement' of subordinate social groups. In this respect, Paul Willis (1980) argues it is the 'culture' agents bring with them to school, rather than the ideological message of the school, which is determinant in this process. Althusser is prohibited from taking account of the cultural contexts and self-descriptions of agents as such a move could be construed as a form of humanism. Althusser is leaving aside many of the things social theory should be seeking to explain. Such an approach when applied to a culture other than one's own or a different historical period, would undoubtedly reproduce the assumptions of the social theorist. Not because he or she was not attending to 'the facts', as Thompson stresses in his account, but more importantly because the writer was not connecting with the beliefs, feelings and desires of agents.

The second model Taylor wants to avoid is one that treats the self-understanding of agents as sacred. This is because the social sciences are in the business of challenging the beliefs of agents, and unless the practical consciousness of social actors is treated in this way, it would hold little, if any scope, for a concept like ideology. This is obviously what Althusser was trying to do. However he did so in such a way as to completely ignore what agents themselves would accept as what was 'really going on'. How then could one legitimately seek to understand a culture different to ones own? Taylor argues:

> This would be in a language in which we could formulate both their way of life and ours as alternative possibilities in relation to some human constants at work in both. It would be a language in which the possible human variations would be so formulated that both our form of

life and theirs could be described as alternative such variations. Such a language of contrast might show their language of understanding to be distorted or inadequate in some respects, or it might show ours to be so (Taylor,1985c,p.125).

This is related to Gadamer's views on the cognitive dimension Bildung (Gadamer, 1975, p. 320). Put briefly, individuals and cultures could be said to be in the possession of Bildung, the extent to which they retain an openness to other forms of life. Bildung, or learning from others, while opening oneself up for experience, is opposed to dogmatism. Gadamer argues that our 'prejudices' are necessary to our forming an understanding. Prejudice does not mean, as it usually does in ordinary language, the refusal to accept the rational arguments of another in favour of that which has no justification. Prejudice is instead, in Gadamer's terms, those cultural horizons through which understanding is made possible. One sees through the horizons of one's cultural tradition in such a way as to reveal, draw comparisons with, and reflect critically upon, past historical periods and other cultures. By merging horizons with other 'experiences' both sets of cultural presuppositions are brought into question. To write in a spirit informed by Bildung is to be aware that the historical horizon one finds oneself embedded within, is not a fixed final point. This involves the recognition that different generations and different authors will necessarily ask different questions of history and culture. No doubt Althusser and Perry Anderson would be uncomfortable in that Bildung leads to a form of relativism. This concern does not seem justified, as to accept Bildung, does not necessarily entail a relativistic conclusion that all culture and forms of life are of equal value. The writer, alternatively, should engage with others in argument and debate developing insight into the 'truth' (Warnke, 1987).

To briefly summarise the argument thus far. The theoretical short comings of Althusser's writing led to the relativist position defended by Hindess and Hirst. Further Althusser can also be accused of theoretical dogmatism by excluding the self perceptions of agents. I have also suggested that the notion of Bildung, defended by Gadamer and Taylor, could help one avoid the theoretical difficulties of Althusser and his followers. This seems to be particularly true if we apply these arguments to history. Hindess's and Hirst's impoverished view of historical writing simply saw the end result as being determined by the theoretical context of the historian. What the post-structuralists, in this context, do not seem to be able to allow for is the intellectual space for what Thompson might describe as the voices and ethical perspectives of others. The historian, by connecting with social actors of the past, must be prepared to have his or her expectations challenged by entering into a dialogue with those who do not share his or her position in time and space.

Thompson, despite the polemical nature of his political writing, comes intellectually closer to the spirit of Bildung than any of his rivals. His unique ability to bring the past and present into dialogue with one another is best demonstrated in his famous essay *Time, Work-Discipline, and Industrial Capitalism.* (1982a). In this essay, Thompson argues, that along with the industrial revolution came a redefinition of 'time'. Time in preindustrial civilisation is task oriented, as the day is divided around the length of a given task, or what Thompson calls 'natural work rhythms' (Thompson,1982a, p.302). Three main points can be made about preindustrial societies with reference to time. Firstly, the task oriented nature of work allows for a certain amount of autonomy. In more modern periods the life of an undergraduate could also be thought of as 'task oriented'. The student may be given a week to complete an essay, but it is up to his or her discretion as to precisely when the work is completed. In Thompson's account he focuses on the work patterns of hand-loom workers prior to the industrial revolution, where similar to many students, their work practices are organised around prolonged periods of rest followed by intense stints of activity. Secondly, task orientation does not tend to maintain such a rigid separation between work and leisure, when compared to industrial relations of production. Thirdly, to those who wish to quantify time at work by the clock, the 'natural work rhythm' would seem inefficient and wasteful. Time and labour, therefore, becomes an abstract and instrumentally calculable phenomena under capitalism. Thus capital attempts to reconstruct and discipline the work force into a authoritarian and calculable work regime, although this project is continually resisted by living labour.

Thompson ends the essay by speculating that given the productive forces that would be 'released' under socialism, then necessary working time could be substantially reduced and collectively redefined. Thompson concludes:

> men might have to re-learn some of the arts of living lost in the industrial revolution: how to fill the interstices of their days with enriched, more leisurely, personal and social relation; how to break down once more the barriers between work and life (Thompson,1982a,p.309).

Thompson, in this example, is struggling to find the language where the life-worlds of past and present can be brought together to foster a more critical understanding. Similarly, in E.P. Thompson's only novel *The Sykaos Papers* (1988), he again brings together two very different cultures. This often very comic work has an underlying seriousness, which investigates the problems of translation between different cultures. The novel is supposedly the record of a poet called Oi Paz who has come to earth as his own planet Sykaos is on the brink of an ecological disaster. Oi Paz encounters a series of cultural misunderstandings where he is mistaken as a Russian agent and later becomes an intelligent game show host. Real understanding is only arrived at when Oi Paz forms a close relationship with an anthropologist. After a long period of discussion between the two, the culture of Sykaos, and contemporary British society are drawn into sharp contrast. For example, the anthropologist discovers that Oi Paz has evaded the process Althusser describes as interpellation. Oi Paz has little sense of himself as an individual apart from a collective which completely sustains his identity. Further, he does not seem capable of personal human feelings such as love, or a personal sense of difference from other members of his tribe on Sykaos.

Alternatively Oi Paz poses questions on the rationality of a civilisation that wastes much of its resources on weapons of mass destruction. That neither the anthropologist nor Oi Paz are ever capable of understanding in other than their own terms is due to their existential rootedness in different cultures. However, Thompson represents this cultural difference, as both tragic in terms of the failure to reach mutual comprehension, and productive as through their relationship the life-worlds of the anthropologist and Oi Paz are sharply and comically contrasted.

So far I have stressed that Thompson can be brought into line with the writing of Taylor and Gadamer, where as the Althusserians cannot. Much of Thompson's best historical writing attempts to get in touch with the cultural contexts, values and beliefs of those he is writing about, in order to bring them critically to bear on the present. Yet I would argue that whileThompson was justified in rejectiing the relativist conclusions of Hindess and Hirst, he was wrong to seek a corrective to this position in a purely factual domain. Instead, as Thompson's own writing bears out, the historian should lay himself open to the life-worlds of historically contextualised actors. Following the arguments of Taylor and Gadamer, around the concept of Bildung, would seem to be the most fruitful way of capturing other historical periods while recognising ones own historicity. This procedure should hold out the prospect of the presumptions of the historian being challenged, in a way that Althusser's internalist notion of truth would not allow. If Thompson's writing on the determining realm of the factual was misleading, he was closer to the truth when he argued that Althusser lacked a theory of reference. As Gregory Elliott (1987,p.111) has written on Althusser: 'theory dependent knowledge of the real world is transmuted into reality-independent theory '.

On a different question, Stuart Hall (1981) has argued along with Althusser, that theory must be considered as being at least relatively autonomous from the historical period in question. For one could ask, as Hall does, where do theoretical categories emerge from? Rationally they can not come from the facts under scrutiny, as this is what the evidence is in Thompson's own terms tested against. Similarly, the tradition or intellectual horizon one finds oneself embedded within must, in the final analysis, also escape the ultimate testability of hard evidence. Thompson, in other words, in order to be consistent, would have to allow for a dimension of theoretical and intellectual practice that can not be directly refuted by historical evidence. In principle, historian's prejudices could be revised through argument or countered by the ' voices ' uncovered through research, but the theoretical concerns of the writer of history could not ultimately be determined by a factual dimension. In this context, the work of Philip Abrams (1982), has convincingly demonstrated that theoretical categories can be reflexively applied to the study of history. Abrams argues, that history and sociology, should not be thought of as separate disciplines posing distinct questions. By focusing on the 'event', one can come to see how the theoretical concepts such as 'action' and 'structure' can be utilised to enhance understanding. Abrams, like Thompson, wants to view history as a process that avoids reificatory forms of representation. An 'event', for Abrams is:

> a moment of becoming at which action and structure meet. The designation of a happening as an event indicates that the meeting has been judged peculiarly forceful (Abrams,1982,p.193).

Abrams argues events are conjunctures between action and structure. This opens up the possibility of producing historical knowledge that is characterised through a notion of process. Thus historical process is dependent upon the way it is captured by the relation between agency and structure, not upon the historian's distance from theoretical concerns. It is through theoretical concepts like agency and structure that the past becomes illuminated. As the 'facts' themselves cannot directly refute theoretical categories, they must be open for discussion. This will enable historical writing to become a reflexive practice free from some of the evasions discussed in this section.

Paul Hirst and the nature of the subject

So far we have seen how in Althusser's writing the subject is formed through a dominant ideology. This gave rise to Thompson's justifiable objection that Althusser cannot account for a notion of agency. However of the responses to Thompson's essay under discussion, it is Hirst who has the closest affinity with the writing of Althusser. Paul Hirst, along with his colleague Barry Hindess, came to represent, albeit for a short period, British Althusserianism. The crux of Hirst's objection to Thompson's essay was his humanism, according to Hirst:

> Thompson supposes a universal human subject. This being has the same essential attributes in all its incarnations: it is unitary within the 'single space' of its self experience, and all the members of its class have the common faculties of 'consciousness' and 'reason'. These faculties have a generality which transcends any definite forms of their organisation (Hirst,1985,p.73).

According to Hirst, it is characteristic of humanism to represent the subject as having a capacity for self-knowledge that is made available through reflection. The subject, in Thompson's reading, is ultimately transparent and capable of rational form of self-understanding. Hirst, goes on to argue, that such access to forms of self awareness and appreciation can only be an illusion. This is because the subject is constructed through language and symbolic processes, with the unconscious continually interrupting attempts to position the self rationally. In a similar vein to Althusser, Hirst's aim is to radically de-centre the notion of a free choosing autonomous subject, and argue such a formation is a humanist illusion. While there are of course important differences between the positions adopted by Hirst and Althusser, for our purposes at least, there also seem to be large areas of agreement.

I would agree with Hirst that Thompson does not appreciate the importance that language and the unconscious have for a conception of the subject. The admission of such concerns for Thompson would undoubtedly have posed important political and theoretical questions he left unaddressed. For example, given that men and women can never achieve absolute self-knowledge and control over the social world, this would inevitably impinge on the traditional socialist aim of a more consciously controlled rational society. Althusser and Hirst are surely right to argue that men and women do not preside over an ultimately manipulable reality, of which they can come to have absolute knowledge about and complete control over. With the denial of complete self-knowledge would come the conclusion that societies are always based upon conflict rather than harmony, and not upon atomised consciously controlled selves who occupy a transcendental position. The utopian vision of Williams Morris, that Thompson (1955) formed such a strong attachment to, represented a society where the state had withered away, and where the needs of individuals had become harmoniously reconciled with society. Such a vision, one could argue, presupposes a society where agents have a privileged access to their wants and desires, and where they never come into conflict with the felt needs of other agents. Thus, a more sophisticated notion of the subject, could have led Thompson towards a more critically informed response to some Morris' writing.

This said, Hirst's version of the subject would seem to be as, if not more, limited than that of E.P. Thompson. J. B. Thompson (1984, p. 94-98), has argued it is contradictory to link a conception of the subject determined by ideology, to a historical materialist project that is dependent on working-class agency. Agents may not act in conditions they fully understand, or following Marx, in conditions of their choosing, but one must accept that agents are capable of acting reflexively and creatively in order to alter their social conditions. That Hirst is not taking a conception of agency seriously enough becomes apparent when he likens the subject to a 'trace' in language. The subject, for Hirst, is 'written' by social processes that are continually interrupted by unconscious desires. Problematically, I would argue, it is one thing to argue that there are limits to self-knowledge, and another to suggest that such attempts, are always by their very nature, illusory. Here Hirst seems to be making three related errors. First, while he discusses the formation of the subject through social structures, he provides little reflection on the relation between agency and structure. This is odd given that a major component of Thompson's critique of Althusser is focused on questions of agency. Second, unlike Raymond Williams and E.P. Thompson, Hirst does not find it necessary to discuss what they call 'practical consciousness'. For Williams, as we saw, this implies a domain of everyday know-how that can be reflexively called upon in differing social contexts. Thus Williams's and Thompson's discussion of practical consciousness is obviously connected with their belief that culture is not an interchangeable category with that of ideology. As Thompson says of Althusser's 'subjects', none of them seem to be capable of either learning from experience, or of experience that is not in some way ideological. Third Hirst's attack on humanism means that he is unable to account for human agents or subjects as being preoccupied with ethical questions. As Charles Taylor (1985a) argues fundamental to our conception of a person is the belief that one can be held responsible for ethical decisions. This does not necessarily or automatically lead to a view of the subject as being transcendent over the social, or to a view of the subject that is not dependent upon a cultural context. Humans are relatively self-determining animals only by virtue of a shared socio-historic context; as by changing the criteria by which we judge a specific action, the act itself can take on a different meaning. But, while informative, Taylor's description of the ethically self-reflexive subject surely retains a deep connection to humanist forms of voluntarism. For example, we may recognise the extent to which we have been socially constructed in terms of our gender relations, but despite demands made by our partner, remain resistant to change. Kate Soper makes this point when she writes:

> we frequently confront situations where an acute sense of responsibility for self-change goes together with a no less acute understanding of why this cannot be viewed simply in terms of an existential project, and why it would be too purely voluntarist to suppose it could (Soper,1991,p.75).

Yet as Soper would surely agree, to say that the self is not consistently manipulable, would not imply that subjects are incapable of reflexively taking up the challenge of becoming different persons with due consideration to social context.

English Marxism and Agency

Perry Anderson's *Arguments in English Marxism* (1980) is dedicated to the work of E.P. Thompson. The book should be read both as an attempt to heal the personal rift between himself and Thompson, and as a defence of some of Althusser's theoretical ventures. Anderson, on questions of agency agrees with Thompson, but only up to a point.

Both writers contend that Althusser does not allow for an adequate conception of agency. They differ from one another in that Anderson finds Thompson's account of agency lacking in any theoretical depth. Anderson himself uses the term agency to signify conscious, goal-directed activity. Thompson's inability or unwillingness to give agency a rigorous definition, according to Anderson, means he conflates three types of 'goal'. This can be characterised in the following manner:

1. The first form of conscious agency described by Anderson is that of 'private' goals. Private goals are pursued by agents on a day to day basis, and form the main level upon which existing social relations are reproduced. This form of conscious activity ranges from choosing a partner, to catching a bus to work each morning. They are not private in that they could be thought of as shut away from the social world, but are dependent upon the conscious action of the individual.

2. The next distinctive level of goal directed activity discussed by Anderson is a more collective form of agency, and can not be conceptualised in terms of individual projects. He calls this type of agency collectivist reformist. Despite operating on a collective level, this form of goal directed activity has for Anderson a somewhat limited character. Instead of challenging whole social structures, proponents of collectivist reformism have formulated goals on the basis of already taken for granted assumptions of social actors. Anderson would probably want to characterise the British Labour party in these terms, as by working within the dominant assumptions of capitalism they have not sought to transform the central class relations of our society.

3. Lastly, Anderson describes another form of conscious collective practice which he argues is 'an unprecedented from of agency' (Anderson,1980,p.20). Unlike the reformist approach this particular form of agency has a common goal which emphasises the total transformation of society. The goal of revolutionary praxis is an emancipated society. This form of agency inevitably challenges the way in which collective activity has been hegemonically defined. Anderson, goes on that, Thompson erroneously assimilates agency to choice, will and decision, and that what is missing in his writing is 'knowledge'. Agency, for Anderson, is dependent on the knowledge one has at one's disposal, as the proletariat cannot come to master a society through an act of will alone. What the peasants and workers in the Russian revolution needed was knowledge of their subordinate position in the class structure, and of their potentiality to act as an agent of change.

Anderson pursues these points by arguing that Thompson's agents are both non-reflexive and exist outside of any recognisable social structure. Such a view is caught up with Thompson's arguments around 'experience'. Experience, in Thompson's writing, is a mediating term between social being and social consciousness. Social being usually signifies for Thompson the values and beliefs of social actors, while he often uses the term experience in connection with emotion and feeling. But, Anderson argues, the distinction between social being, experience and social consciousness has led Thompson to adopt a voluntaristic idea of class formation. As we will see later, in *The Making of the English Working-Class* (1980), classes only come into being when large groups of individuals share common experiences. Anderson, rightly argues, in opposition to Thompson, that social orders in modern or past societies cannot be explained in terms of shared values and beliefs. Instead of focusing on the atomised wills of individuals and groups one must, if we follow Anderson, look to the dominant mode of production to explain the cohesiveness of a social formation. It is, for Anderson and Althusser, the economic structure that allots agents to positions in the social structure, not the wills of agents that form the mode of production.

While Anderson provides a provocative corrective to Thompson's utilisation of agency, he has evaded some of the central problems that can be associated with notions of agency. Thompson's main error was to conceive of action and structure as separable theoretical problems, and that Anderson highlights this is the main point he has to make against him. But, while Anderson discusses both agency and structure, his arguments are not particularly convincing. The theoretical difficulties involved in conceptualising agency and structure as a 'duality' cannot be resolved by appealing to the dominant mode of production. In what follows, I will question Anderson's writing on agency, and the soundness of his arguments against Thompson. This will be followed by what I consider to be a more convincing account of agency and structure.

Firstly, Anderson's definition of agency as being conscious and goal directed is misleading. It remains doubtful whether this conceptually thin definition captures the many diverse aspects of agency. To be an agent is not simply dependent upon the cognitive consideration of goals, as such a description could not account for social action that is either ritualistic or unconscious. Further, Anderson's claim that Thompson does not fully take account of the extent to which social agents and collectivities act knowledgeably is similarly misleading. For Thompson, that agents are capable of acting knowledgeably and reflexively is one of the defining qualities of being a human agent.

This quality may have been lacking from his historiography but it was certainly present in his writing on socialist humanism (Thompson,1957). In the making of history men and women, in specific social contexts, draw critically on contextualised moral considerations that are connected to cultural and political formations. Finally, I want to reject Anderson's argument that definitions of social classes need not appeal to an experiential dimension. As many sociologists have argued, including both Marxist and non-Marxist writers, unless one understands class in terms of the interconnection between common experiences and objective relations, it becomes difficult to understand how a sense of class belonging or solidarity becomes engendered (Bourdieu, 1987; Giddens, 1973; Poulantzas, 1983). Anderson's definition of class is overly economistic, and has been defined in opposition to Thompson's perceived culturalism.

Anthony Giddens and structuration theory

Structuration theory has been the hallmark of the writing of Anthony Giddens. His theory of structuration is designed precisely to avoid the sort of polarisation we encountered in the Anderson/Thompson debate. Anderson rightly emphasises the importance of social structure in seeking to explain the persistence of modern social relations, but what he could not do is interlock this emphasis with a notion of agency. Althusser, as we have seen, similarly put the stress in his writing on the importance of social structures. Alternatively, Thompson's writing portrayed social agents actively involved in culturally shaping the world they inhabit. Yet where as Althusser cannot account for agency, Thompson encounters a similar problem with structures.

Giddens refuses to see action and structure as separate terms of analysis, instead he represents them theoretically in terms of dualism, or what he calls a 'duality'. Agency is normally thought of as the capacity to do otherwise to that which one has done. But social theorists need to forego the temptation of opposing this sense of agency to determining structures. Instead, as the term duality suggests, agency and structure are best thought of as interdependent theoretical categories. Giddens writes:

> Understood as rules and resources implicated in the 'form' of collectivities of social systems, reproduced across space and time, structure is the very medium of the 'human' element of human agency. At the same time,

117

agency is the medium of structure, which individuals reproduce in the course of their activities' (Giddens,1987a,p.p.220-1.).

Similar to Thompson's discussion of experience in *The Poverty of Theory* (1978a), Giddens wants to highlight the extent to which agents know a great deal about the social world they are caught up in. But, unlike either Thompson or Anderson, Giddens gives us a theoretically precise definition of agency. Not all agency has the clear intentional goal orientation that Anderson describes. Agency is only purposive the extent to which actors continually monitor what they are doing in differing social contexts. Thus agents are knowledgeable as they are capable of offering cogent explanations of their conduct.

Giddens, for me at least, best illustrates his theory of structuration through his discussion of language use. The rules of language (langue) are drawn upon in the actual production of speech (parole). Hence one of the unintended consequences of language use is the reproduction of langue. The a fore mentioned rules of language may of course also change, as a result of actual practice. Language, as a set of rules and resources, cannot be thought of as produced by or for any one agent. Instead langue pre-exists parole and is a precondition of language use, not a direct product of it.

In summary we have seen how the position of Althusser, Anderson and Thompson could have been bettered had they approached questions of agency and structure as a duality. While Giddens's theory has attracted critics it would seem to avoid many of the theoretical errors of its rivals (J.B.Thompson 1984, Callinicos 1987). This said, E.P.Thompson's view of agency as possessing an ethical dimension should also be sustained.There seems to be no immediate contradiction between structuration theory, and the idea that agency has a moral component. Both theories stress the reflexive character of human praxis within determinant social structures. It is towards the issues of agency and ethics I want to turn to again in a later section.

Culture, value and ideology

Thompson, throughout *The Poverty of Theory* (1984a), raises a number of objections to Althusser's writing. Many of these have already been discussed, such as Althusser's treatment of agency. However, there are a number of other related problems that Thompson raises with respect to Althusser's contributions on ideology and culture. I shall now unpack some of these items.

Thompson identifies a connection between Althusser's Leninism and a form of intellectual elitism. If the masses are prevented from developing a revolutionary consciousness through their position in the social structure, then they must be, in Althusser's terms, the victims of a dominant ideology. The emergence of a class for itself from a class in itself will not arise spontaneously, which justifies the existence of an elite group of party intellectuals. In early Leninist (1964) theory it was the function of the party elite to implant a revolutionary ideology externally into the consciousness of the proletariat. Althusser, on this score, openly admits his admiration for the political philosophy of Lenin. Althusser, Thompson would argue, through theoretical practice is creating a similar social space for the operation of an intellectual vanguard. Althusser adopts a position similar to that of Lenin by arguing that the relationship between the proletariat and the scientific discourse of Marxism is one of 'exteriority'. Other writers who belong to a radical post-structuralist tradition, while rejecting the science/ideology distinction, occasionally talk in similar terms. Theresa de Lauretis (1987, p.17) while accusing Althusser of being gender blind, recommends that progressive intellectuals ' implant' new objects, and modes of knowledge in individual subjects'. Quite clearly, a point that Williams and Thompson would both want to make is that the afore mentioned writers are ignoring the cultural contexts of reception. Thompson, on the other hand, argues for a socialist theory that forms connections with the social experience of the people, and suggests that the root of the Althusser's elitism lies in the:

> characteristic delusion of intellectuals, who suppose that ordinary mortals are stupid. In my own view, the truth is more nuanced: experience is valid and effective but within determined limits: the farmer 'knows' his seasons, the sailor 'knows' his seas, but both may remain mystified about kingship and cosmology (Thompson,1978a,p.199).

The development of political projects, in Thompson's writing, bears a striking resemblance with the social practice of the historian. Just as the historian retreats into a form of 'scholasticism' the moment he loses touch with the facts, so socialist intellectuals risk forms of authoritarianism once they become detached from the experience of ordinary people. But again, just as Thompson argued that facts had a determining relation in the writing of history, the experience of ordinary people plays a similarly decisive role in the formation of political projects. In Thompson's *Open Letter to Leszek Kolakowski*

119

(1978b), he counterpoises a detached elitist intellectual culture, to those values he has learnt through active engagement in politics. While he retains a commendable openness to the 'experience' of others, any serious theory of political mobilisation could not be determined through the primacy of people's experience. Thompson with his political ear to the ground, allows himself to be constructed in opposition to Althusser, whose political theory completely ignored the self-descriptive categories of agents. To argue, as Thompson does, that experience is somehow primary, could have the unintended consequence of mystifying the relationship between political organisations and the social groups it is meant to represent. Representation is never simply a matter of drawing upon the direct experience of the people: if it was, how could we explain the attraction of the peace movement for those with no first hand knowledge of nuclear warfare. Thompson's 'dialectic' also begs certain questions related to how representatives are chosen, elected, and what kind of forums they can legitimately operate in. This links onto my second point, that politics can never be reconstituted so that it reflects the experience of certain oppressed social groups. The political is not given, or read off from class position, but must on some level become materially and symbolically constructed. This is not to say that the 'experience' of social actors does not play a part in forms of political identification and support. As Thompson's historical studies continually reveal knowledgeable human agents are capable of reflecting on their 'experience', while seeking to mobilise others in the struggle for a 'better' society. But again this does not entail politics simply flows from experience, or that communities exist ready made for mobilisation outside of their political and symbolic forms of construction.

That Althusser treats the cultural and the ideological as interchangeable categories was criticised earlier in my discussion of cultural materialism. Ideology is not, as Althusser argues the case to be, simply representative of the symbolic dimension, but is the means whereby contextual meaning is mobilised to uphold relations of domination. The writing of E.P. Thompson, as we will see later, contains a similarly 'critical' conception of ideology. For Thompson cultural traditions and processes can either be ideological such as Methodism, or potentially liberatory such as the tradition of 'the free-born Englishman'. Dominant ideologies are not represented, by Thompson, as 'total' and all encompassing in the way he perceived them to be in the writing of the early Frankfurt school and Althusser. Thus, it was not the sole responsibility of politically militant intellectuals to find some means of transcending ideology, as this will already have been achieved through current political protest and older radical traditions. I shall return to these questions later.

Anderson repeats the often made criticism of Althusser that his theory of ideology makes it difficult to account for the class struggle. Althusser's functionalism, as other writers have mentioned, leaves very little space for the construction of oppositional cultures and political movements. This is partly because in Althusser's writing the ISA's seem to cover everything from trade unions to nursery schools. As we have already seen, for Thompson and Williams, as well as Anderson, civil society does not possess the sort of ideological unity that is evident in Althusser. Thompson however takes this argument one stage further by insisting that civil society is not only ideologically open in that dominant ideologies are never permanent and fixed, but also that the domain of civil society has an emancipatory content.

The final chapter of *Whigs and Hunters* (1977) can be read along with the essay *Poverty and Theory* (1984a) as a defence of Thompson's historical method against structuralism. Thompson's study of eighteenth century society pertains to reveal the cynical manipulation of the law by the Whig government. This was particularly evident in the Black act. The infamous Blacks, according to Thompson's account, effectively challenged the hegemony of the Crown and the Whigs during the 1720s. Such was the perceived threat to the status quo by the Blacks (who were those from 'middling' orders of the forest refusing to give up their rights under old customary agreements) that the interests of the old ruling elites effectively merged in opposition to the threat to private property. Hence Thompson accepts Anderson's and Williams's arguments about the so call ISA's being the site of conflict. But, what he also illustrates, is that the 'law' was always more than the outcome of the specific relations between class forces. The institution of legal practice has its 'own characteristics, its own independent history and logic of evolution' (Thompson, 1977 p. 262). It seems to have escaped Thompson's attention that Althusser's writing on the relative autonomy of the economic, political and the ideological, wants to make a similar point on the structural specificity of these spheres. But, it is fair to suggest, Thompson draws differing conclusions from those of Althusser regarding this insight. While the rule of law can be ideological; it can simultaneously be represented as 'a cultural achievement of universal significance' (Thompson,1977,p.265). Here Thompson ingeniously attempts to merge both liberal and Marxist theory. He argues that it is not necessarily contradictory to propose that the law has both an ideological function, as well as acting as a limitation upon the power

121

of the state. The law has historically been used, often unsuccessfully, by citizens to either defend old historically won rights, or claim new ones. Despite the role the actual practice of the law has played in legitimating differing forms of domination, it can be considered an achievement the extent to which it holds 'equal treatment' as a human good. While Thompson would hardly be able to describe himself as a Marxist if he did not recognise that the law systematically discriminates in favour of powerful social groups, this does not mean that the law can be simply considered superstructural. The law, while it attains towards treating persons equally, which Thompson identifies as a socialist principle, resists the one dimensional characterisation often attributed to it by many Marxists.

Thompson's main point is not simply Marx's argument, that within the present there must exist the kernel of the future good society, but that institutional structures are the embodiment of certain moral values. The values that are rooted in institutional practices such as law open up a theoretical space for a form of immanent ideology critique. The institutional practice of law can be confronted and called into question in terms of its own expressed values. This particular process of critique would also apply to future socialist institutions, where Thompson writes:

> Everything will depend upon men being able to create the institutional devices through which antagonisms of interest can be disclosed and rationally reconciled (Thompson,1977,p.170).

Thompson continually reminds the reader that conflicts of interest are always conflicts of value. These disputes can only be resolved in a socialist society which enabled open democratic and rational discussion. Hence *Whigs and Hunters* (1977) reaffirms and uncovers the values encapsulated in the law as a means of writing about the relations of domination in the eighteenth century. While recognising the historical distance between himself and the eighteenth century, he forms intellectual connections with the past by identifying with certain values that continue to inform the present. These values are not only found in institutions, but in social movements and social practices. Part of the project, as we shall see, of 'history from below' was to rescue those voices that had been ignored by more traditional historical writing. Thompson's hope was that similar values that had formed the radical culture of the labour movement, could having been recovered from the past, form a similarly critical function in the present.

Stalin, Althusser and socialist humanism

Perry Anderson (1980) can be forgiven for treating Thompson's comparison between Stalin and Althusser as absurd. For Anderson, the grouping together of Althusser and Stalin, marks an odd lapse for a historian with E.P. Thompson's obvious credentials. Thompson does not situate Althusser's writing in any kind of historical context, and completely ignores his political writing on the Soviet Union, nor does he investigate Althusser's complex relationship with the French Communist Party. While Anderson is right to argue Thompson should have researched Althusser's writing more thoroughly, he does seem to have misunderstood what I take to be the point of Thompson's comparison. Kate Soper, writes that alternatively, Thompson may have a case to be answered. She says perceptively:

> while it is true that Thompson misjudged the real target of Althusser's polemic, it is not clear why Anderson should suppose that in revealing Althusser's Maoist leanings he has vindicated him of the charges laid against him by Thompson (Soper 1990b, p. 217).

These 'charges' were a culturally reductive attachment to the base/superstructure model, their joint 'scholasticism', and their rejection of a moral dimension in politics. Here I intend to bypass yet another discussion of base and superstructure as these issues were largely dealt with in the earlier chapter on cultural materialism. Also, as I have already discussed Althusser's so called idealism, I can deal with this point quickly. Earlier I argued that while it remained doubtful whether theoretical categories could be empirically refuted, they should at least attempt to establish a relation between theory and reality. I suggested, following the writings of Gadamer and Taylor, that this might be best achieved through the self-descriptive categories of agents, rather than constructing 'facts' in external constraining relations. Thus, Thompson does have a point, if he is merely emphasising that political theory should not be cut away from the actual lived cultural experience of the people, that is bound up with, as we saw, the self-descriptive perceptions of agents. Both Stalinism and Althusserianism, I would argue, could be said to exhibit similarly authoritarian qualities. Stalinism did not subject itself to democratic control, or respect the relative autonomy of civil society, instead the regime proceeded as if it had a monopoly on truth. Likewise Althusser's connection with Leninism revealed an authoritarian tendency bent on 'implanting' ideologies irrespective of the beliefs and concerns of social agents.

On the final point, Thompson would surely be correct in wanting to maintain a link between politics and ethics. An authoritarian regime bent on human devastation, such as those that can be associated with the practice of genocide, would have to find a way of preventing the emergence of moral objections. Zygmunt Bauman writes:

> The first thing a power bent on genocide must do is substitute impersonal rules for moral (or for that matter immoral) drives and intuitions. And such powers can do this because of the unique capabilities offered to them by modern social organisation (Bauman,1990,p.722).

Anderson, as we saw, accuses Thompson of neglecting social structures in favour of a concern over values. This, Anderson claims, acts as a form of moralism in his writing and does not fully appreciate the structural limits that are placed upon social agents. Anderson however does not appreciate that morality and differing forms of domination are intimately bound up with one another. Social forms of domination as diverse as Thatcherism and Stalinism, for example, attempt to hegemonically secure their definition of ethics as the dominant legitimate code. Part of my argument against Althusser was that he did not fully appreciate socialist humanist arguments around human nature. Both Williams and Thompson represent human-nature as mediated by social context. This arguably makes the point that human-beings are not as plastic as the structuralists supposed them to be. For Williams, as we saw, human-beings are creative beings who depended upon the support of social institutions. Thompson, like Williams, also recognised that human-beings had an intrinsically material nature which delivered them with certain needs. Yet, on the other hand, he tallks of them in terms of historically mediated potential. Here Thompson writes:

> what has been potential in history has not been one single 'fully human' essence of womanliness, but precisely the potential of feminine self-determination within changing historical contexts; of freedom from being conditioned and limited by a masculine definition of her role and nature (Thompson,1978b,p.154).

This is a view of human nature that I would wish to defend. Human-beings by virtue of their capacity to forge connections with one another and act creatively are thus able to realise their potential in different social contexts. However, our need for self-determination, can not be generated from our inherited biological structure. This is the product of a specifically social imaginary dimension. What is emphasised is that our 'natures' are the result of social contexts and human agency. Resting on the previous discussions of Heller and Taylor, we have already seen how human subjects are historically contextualised, relatively self-determining agents. Similarly a radical politics, as Heller in particular stresses, would have to recognise a hierarchy of values that is compatible with a democratically held view of human nature. For example, a concern for socialist politics, would where possible, prioritise the value of democracy over efficiency criteria determined by economic reason. We are now in the position, I would want to stress, to see why the notion of a self-determined society relies on a particular view of human nature. Williams,Thompson, Heller and Taylor would all agree that societies are to be judged to the extent they allow for social development in accordance with certain values. While Thompson conveys a belief that the social can be completely determined by moral values that I do not share - I would go along with the main emphasis of his argument. Thompson writes:

> the potentia is exactly the human potential to act as rational and moral agents, to enter an age in which human wills and aspirations take charge and are no longer subservient to economic necessity and the law-bound inevitability of the past (Thompson,1978b,p.155).

This view of human nature is historically dependent. The idea of self-determination would not be available to us as subjects without a shared inter-subjective realm that accepted common terms of reference such as language of rights, democracy and equality. Hence the idea of self-determination is dependent on a shared historical context of background meanings, while the capacity of human subjects to practice self-determination is also reliant upon social institutions being organised materially along these lines.

A word of caution is perhaps necessary at this point. What is not being suggested is that society is ultimately subordinate to the will of the people, that Thompson is caught up with this view is undeniable. However, I see no inherent reason why the value of self-determination can not be accepted, along with a recognition that it is never absolute. Although Thompson still wants to talk in traditional Marxist metaphors of moving from a society dictated by 'necessity' to one that enters the realm of 'freedom', the claim being made is that these institutions and practices need to be opened up, as far as is possible, to the idea of democratic self-determination.

Thompson did not make the connection between humanism and a self-determined society in quite the way I have done, but I would maintain the way I have presented the argument is in accordance with the informed spirit of his writing. His commitment to a view of human nature as relatively self-determining provides him with the criteria upon which he can strongly 'evaluate' differing forms of social organisation. Thompson is therefore in a position to morally assess the failure of 'actually existed socialism', in a way that Althusser was not. Where Althusser sees state apparatuses functioning as ideological terminals, Thompson through the value he places on the realisation of historically grounded human potential, can argue one state is more repressive than another. Such a view is an essential characteristic of a normative critical theory.

4 Robust Englishmen, Marxism and exterminism

The early writing of E.P. Thompson united the study of sociology and history. His particular contribution is usually referred to as 'history from below'. Instead of constructing a notion of history around the actions of great men and social elites; history from below concentrated on the social and economic activity of subordinate social groups. History from the bottom up sought to redress the balance by bringing into the light the activity of social groups whose presence is rendered invisible by more conservative historical narratives. One of Thompson's concerns was to avoid writing the history of social groups in isolation from one another; instead the historian should seek to uncover relations of cultural domination and the distinctive patterns of emerging ways of life. Thompson, rather like the Annales school, opened up the life-worlds of social actors that informed the everyday as much as the exceptional event. While Thompson has been criticised for his cultural definition of class, his early and later writing conceptualises classes as sites of symbolic struggle. His focus on the symbolic dimension of class struggle enabled him to represent the working-class as creatively shaping the early modern world. *The Making of the English Working-Class* (1980) represents class not as a static structure imposed from the outside by the industrial revolution, but as the product of the conscious self-activity of the working-class. Thus the working-class, in his account, were formed not only through the rise of capitalism, but more importantly in relation to their own radical cultural and political institutions.

Culture and the making of the English working class

E.P. Thompson's *The Making of the English Working Class* (1980) is a classic of post-war social history. Along with Williams's *Culture and Society* (1961), it was one of the founding texts of the British New Left and cultural studies generally. Thompson's narrative pertains to give a detailed account of the social and political formation of the working-class between 1780 and 1832. The main aim of the text is to deconstruct the argument that the making of the working-class arose exclusively out of structural changes in the economic base, and that history can be understood through grand narratives of progress. Thompson wrote:

> The changing productive relations and working conditions of the Industrial Revolution were imposed, not upon raw material, but upon the free-born Englishman - and the free-born Englishman as Paine had left him or as the Methodists had moulded him. The factory hand or stockinger was also the inheritors of Bunyan, of remembered village rights, of notions of equality before the law, of craft traditions. He was the object of massive religious indoctrination and the creator of political traditions. The working-class made itself as much as it was made (Thompson, 1980a, p. 213).

I have already criticised Thompson's writing on class formation through the work of Perry Anderson (1980). In this chapter, I will in part concentrate on the role culture plays in Thompson's early writing. If the previous quotation is read carefully, one could easily interpret Thompson's writing as an example of how the working-class were actively involved in shaping their own culture, rather than in voluntaristically making themselves as a class. The cultural relations that working-class enter into within its own class and with other classes, I would suggest, says something central about its historical character. If Thompson's writing is read as making this lesser claim, as I believe it should, then it maintains a radical cutting edge against other perspectives.

E.P. Thompson traced the cultural origin of the 'free-born Englishman' to the constitutional settlement of 1688. These liberties included equality before law and limited entitlements to freedom of conscience and freedom of speech. The constitutionalism of 1688 was later combined with the more egalitarian sentiments of Tom Paine and Jacobinism, which helped form a consensus around the defence of certain civil rights. The early Jacobin radical societies expressed forms of independence in keeping with the spirit of the 'free-born Englishman', as Thompson says, the 'bawdy debates' (Thompson 1980a,p.172) of the artisans, took the arguments of Paine and Jacobinism, 'to the borders of Socialism' (Thompson 1980a,p.175).

The culturally inherited figure of the robust 'free-born Englishman' went on to inspire the future leaders and followers of the radical working-class movement. In his biography of William Morris, Thompson (1955) writes as though his hero is the embodiment of this tradition. For Thompson, William Morris provides the intellectual link that transformed the romantic movement from a heart felt protest over industrialism, into the hope for the liberation of the working-class. Like Williams, Thompson discovered in the Romantic tradition not only a critique of individualism, but a concern that can also be found in the early Marx, that capitalism does not enable men and women, due to its oppressive nature, to realise their historically given potential. But, as was the case with Williams, Thompson's adoption of historically inherited cultural traditions enabled him to ask some pertinent questions, while seemingly blinding him to others. In this context, the idea of the 'free-born Englishman' and its connection to romanticism is not only ideological, but could also, I shall argue later, have prevented the British Left from taking up ideas related to a rights based citizenship.

One of the issues Thompson's romantic Marxism or socialist humanism predisposed him towards were concerns related to the 'quality of life'. Thompson's (1955) historical interest in the quality of human experiences is juxtaposed with what he calls Podsnapism. Podsnap was a character in Dickens's story called *Our Mutual Friend*, who upheld the Victorian virtues of self-help with the belief that statistics could tell us all we need to know about the life-worlds of men and women. Thompson argues, to overly concern one's self with changes in material consumption, represses equally important questions around the nature of the good life. He wrote:

> It is quite possible for statistical averages and human experiences to run in opposite directions. A *per capita* increase in the quantitative factors may takace at the same time as a great qualitative disturbance in people's way of life, traditional relationships, and sanctions. People may consume more goods and become less happy and less free at the same time (Thompson,1980a,p.231).

Thompson, along with other British Marxist historians like Eric Hobsbawn (1964), wants to resist revisionist trends in social and economic history that would reduce questions concerning the social condition of the early working-class to abstract issues of economic well being. Hobsbawn argues, in this context, that many of the statistics from the industrial revolution do not adequately appreciate that periods of employment are often mixed with intervals of unemployment, and that this gave rise to a culture of 'uncertainty' that obeyed different rules to rational economic assessment. Here Thompson's identification with the radical culture of the time led him to consider broader questions around the social prospects for freedom and autonomy. Through the radical culture of the 'free-born Englishman' Thompson is able to offer a moral assessment not only of the opponents of the nineteenth century workers movement, but of more contemporary defenders of capitalism. The task of the historian is not simply the restoration of historical documents to given contexts, but inevitably involves their moral judgement and evaluation.

The road to a radical working-class culture is an uneven and historically discontinuous process in Thompson's account. Methodism, for example, is skilfully treated as an ideology that legitimated the interests of the industrial bourgeoisie, as it was able to divert and infiltrate the revolutionary energies of the people. But it was not only ideological beliefs that prevented the emergence of a revolutionary consciousness, as there was a hegemonic struggle between a labour aristocracy and other members of the working-class over certain 'ways of life'. Irish workers, according to Thompson, had a more oppositional and 'fiery' cultural disposition than their more reserved English counterparts. For Thompson, such was their temperament, that the Irish found it difficult to learn skilled jobs. Here Thompson would certainly be guilty of racial stereotyping in this description and an underestimation of the power of imperialist ideology. Yet he recognises that cultural and material differences existed in the working-class. The working-class, therefore, could not, for most of the period that Thompson addressed, be thought of as a culturally homogeneous and hermetically sealed group. But while Thompson recognises cultural difference, he also wanted to argue, particularly from the 1830s, that there exists a common intellectual culture that was able to connect with a common experience. The common radical culture, was, through writers such as William Cobbett and James O'Brien, able to bring together different occupational groupings into a common discourse with one another. Thompson wrote on this theme:

The working-class ideology which matured in the thirties (and which has endured, through various translations, ever since) put an exceptionally high value upon the rights of the press, of speech, of meeting and personal liberty. The tradition of 'free-born Englishman' is of course far older (Thompson,1980a,p.505).

The radical culture of the 1830's was the result of the combination of diverse intellectual traditions such as socialism and Jacobinism, which were able to meet the political needs of the present. Thompson describes the passionate political culture of the working-class in the 1830's as the 'most distinguished popular culture England has known' (Thompson 1980a, p. 914).

There does however exist a tension between Thompson's recognition of cultural differences within the working-class, and what he calls 'a common available experience' (Thompson,1980a,p.823). Yet this common experience cannot be the cultural inheritance of the 'free-born Englishman'. This was because it was a previously formed common experience that allowed the oppressed to identify with this tradition in the first place. Thompson, in the chapter called *Exploitation*, makes very clear to the reader that one cannot talk of the common experience of factory discipline, as by the 1830s, 'cotton hand loom weavers alone still outnumbered all the men and women in spinning and weaving mills of cotton, wool, and silk combined' (Thompson 1980, p. 211). Indeed, such was the localised fragmentation of the working-class, that representatives from differing communities were often unable to understand one another in face to face communication. What Thompson is arguing is that despite the cultural differentiation of the working-class, there is an available shared experience, but without ever explicitly drawing out what this experience is centred around. In fact Thompson's writing seems to demonstrate the opposite conclusion. But, as we shall see, his attachment to a collectively produced radical culture ultimately meant other forms of cultural combination were written out of Thompson's account.

Nowhere in *The Making of the English Working-Class* (1980) does Thompson say what he means by the term culture. The impression one gets from this work, and from his historiography in general, is that culture is a prime site of contestation and social struggle. A view that is undoubtedly necessary to any theory of cultural domination and hegemony. In Thompson's (1961) essay on *The Long Revolution*, Williams is criticised for conceptualising culture as an impersonal abstraction, that could not be contextually related to an active sense of agency. Thompson represented culture as a privileged site of agency and moral choice as it 'is performed by active agents both for and against something' (Thompson,1961,p.29). Culture, as it is in the writing of Marx, is associated with sensuous forms of praxis and conscious activity. The continuation and reinvention of radical traditions are dependent upon men and women drawing upon, and contributing to those traditions, as they aim to give a voice to their own oppression. The project that can be associated with 'history from below' is reliant upon the self-activity of ordinary people who realise their own cultural inheritance in the struggle for a better life.

Problems of ideology and hegemony; past and present

In contrast to Williams, the need to develop a 'critical' theory of ideology remained a concern of Thompson's. In his first major work, the previously mentioned biography of William Morris (1955), he provides a thought provoking analysis of cultural domination that pre-dated his later writing on hegemony. Here his writing is best represented, as we saw, through the theme of Podsnapism, which embodied a middle-class world view assembled around an ideological belief in the virtues of self-help. Podsnapism aimed to explain away the extreme material poverty of Victorian society, through the implication that the poor could improve their social conditions by morally reforming themselves. Hence Podsnapism is ideological as it legitimises the existing relations of class domination. Further, while the ideology of self-help was structurally produced by the middle class, inevitably it escaped the location of its original conception.

> it resembled a poison seeping through the veins of society, and yet continually resisted by the forces of life (Thompson,1955,p.177).

Later on in *The Making of the English Working-Class* (1980), Thompson discusses the cultural struggles that were fought over differing 'ways of life'. These struggles, as we have seen, took place not only between the middle and working-class, but within the working-class itself. In Thompson's account, cultural conflicts erupted once the existing 'moral consensus', that had existed between dominant and subordinate groups, had become historically redundant. As Thompson wrote, within social relations determined by the cash nexus:

132

There is no whisper of the 'just' price, or of a wage justified in relation to social or moral sanctions, as opposed to the operation of free market forces(Thompson,1980a,p.222).

In a later article *The Peculiarities of the English* (1978c), one finds the first clear attempt by Thompson to develop a general theory of cultural domination. This essay, along with *Whigs and Hunters* (1977), helps to make up Thompson's mature writing on the subject of hegemony in connection with problems of historiography. *The Peculiarities of the English* (1978c) is an extensive critique of the view that the stability of capitalist society is maintained through the socialisation of subordinate groups into a dominant value system. This particular version of the incorporation thesis was propagated by Nairn (1964) and Anderson (1964), who argued, like Williams, that the dominant value system was inherently ideological as it sought to symbolically dominate any socialist alternative. Thompson, on the other hand, developed a theory of hegemony that differed from the Nairn/Anderson thesis. Harvey J. Kaye writes sympathetically:

By hegemony (and this is important) Thompson does not mean consensus. At least in the eighteenth century, he says 'hegemony does not entail any acceptance by the poor of the gentry's paternalism upon the gentry's own terms or in their approved self image. Rather it refers to an order of struggle that is constantly being disputed and negotiated, but does not become revolutionary conflict, nor entail the continuous use of physical force or coercion by the state (or similarly authority) to maintain the social order (Kaye,1984, p. 197).

After *The Making of the English Working-Class* (1980a), Thompson seemingly relied less on the idea of a moral consensus, and more on historically shifting hegemonic formations. But, despite his formal rejection of the Nairn/Anderson thesis, later Thompson adopts a similar position himself. This is less in evidence in his historical writing, than it is in his work on Exterminism and the state.

For Thompson the dominant ideology of the Cold War is deterrence theory. Put simply, deterrence theory was an ideological explanation that sought to justify Western nuclear dominance during the Cold War. Under deterrence theory nuclear weapons took upon a mostly defensive function, as the argument ran, that in order to 'deter' one side from launching a nuclear assault, the opposing side

133

should maintain sufficient nuclear force to ensure the entire destruction of the other. Thus, for deterrence theory to work, the 'other' must believe that any attack would by necessity ensure their own destruction. This strategy was often referred to as mutually assured destruction, or MAD for short. There were two possible outcomes for deterrence theory, with the desirable one being that both sides in a conflict would, out of fear of retaliation by the other, not resort to aggressive means. Obviously if deterrence theory failed this brought forward the distinct possibility of a nuclear holocaust.

Deterrence theory for Thompson was ideological as it legitimised the drift towards Exterminism. The growth of an authoritarian secret state was linked to deterrence theory; should the 'enemy' gain an understanding of the others defence plans, it could lead them to believe that a 'first strike' would be capable of cancelling out any capacity for retaliation. Unless large amounts of scientific research are geared towards the improvement of weapon technology there is the possibility that the other side will come to believe it can win a conflict in one blow. With this in mind, Thompson represented deterrence theory as a form of scholasticism, similar to that of Stalinism and Althusserianism. He wrote:

> Like all scholasticism's the practitioners are trapped within the enclosed circularity of their own self-validatory logic. Every conclusion is entailed within the theory's premises (Thompson,1982b, pp. 10-11).

One of the arguments put forward by deterrence theory was that the reason there had not been a major European war since the Second World War was largely due to the deterrent. According to Thompson, this argument could be either true or false as it was not empirically refutable. However, the ideology of deterrence retained an essential difference from other forms of scholasticism; it could not be refuted in the way that Stalinism and Althusserianism could by making a critical reference to 'common experience'. Thompson comments:

> In the case of internal ideological systems, the public normally have some experiential means of checking the ideology's veracity. Thus monetarism may appear as a superbly-logical system, but we still know what prices are in the shops, which of our neighbours are unemployed, and who has gone bankrupt. But in the case of deterrence theory, the ideologists control both the intellectual system and the informational input (Thompson,1982b,p.19).

Defence decisions are dependent upon remote expert systems; the information from which are processed by the central state apparatus. This inevitably meant that democratic decision making could be easily bypassed, and replaced by more secretive and autocratic processes. Thompson argues in a healthy democracy one might expect the media and intellectual opinion generally to challenge the way the state was seeking to stage manage current political debates. This expectation however was misplaced. Much of Thompson's political writing from the sixties onwards pertains to reveal the extent to which intellectuals often 'slavishly' conform to the way in which the political agenda is being constructed. Characteristically, Thompson argues in his essay *The Heavy Dancers* (1985), that:

> this delicate innovative area of our culture is in some ways more manipulated - more marginalised than for a long time. New ideas still do arise, but they are either co-opted into a manipulated 'consensus' or they're pushed out into the margin of public life, where people can still march around with banners in their hands (Thompson,1985,p.1).

The politics of peace

How did a key defender of socialist humanism become one of the main theoreticians of a non-class based movement like the peace movement? This is the central question I want to ask in the following section. That the so called new social movements are of a fundamentally different type in terms of membership, organisation and levels of 'commitment' from more traditional socialist forms of organisation, never properly enters the foreground of Thompson's writing. Yet this does not mean that Thompson believed, as Williams certainly seems to have done, that the new social movements could be ultimately reduced to a form of class politics. Instead, I would argue, that one would need to take a biographical approach to Thompson's writing in the context of New Left discourse, in order to unravel the complexity of his position.

During the early sixties, Thompson began to write less about a struggle that could be theoretically constructed around the workers and the ruling class, than around the people and a repressive bureaucratic state. Thompson's suspicion of the base/superstructure metaphor meant that the working-class could neither be assumed to have intrinsic interests in socialism, and nor could their existing 'consciousness' be constructed unambiguously in line with revolutionary aims. In one of his early *New Left Review* articles, *Revolution Again, Or shut your ears and run* (Thompson 1960), he argues that the division between the traditional labour movement and younger workers in what he referred to as 'human services', coupled with Britain's ideological attachment to NATO, made it difficult to mobilise the people for change. In a later essay *The Peculiarities of the English* (1978c), socialists are urged to work upon the consciousness of the working-class as it actually is, rather than assuming that it is already constructed in favour of radical social change. Consciousness, in Thompson's writing, is historically shifting and at no point becomes 'fixed' for all time. Thompson, under the influence of Gramsci, realised sooner than many on the Left that political mobilisation for change was not teleologically guaranteed. Instead, in the fifties and sixties, it was dependent upon the labour movements ability to construct a general interest that articulated the cultural insights and common sense of the people. The construction of an alternative political programme inevitably would have to challenge the dominance of NATO and capital, while accepting certain limitations due to the failure of European socialism.

During the seventies Thompson virtually gave up on the writing of history to concentrate on a cluster of issues which involved the erosion of the civil liberties of 'free-born Englishman'. For example, the judiciary, according to Thompson, should embody the principle of public participation in such a way that has the opportunity of expressing a will which is opposed to that of the establishment. Thompson's investigation of the legal system in the seventies reveals, particularly with reference to Northern Ireland, attempts made by elite groups to rig the judicial system in favour of certain results (Thompson,1980b). It is during the late sixties and seventies, that Thompson begins to view consciousness, less immediately arising out of experience, and more through the manipulation of the media and the state. While in the sixties and early seventies the dominant ideology is dismantling the cultural tradition of the 'free-born Englishman', in the late seventies, it is pushing human civilisation ever closer to its own destruction. Thompson refers to the logic of this process as Exterminism. Thompson wrote:

> Exterminism designates those characteristics of a society - expressed, in differing degrees, within its economy, its polity and its ideology - which thrust it in a direction whose outcome must be the extermination of multitudes (Thompson,1982c,p. 64).

Exterminism, as a concept, was developed in opposition to the two predominant critiques of the Cold War that existed on the Left. The first of these argues that the arms race should be analysed solely in terms of the economic interests of those who profit out of large defence contracts. While Thompson does not deny this, the Cold War, for him at least, was not reducible to an economic base. The second related argument was that the arms race was mainly fuelled by Western imperialist attempts to defeat a bureaucratically deformed socialism. Again, Thompson alternatively argues, that the arms race had a reciprocal logic that hegemonically secured the position of both superpowers over their respective allies.

While Exterminism was economic and political the most important component in its make up was ideology. Thompson suggested:

> In both camps ideology performs a triple function: that of motivating war preparations, of legitimating the status of the armours, and of policing internal dissent (Thompson,1982c,p.67).

Both East and West were involved in an ideological mirror-stage, where the threat of the other legitimated internal policing and intellectual control. The polarisation of East and West into two antagonistic blocs meant that the real or imaginary threat of the other was necessary for the maintenance of the ideological consensus. Hence the ideological relation between East and West unintentionally resulted in the mutual reinforcement of the hegemonic dominance of NATO and the Warsaw Pact. Thompson expresses the way in which both the East and West had been shaped by the logic of Exterminism, in his pamphlet *Beyond the Cold War:*

> The United States is the leader of 'the Free World' and the Commies are the Other. They need this Other to establish their own identity, not as blacks or Poles or Irish, but as free Americans (Thompson1982c,p.172).

In order to mobilise people against Exterminism one needed to appeal to a broad cross section of the population. For Thompson 'exterminism itself is not a 'class issue': it is a human issue' (1982c p. 74). The peace movement, Thompson observed, should build alliances across the blocs in order to promote cultural understanding and intellectual exchange. Given that the political elites of East and West are effectively locked into the ideology of deterrence; the agency for change would have to come from below. What remains important in Thompson's account is his realisation that the peace movement needed to create the social context for a new detente, as the two superpowers could not be relied upon to conceive of such a strategy. Here Thompson's writing has an affinity with Gandhi's concept the 'satyagraha' (Parkeh,1989). The satyagraha was the recognition that without the symbolic and material conditions for reflexivity simple appeals for rationality from those in structurally powerful positions would most likely have no positive effect. While Gandhi certainly overstates the transformative capacity of moral power, he shares with Thompson the argument that the conditions for a constructive and receptive dialogue have to be socially and morally created. This was essential, for in Thompson's words, 'Humankind must at last grow up. We must recognise that the Other is ourselves' (Thompson,1982c,p.188).

In some of his final work, Thompson acknowledges that the single most important reason for the collapse of the logic of Exterminism was the coming to power of Gorbachev in 1985 (Thompson and Halliday, 1990a). The peace movement, in Thompson's assessment, made a significant contribution to the dismantling of Cold War ideologies. They did this by helping to create the cultural space for Soviet peace initiatives. Conversely, the continued icy rhetoric of the New Right, has hindered the prospective chances for the demilitarisation of Europe. Since the Eastern European revolutions of 1989, Thompson has, not surprisingly, written cautiously on the tasks that a democratic 'new world order' should address. The socialist tradition is no longer conceived of as playing the leading role that he originally believed it would at the beginning of the eighties. Although, in the wake of a victorious liberalism, he would not accept Fukuyama's (1991) famous remarks that history had reached an end point, and that consequently the socialist tradition was a spent force. On the future of radical politics he has written optimistically:

> the struggle to bring greed within moderate control, to find a low level of growth and satisfaction that is not at the expense of the poor, to defend the environment and prevent ecological disasters, to share more equitable the worlds resources and to ensure their renewal - all this is agenda enough for the continuation of 'history' (Thompson,1990,p.120).

Thompson; the nostalgic Englishman

The polemical orientation of much of Thompson's writing meant that it is as important to discover what he is writing against, as it is to uncover those positions he is seeking to uphold. As many of Thompson's critics recognise, his open commitment to an English romantic culture has meant that he did not ever adopt the sort of theoretical readjustments that are characteristic of Williams's writing. Just at the point when Williams was developing his theory of cultural materialism, Thompson wrote:

> Take Marx and Vico and a few European novelists away, and my most intimate pantheon would be a provincial tea party: a gathering of the English and the Anglo-Irish. Talk of free-will and determinism and I think of Milton. Talk of man's inhumanity, I think of Swift. Talk of morality and revolution, and my mind is off with Wordsworth's Solitary. Talk of the problems of self-activity and creative labour in socialist society, and I am in an instant back with William Morris (sited by Kaye,1984,p.267).

Thompson's commitment to a form of cultural Englishness had an enduring impact on his writing. While Williams is also implicated in this tradition, he recognisably sought to incorporate more continental theory into his work, while his Welshness, especially in his later writing, came increasingly to the fore. Much of what follows is concerned to map out Thompson's relationship with an English radical culture, while commenting critically on its impact on his writing.

Thompson's romantic form of socialism is a Janus-faced phenomenon. If romantic humanistic socialism is understood as it is represented in Marx's *Paris Manuscripts*, (1961), then as modern political project it has surely run its course. Here the private ownership of the means of production was the root cause of the worker's alienation from his or her self, their fellow human beings and the product of their labour. The socialisation of the means of production would restore human society's control over its own production and reproduction. In more humane communities, men and women become reconciled with themselves, the rest of society and with the creative goods produced by their labour power. While Thompson nowhere explicitly attaches himself to such a project particularly after 1956, the residue of such beliefs, I shall argue appears in his critical defence of William Morris. Yet, while I feel compelled to reject such an argumentative srategy, I woould also hestate before dismissing some of the insights that can be attributed to Thompson's romantic socialism. This ambivalence is evident in the discussion.

Some of the more negative consequences of a commitment to a romantic cultural tradition came out earlier in the cultural idealism of Raymond Williams. Particularly evident in Williams's early writing was a belief in the perfectibility of human society through an aesthetic dimension, a teleological account of the long revolution, and a considerable measure of cultural conservatism. On the other hand, Williams's romanticism led him to take human feelings and emotions seriously, while articulating a theory of human nature. This meant that a cultural dimension could not be reduced to issues related to political economy, or to a private realm like the family. In this sense I argued that Williams's cultural idealism should be treated dialectically.

The figure of the preindustrial craftsperson is one that stalks much of Thompson's early writing. His essay on *Time,* as we saw, unfavourably compared the disciplined wage labourer, with the skilled independent artisan that was threatened by capitalism (Thompson 1982a). A nostalgic attachment to the skilled artisan comes to Thompson through the Romantic movement generally, and in particular from William Morris. It is difficult not to read Morris's utopian novel *News from Nowhere* (1970), as anything other than a literary argument that upholds the virtues of premodern forms of community and artistic practice, against a deformed industrialised world based on machine production. This can be said while keeping to Thompson's reasoned arguments that Morris was neither anti-machinery, nor was he producing a blue-print of a future feasible society. In the fictional utopian land of 'Nowhere', the populace, other than a few 'grumblers', spend their time creatively without the constraint of a fixed task that characterises the wage labourer. There is seemingly a direct correspondence with Morris's detailed description of 'Nowhere', and Marx's famous utopian remarks on what a future Communist society could be like. Marx, Morris and Thompson all commit themselves to the argument that human creative capacity would be enhanced by the socialisation of the means of production. Culturally this argument displays a familiar distain for popular culture. In a familiarly polemical moment Thompson wrote:

From Paris to Berkeley, from Munich to Oxford, the 'West' offered a supermarket of avant guard products, some branded as 'Marxism', each cutting the price against the other. But how many of these products, when unpackaged, contained only old and discredited arguments under a new label, or a horrific make up-hit for the revolting young bourgeoisie (a fast sports-car, a villa in the Appenines and the thoughts of Mao-Tse-Tung) (Thompson,1978b,p.99).

While the above quotation is partly critical of the failure of the New Left to learn its lessons from an older wiser Left, it also exhibits a similar form of cultural conservatism to that of Williams. Both Williams and Thompson, at various junctures in their writing, juxtapose the popular culture of a more authentic, radical past against a depthless commodity ridden present. Our inherited radical traditions, for Thompson, have not only been undermined by an authoritarian state, but have been displaced in the popular memory by the desire for commodities. The commercial culture of the present, that often imitates the more substantial radical culture of the past, has been seized upon by an unsuspecting younger generation. Of course Thompson's dismay at the enthusiasm of the younger generation for new brands of Marxism, can also be related to his own disagreements with Perry Anderson and Althusser. It is Thompson's duty, as the keeper of the spirit of the 'free-born Englishman', to persuade the new generation of Marxist intellectuals to yield to his fatherly advice. This new generation had not only forgotten the discipline of historiography developed by Thompson and other Marxist historians, but had turned away from their own home grown cultural traditions. What is evident here, until the rise of the peace movement in the late seventies, is an intense sense of political isolation, that retains both critical and ideological implications.

His story

Some recent contributions from feminist historians have suggested that *The Making of the English Working Class* (Thompson 1980a) obscures the cultural practices of those who are not 'actively' involved in shaping of the radical culture. Feminist historian Catherine Hall (1990) has argued that Thompson's account uncritically reproduces the ideological aspects of the radical culture he was writing about. In terms of the formation of a radical working-class culture, men are positioned as agents, and women as their hidden supports. While this can be partially attributed to the exclusion of women from the nineteenth century public sphere, Thompson colludes with this 'fact' as he does not consider it worthy of mention. Hall also uncovers historical evidence challenging middle-class definitions of domesticity, that Thompson, and the romantic radical culture presupposed. If historical actors were not upholding cultural traditions in a masculine public sphere that either detracted from or added to the making of a radical popular culture, they were marginalised by Thompson. Thompson's intellectual reliance on the culture of 'free born Englishmen', it would seem, entailed that he was only able to construct the cultural experience of the people, the extent to which they upheld the ideals of a forceful and independent morality. As the 'commonly' held radical culture was what actively formed the working-class into a class, one might ask whether women, in this analysis, can be located in class relationships? This is not a rhetorical question, as if 'class' is the result of a common cultural experience, that is itself the product of 'free-born Englishmen', then others such as women, either belong to a different class, or occupy a non-class position. Hence Thompson's construction of class formation denies women any recognition as cultured subjects. While tracing this argument through, it should also be apparent from my previous remarks, that similar arguments could be applied to Thompson's treatment of race. As Irish men and women are obviously not 'Englishmen', their cultural experience is also excluded from proper consideration, or treated in an ethnocentric manner by Thompson.

Sally Alexander (1984) has also written on the working-class movement of the 1830s and 1840s. Alexander provides evidence that women, contrary to the impression created by Thompson's account, actively participated in the birth of the labour movement, but were often excluded when radical movements sought to standardise a formal democratic structure. There are two main reasons for this, they are; the separation of a predominantly masculine public sphere from a femininely defined private sphere, and the tradition of the 'free-born Englishman'. I shall address the question of the often made distinction between gendered public and private realms later; for now, I want to look at the second strand of Alexander's critique. Alexander writes on the tradition of independent Englishmen that:

> The legal, political and economic subject in radical popular speech reaching back to the seventeenth century Levellers, was the propertied individual, and the

propertied individual was always masculine (Alexander,1984,p.12).

The vocabulary of grievance of the early free-born Englishman was shaped by the language of disinheritance, which the working-class movement connected not so much with private property, as economic and sexual authority. The 'free-born Englishman' through his attachment to the Chartist movement was not only protesting against a lost economic independence, but also the erosion of the dominance of the patriarchal head of the family. Hence the Chartist movement opposed the factory system due to it's link with de-skilling processes, and because it provided a challenge to the natural social unity of the family. Elsewhere, Michelle Barrett (1980) has built on this argument and described how the workers movement, along with the owners of capital, sought to exclude women from the public sphere in the mid-nineteenth century. To represent the morally independent Englishmen of this period as the embodiment of a tradition that maintains a contemporary critical purpose, in the way that Thompson does, is to ideologically collude with male domination over women both past and present.

According to Carole Pateman (1982), feminists have traditionally challenged the distinction made in social theory between a public and private sphere, as it obscures the social subjugation of women. Traditionally, liberal theorists have distinguished between a public sphere based upon universal criteria, and the family which was the domain of so called natural relations. In more general terms women's connection with the 'natural' comes through child bearing, that proscribes their social position in the family. Michelle Barrett and Mary McIntosh (1991) call the assumption that women should bear the sole responsibility for the social rearing and early care of children the ideology of naturalism. Pateman, goes on, that the division between the two spheres that are predefined as either masculine or feminine, means that men tend to be identified with 'culture' and women with 'nature'. This distinction has also been brought out by other feminist writers such as Jessica Benjamin (1988) and Nancy Chodorow (1978, 1989) who adopt a more obviously psychoanalytic approach to the construction of masculinity and femininity. While this is not the occasion to do justice to their respective accounts both Benjamin and Chodorow conclude that the construction of masculinity is particularly traumatic for the male child. This is because the gendering of the male subject involves the separation from the initial bond with the mother, and identification with the patriarchal head of the family. The process of psychic identification with a masculine father figure, in more political terms, involves the rejection of a biologically natural private sphere, in favour of a public sphere that represents masculine forms of freedom and independence.

Roslyn Bologh (1990), following this account, describes the masculine public sphere in the writing of Max Weber as embodying a subject who espouses a masculine ethic. The masculine subject is characterised by Bologh as:

> the strong, stoic, resolutely independent, self-disciplined individual who holds himself erect with self-control, proud of his capacity to distance himself from his body, from personal longings, personal possessions and personal relationships, to resist and renounce temptations of pleasure in order to serve some impersonal cause - a masculine, ascetic image (Bologh,1990,p.12).

Weber, makes a conceptual split in his writing between a public (masculine) world and a private (feminine) domain. His portrayal of the social world separates the strong and independent public world, from a private familial domain of attachment and love. Thompson comes closest to a similar form of masculine representation in his biography of Morris. In the first edition of his biography on Morris, Thompson discussed his hero as being attracted to Icelandic literature due to the qualities of 'manliness and independence' (Thompson, 1955, p. 222). Also, according to Thompson, it is these values that inspired the early socialist movement, through the stance taken by its leaders and early moral founders. The virtues of manliness and independence were precisely those values that the present generation lacked. Academic work, according to Thompson, in the fifties was caught up in a culture of:

> intellectual self-questionings, that lack of confidence in man's life and in human ambitions which has become part of the intellectual climate of a class in decline.(Thompson,1955,p.745).

But, despite the preceding comments, Bologh's writing on Weber cannot be directly transplanted onto Thompson. While Thompson does display an early indifference to the subjugation of women through his celebration of heroic forms of masculine agency, such an objection does not address the full complexity of his writing. Some of Thompson's more historically 'thick' writing resists the representation of subjects in line with what Bologh calls the masculine ethic. The masculine ethic has a pronounced tendency, she argues, to represent the subject as self-determining and the author of his social destiny. While Thompson certainly has a tendency to lapse into a form of masculine voluntarism, he also portrays agents as dependent upon cultural contexts and traditions, that they contribute towards, rather than directly author. Agency for change, in Thompson's early writing, is not simply dependent upon masculine forms of discipline and self-control, but on a supportive culture and tradition that seeks to meet the needs of an urban community in certain historic social relations. For Weber, according to Bologh, one's values are not scientifically secured, but are dependent upon the individual choice from those historically available in a public sphere, which is dominated by instrumental forms of rationality. Where, as for Thompson, our values are also a matter of choice, they are simultaneously creatively realised by social agents embedded in culturally defined communities. While Thompson, it is true to say, excludes a discussion of the relations of domination between men and women in the public and private sphere, his writing cannot be unambiguously assimilated to a discussion of a masculine ethic.

Jardine and Swindells (1990) add support to Hall's and Alexander's contention that women are treated as 'supports' by Thompson, in the historical creation of a radical culture. This has less to do with the masculine terms that Thompson often uses to describe agency, but can be firmly connected with the culture of romanticism itself. Romanticism is the product of a reactionary ideological formation as it draws its ethics from the medieval period, while aesthetising the relations of domination between men and women. The dream like utopia of 'Nowhere', argue Jardine and Swindells, is dependent upon an idealised representation of the modern nuclear family. Women, in Morris's account, find their sense of purpose through housework and motherhood, while men are more actively involved in skilled artistic production. Thompson's and Morris's medievalism enable them to contrast an ugly conflict ridden present, with images of a more integrated and harmonious premodern social order.

Jardine and Swindells illustrate their argument through the way in which Morris's wife Jane Morris has been represented by Thompson. Thompson writes about Jane Morris as an aesthetic object in such a way that denies her a position in class and gendered social relations. The male biographers, they argue, tend to uncritically identify with Morris's own obsession with her physical beauty, which in Thompson's case is not just due to his underlying sexism, but because such a characterisation allows him to represent Morris as oppositional. Romantic culture is represented as a form of critique as it opposes Victorian barbarism and lack of concern for high culture. Jane's beauty becomes representative of a yearning for a world without conflict, where women are unquestioningly subordinate to men. The aesthetisation of Jane 'paints over' her position in gendered class relations, as it does the position of women generally in the writing of Thompson and Morris.

While remaining sympathetic to Jardine's and Swindells's argument, I would suggest that they have a tendency to assume that the romantic culture of Morris and Thompson is inherently ideological. I would certainly not want to get Thompson completely off the charge of a reactionary form of medievalism, that is undoubtedly related to his lack of theoretical concern over the representation and oppression of women. Yet while Jardine's and Swindells's position is certainly understandable, it seems to blind them to other more critical aspects of Thompson's historical writing. In this respect, Joan Wallach Scott (1988), has argued, that Thompson's and the Annales school's concern for ordinary life has provided the intellectual context for the writing of women's history. Given that women were excluded from traditional narratives of statesmanship and diplomacy, writing about the cultural life-worlds of ordinary people has provided feminists, and other historians, with the conceptual apparatus to make women visible in historical texts. That Thompson is also able to open up questions around the quality of life, morality, feelings and emotions generally, would, despite the limitations of this approach, also seem to be the product of this tradition. Before getting on to these arguments, I want to look at the challenge to Thompson's historiography that has been posed by Gareth Stedman Jones.

Language and class

Gareth Stedman Jones's (1983) *Languages of Class*, can be read as a theoretical attempt to reconsider Thompson's approach to historiography. Stedman Jones admits the considerable intellectual debt that he owes to Thompson, but also acknowledges the part that French post-structuralism has played in his intellectual formation. Thompson's classic work *The Making of the English Working-Class* (1980a), according to Stedman Jones, represents the growth of a more class conscious politics as being the product of the dialectical interplay between social being and social consciousness. However the 'social' in this approach is conceptualised as being prior to language.

146

Language, in Thompson's writing, is produced by particular experiences of oppression in the social order. Stedman Jones wishes to argue that instead of consciousness producing politics, it is politics that produces consciousness. Thus how interests become constructed is dependent upon historical and political alignments; a position Thompson fully accepted in his later writing on hegemony and notions of historical process. But, perhaps more problematically, Gareth Stedman Jones (1983,p.21) seeks to defend a 'non-referential conception of language'.

Stedman Jones takes this to mean that one cannot attribute primacy to a material base of social being, as these determinations are not prior to language. Language cannot be determined by an underlying material process, as it is only through linguistic forms of construction that one has access to being and consciousness. Other post-structuralist writers, like Ernesto Laclau (1977), have similarly argued that the Marxist tradition often theoretically positions a 'material' economic base that acts as a 'constitutive outside' to any antagonistic relationship. Arguably Laclau and Stedman Jones want to look at the way discursive practices construct notions of the political, as well as subjectivity.

More concretely Stedman Jones reappraises Thompson's writing on Chartism. Chartism, contrary to Thompson's account, was not the direct result of the experience of exploitation, but instead: 'pre-existed any independent action by such a class and did not significantly change in response to it' (Stedman Jones,1983, p. 95). He goes on to add that Chartism was not singularly a working-class movement, but was a broad based mass movement. While Thompson was theoretically justified in historically disconnecting the growth of class consciousness from the development of the productive forces, the dialectic between being and consciousness, cannot explain the particular discursive form that Chartism adopted. Chartism, according to Stedman Jones, is best represented as the merging of many discourses that resulted in a political language that was able to 'embed itself in the assumptions of the mass of the people' (Stedman Jones 1983, p. 96).

In Thompson's defence, Stedman Jones does not appreciate the importance that a conception of 'tradition' had for his writing. Thompson does not represent Chartism as being the direct effect of the misery and pain of oppression, but as the result of certain inherited traditions and social practices. In Thompson's account he represents political movements as the combination of inherited traditions and present experiences. Further, Stedman Jones also suggests that a more sophisticated approach to language and culture

147

could ultimately have checked Thompson's voluntarism and culturalism. While this is true, I remain unconvinced that Stedman Jones's approach is necessarily preferable to that of Thompson. The historical actors in Stedman Jones's account are constructed through discursive practices, without the capacity of being able to reflexively monitor their activity. Despite Thompson's relatively unsophisticated theoretical approach he is able to uncover cultural forms of identification bypassed by his fellow historian. Thompson's writing on the independent artisans and Methodism reveals that the culturally complex life-worlds were not only discursively shaped by the radical culture of the time, but were critically acted on by historical actors. That is where as Thompson is concerned to uncover the social context of linguistic practices, Stedman Jones discusses the objectivist features of language games. John Foster (1985) was similarly critical of Jones's attempts to 'de-class' language.

> We may know with perfect clarity what people said. The meaning of the words is altogether another matter, and the main weakness of Stedman Jones's approach is that it does not pose this as a problem. It is solved, quite arbitrarily, by linking specific words into a wider, subjectively constructed language system (Foster,1985,p.40).

Human feelings and moral choices

Thompson's intellectual connection to Morris allowes him to write about feeling and emotion in such a way that can be reconnected to socialist humanism. The value that Thompson places upon forms of human community and understanding against divisive forms of hatred, while remaining connected to certain masculine notions of 'brotherhood', are not simply the product of an ideological humanism. Further, his refusal to reduce human subjects to forms of linguistic construction is not just because he conceived of them as morally and culturally reflexive, but it is also on account of their capacity for feeling and emotion. The way in which this is manifested for Thompson is similar to that of the early Williams. Works of art and culture are the embodiment of certain feelings, that of themselves cannot be reduced to the ideology of a particular class and presuppose an intersubjective dimension. Thompson's stress on the importance of feeling and emotion is probably best illustrated through his writing on Morris's aesthetic utopia. He writes, on Morris:

> His intention was to embody in the forms of fantasy alternative values sketched in an alternative way of life. And what distinguishes this enterprise is, exactly, its open, speculative quality, and its detachment of the imagination from the demands of conceptual precision (Thompson,1976,p.97).

While Swindells and Jardine (1990) were justified in their mutual protest over the social nature of 'Nowhere' it is the aesthetic and investigative nature of Morris's writing that attracted Thompson. The opening up of an imaginary dimension that does not simply restrict itself to the 'possible', is the foundation of Thompson's utopianism. The transcendence of the here and now by the consideration of the 'good life', must always, for Thompson, be coupled with aesthetic and moral concerns. Thompson describes the development of our capacity to feel as 'the education of desire'. Within this perspective, as one moves beyond a pre-given reality, one's desires change; while exploring one's own feelings and emotions, one's view of one's self also changes. Our feelings and emotions, according to Thompson, are changed by being challenged politically, and through cultural interaction generally.

Thompson's emphasis on the reflexive nature of emotions and feelings remains sound, and by coupling these concerns to Morris's utopian writing, he opened up the possibility of a form of ideology critique. Paul Ricoeur (1986), has argued, the attempt to think transcendentally through a notion of utopia is intimately connected with the principle of self-reflection. Utopian strains of thinking urge us to hope for a better world, 'because it is the condition of possibility for doing something else' (Ricoeur,1986,p.251).

By speaking up for the 'emotional' Thompson has not only refused to confine feelings to a private sphere, as he surely would have if he could be comfortably positioned in a purely masculinist tradition, but suggested that human feelings have a critical function. This more critical role consequently cannot be reduced to linguistic constructions or scientific forms of rationality. The recent writing of Agnes Heller (1990a, 1990b) also takes up this question. For Heller there has been a disappearance from our media of a shared emotional language, that would teach us to differentiate our feelings. The cultivation of what she refers to as the 'emotional household', compared to the proliferation of discourses about the body, is relatively impoverished. A more richly textured common emotional language, she reasons, would encourage the development of our own selves, as one becomes increasingly able to differentiate between a wide range of feelings. The more we reflexively investigate our own feelings and emotions, the more sophisticated subjects we shall become, and the greater our contribution to a common emotional language. Yet while remaining sympathetic to the concerns of Agnes Heller and Thompson, they do seem open to question. Here the development of feeling and emotion is primarily the task of a high culture, ignoring the way, that say watching a soap opera, can open up certain emotional responses. Alternatively, the development of a sexual relationship or a close friendship, could also provide us with a more sophisticated vocabulary of the emotions. But primarily, what Heller and Thompson seem to temporarily forget, is that the expression of feeling also takes place in social contexts that are ideologically and culturally penetrated. While neither Heller nor Thompson would seek to deny that feelings are at least partially socially constructed, this aspect seems to drop from view once one becomes overly concerned with a relation between feelings and aesthetics. Raymond Williams more concretely grasps this when he writes on the changing historical definitions of masculinity. Notable exceptions apart, Williams argues men since the Victorian era rarely cry in public.

> What was taught and learned was a new and rigid control, 'self-control' - even weak men not crying and being very stiff and proud of it where much stronger men before them had quite openly wept when the feeling, the impulse was there' (Williams,1985a,p.62).

Further, a concern for human feelings and emotions is related to questions of need that undoubtedly has a material dimension. Put crudely, the development of a human beings capacity to experience a range of emotions, as Heller puts it, is dependent upon a social existence that is not dominated by scarcity. It is difficult for me to develop my emotional household if I am an overworked and undervalued school teacher, suffering from occupational stress. As Kate Soper has written:

> If you are deprived of food, you feel the pangs of hunger; if you are deprived of love, or of opportunities for creative activity, or of the space and the time for any self-development, you do not so much feel the loss as lose the

power to feel - you become the victim of a vicious regress, caught up in a process that numbs your sensitivity in the very act of depriving it (Soper,1981,p.184).

The development of our human and moral feelings remains a profoundly political project. Earlier we saw that in Thompson's analysis the repression of a moral sensibility was what linked Stalinism to the writing of Althusser. Thompson construes the political nature of morality as:

> a task of socialists (his own first task) to help people to find out their wants, to encourage them to want more, to challenge them to want differently, and to envisage a society of the future in which people, freed at last of necessity, might choose different wants (Thompson,1976,p.107).

What is not clear from Thompson's or Heller's writing is the explicit social conditions that would have to be met before a reformulation of needs was possible. Andre Gorz (1989), for example, argues that a reduction in labour time, with a corresponding increase in free time would fulfil this role. The utopia of free-time envisaged by Gorz, allows human subjects the possibility of re-evaluating themselves and their relationship to their corresponding society. Under Thompson's own analysis it would appear 'idealist' not to recognise the common conditions that would have to be satisfied in order that people could critically reconstruct their interests. This is perhaps an odd omission from Thompson's writing, given that the Marxist tradition generally has recognised that social contexts, as free as possible from relations of domination, are necessary for the 'education of desire'.

The manipulated consensus

While remaining sympathetic to Thompson's writing on ideology, I want to stress that such a concept should be disentangled from the possibilities of a socialist society. By tying his analysis of ideological domination to the possibility of a 'good life' Thompson tends to marginalise some of his earlier theoretical insights. In my commentary, I will concentrate on the transition from his writing on hegemony in reply to Nairn and Anderson, to his later contributions on the Cold War. This by necessity leaves to one side the interesting issue of Thompson's progression from the 'moral consensus' to his later adoption of hegemony. This choice has been made to give added focus to the argument, and because it is in this area that I best feel my contribution can be made. In the first part of what follows, I want to present an immanent critique of Thompson's approach to the questions of ideology and hegemony. This will be followed by a short analysis that emphasises the general strengths and weaknesses of his writing on this topic. Here I argue that his earlier writing contains essential elements of a critical theory of ideology that due to the failure of the labour movement to bring about social change became less pronounced during the 1980's.

Once the possibility for a socialist transformation of society has become remote, Thompson seems to place an increasing amount of emphasis on the formation of social subjects through a dominant ideology. Through practices of domination, social consciousness became increasingly the site of manipulation by the apologists of the post-war consensus. Here Thompson has made a significant contribution to our understanding of the relationship between the mass media and the Cold War. Through his discussion of the exclusion and marginalisation of dissenting voices, Thompson sought to explain the maintainence of biopolar structures. But, what is missing from Thompson's writing, is an explanation of how agents form diverse patterns of cultural attachment with the so-called dominant ideology. Thompson's description of Methodism, in *The Making of the English Working-Class* (1980a), sought to explain the sense of identification workers had had with what he called a reactive culture. Methodism was compared unfavourably with a romantic radical culture. For Thompson, Methodism concentrated on the fear of death, rather than the opposed life affirming qualities of love and human fellowship. The indoctrination of the masses took place in socially variable pedagogic relationships that were of themselves capable of transforming the Methodist culture. Also Methodism compensated those who had shifted geographically from the country to the city by alleviating the accompanying culture shock, and gave some of these people a sense of community that had been lost in the process of migration. Further, in perhaps more tradition Marxist terms, Methodism temporarily embodied a personal spiritual solution to social needs, that could not be met satisfactorily through religion, but would only be secured through a revolutionary transformation of society.

While not wanting to enter into the debate around Thompson's treatment of Methodism, his writing displays a concern around cultural forms of interpretation, that is missing from his later political

152

essays. Earlier, in the discussion on Williams, we saw that he explained ideological domination through the incorporation of a central value system. Similarly,Thompson's despair at the prospects for socialism and his cultural conservatism led him to assume that the mass of people were becoming increasingly incorporated into a 'Natopolitan' ideology (Thompson,1978d,p.26). What is missing from his analysis is firstly the cultural reasons why deterrence theory was as popular as Thompson thought that it was, and the idea that all ideologies have to be socially interpreted. I am not arguing that Thompson was wrong to place the importance he did on the ideology of deterrence, but I am suggesting that it remains at least open to question the extent to which people generally would have had their opinions dominated by its logic. This is particularly apparent in Thompson's case, especially given his earlier concern to represent agents actively engaging in the construction of the social world.

Thompson's original definition of hegemony is born out of his early historical writing, and what I dubbed the Nairn/Anderson thesis. Before we get on to Thompson's own response, we should try and more accurately locate the discussion within its original intellectual context.Tom Nairn (1964) and Perry Anderson (1964) argued that the British labour movement had historically developed along reformist rather than revolutionary lines. The reason for this can be traced back to the English revolution in the seventeenth century. According to Nairn and Anderson this event transformed the economic structure, but left the superstructure largely unreformed. Due to the premature and partial nature of the English revolution; the bourgeoisie failed to develop a suitably 'progressive' ideology. The early arrival on the historical stage of the bourgeoisie meant that the working-class movement developed in a reformist direction. Not only had the bourgeoisie failed to develop an ideology of it's own, but likewise the working class lacked a mature Marxist intellectual culture. The culture of the labour movement, according to Nairn and Anderson, had not so much been actively created by the working-class, as it had been inherited from the bourgeoisie. As one would expect, Thompson (1978c) refutes the claim that the cultural inheritance of the working-class was produced from above by a premature bourgeoisie. Moreover Nairn and Anderson, for Thompson, teleologically attributed to the working-class distinct goals it had yet to historically realise. Thompson wrote, in opposition, that one cannot fix definite interests to the working-class that remain with them independently of their historical context. While the working-class remained the main agency for change due to its structural position, one could not, for Thompson, understand its actual consciousness, without addressing the specific set of historically variable hegemonic relations entered into with other social classes. Historically teleological thinking has meant that the Left has been unable to grasp two fundamental historical truths that limited the prospect for socialism. These were the failure of scientific socialism to provide an alternative to capitalism, and the relative success of social democracy in satisfying some of the needs of the working-class.

In opposition to the attribution of class interests, Thompson proposes that one understands domination in terms of hegemonic and counter-hegemonic formations. Hegemony, as we saw, was the continuous intellectual and moral battle that attempted to seal the consent of subordinate classes and social groups to a diverse range of political projects. As I have already written on this particular version of hegemony, I will resist the temptation to say very much more, other than to point to Thompson's eventual retreat from this position. This is evident below:

> the active component of apathy, just as prevailing circumstances have provoked apathy as a passive response. It is an intellectual and cultural fact in its own right - a certain stance in relation to circumstances, a capitulation of centres of agency (Thompson,1978d,p.3).

On the one hand, Thompson was justified in his belief that 'actually existed socialism', in the context of the Cold War, severely limited the labour movements room for manoeuvre. The problem is however that the structures of the Cold War were so monolithic that they divert our understanding from changes in the political and economic sphere. As Thompson would undoubtedly agree the specific content of hegemonic modes of domination has changed considerably over the period since the Second World War. In keeping with his earlier definition of hegemony, forms of ideological domination have to be continually negotiated, reaffirmed and transformed. Thompson's rather static view of the ideology of the Cold War excludes the very notion of historical process he sought to defend against Althusser. A more historical reading of post-war society, that effectively incorporated a more detailed analysis of economics and politics would necessarily concern itself with the failure of social democracy and the rise of the New Right. Had Thompson maintained his earlier approach to hegemony, that was critical of the incorporation thesis, he would not have so readily assumed that the ideology of the Cold War was the most distinctive and important ideology of the epoch.

Clearly a theory of hegemony, that sought to explain relations of domination in post-war society, would have to concern itself with the shifting patterns of East/West relations, but would also focus more concretely on institutional relations of power at international, national and local levels.

Related to my two previous points, I would argue that E.P. Thompson, systematically overestimates the power of militaristic ideologies. Michael Mann's (1988) has made a useful contribution in this respect. Roughly speaking, for Michael Mann, war as a social practice can be cautiously described as rational up to the end of the Second World War. Until this point, war could be legitimated by ruling elites as being necessary to either preserve or achieve a 'better way of life'. The widespread ownership of nuclear weapons, however, has meant that it is irrational to mobilise one's nuclear resources against another as the probable result is mutual destruction. As Thompson has shown, the ownership of nuclear weapons tends to lead to an increasingly secret state, where the nation can no longer be reaffirmed economically and culturally through a world-war. This has led, according to Mann, to the rise of more limited conventional wars, that are not dependent on the mobilisation of the population, in a similar way that of the First and Second World War's. The West now has the privilege of a largely de-militarised culture. As the limited war does not involve personal sacrifice other than by professional soldiers, modern war is generally experienced as a spectator sport. The nation is mobilised through relations of distance that enable the state to legitimate such a conflict, within certain cultural constraints.

Generally the commitment to military manoeuvres is not deeply held. Once the population at home is expected to demonstrate personal sacrifices, it is unlikely that a firm commitment to military ventures can be sustained. In addition, professional soldiers are still thought of as citizens of the nation-state, and must not be sacrificed without 'good' reason. Mann's analysis is surely correct, that in the West at least, there are cultural restrictions that impose themselves upon modern militarism. However a similar recognition would often seem to be absent from Thompson's writing. In his essay on the Falklands war, Thompson is very attentive to the imperial imagery used to symbolically represent the conflict, but there is no sense that the initial outburst of national fervour could have been a limited phenomenon. Thompson wrote that the:

> Falklands war has shown us at least this - how close to the surface our even-tenored life the atavistic moods of violence lie (Thompson,1982d,p.195).

Of course Thompson could not be expected, in the often immediate fashion he had to write his articles on the Cold War, to have always been as precise as he might. What I would insist is that the failure of the labour movement made him more cynical than he might otherwise have been.

One of the reasons that Thompson evidently feels it is important to write about the ideology of deterrence is that like Stalinism and Althusserianism it is a form of scholasticism. Earlier I argued that it was a general condition of studies of ideological domination, that what Thompson assumed to be the immediate presence of experience, had to be linguistically and politically constructed. Just as the knowledge that small businesses are closing down does not necessarily determine our politics, so that living near Greenham Common does not make us supporters of CND. This of itself was not taken to mean, as perhaps certain post-structuralist writers have implied, that human agents are incapable of moral and political reflexivity. But, it does entail, that one cannot pit a concern for experience that is self-evident, against forms of ideological domination. Yet, as Thompson realises, dominant ideologies often involve falsity in that they are empirically refutable. However, it is not the case that certain perspectives become ideological by virtue of the fact that they evade empirical controls. Such a formulation severs the link between ideology and domination. As Terry Eagleton (1991, p. 28) has argued a person may recognise that capitalism involves injustice and oppression, but believe that it is on the whole preferable to democratic socialism. This position from Thompson's standpoint would be ideological as it justifies relations of domination, but one could hardly rank this as a 'false belief' given the actual record of scientific socialism. Hence deterrence theory was not ideological because it could not be empirically refuted as Thompson sometimes claimed. It should alternatively be considered ideological as it served certain relations of domination that sought to symbolically 'close down' more peaceful and democratic alternatives to the Cold War.

Exterminism, state and civil society

E.P. Thompson has made a substantial contribution to social theory in his writing on the state and modern forms of militarism. Much Marxist writing has concerned itself with the state's superstructural role in the economic sphere, and in the political oppression of dissent. In distinction, liberal writing on the state, has concentrated on the separation of spheres, and the rights and obligations of citizenship. What is striking about Thompson's writing on the state is that he combines a Marxist and a liberal approach through the idea of 'the free-born Englishman'. Interestingly, for someone who places himself in a Marxist intellectual tradition, he has little to say on the state's role in securing the social conditions for the accumulation of capital. There would seem to be two reasons for this; firstly, Thompson is resistant to the idea that the economic sphere is theoretically separable from cultural concerns, and secondly, he argues, that the good society could not be immediately secured through the socialisation of the means of production. What neither Stalin nor Althusser allowed was the theoretical and social space for an active independent civil society. Thompson's writing in this respect could be thought of as pre-dating later attempts to combine and bypass Marxist and liberal interpretations of the state. This will be illustrated in the following points.

1. Many Marxists, following Marx, have not only neglected issues related to citizenship, but have underestimated the impact of militarism on the modern world. Marx assumes that along with globalisation of capital would come a decline in national allegiance. The worker was literally thought to have no country. Thompson's writing on Exterminism stressed that the Marxist categories that are usually deployed to explain militarism were largely redundant in the nuclear age. More traditional forms of Marxism represent militarism as having economic rather than ideological and political roots. It is to Thompson's credit that in his analysis of the Cold War, he stresses the former over the latter.

2.Thompson wants to demythologise the operations of the British state by drawing our attention to the surveillance practices that concentrated mainly upon the political Left. Thompson's writing can be connected to Marxist theories of the state that stress the management and control of internal opposition. Thompson wrote on the secret state:

> It would amaze many British citizens to learn that these and other organisations are only at the end of a long historical line of ruling-class institutions, with agents or informants in trade unions, educational institutions, and political organisations (especially of the Left), and less subject to ministerial or parliamentary control than they have ever been (Thompson,1980b,p.150).

While this argument has some persuasive force, Thompson ignores the need to place the centralisation of the means of surveillance in a more historical perspective. Anthony Giddens (1987b) usefully reminds us that both liberal and Marxist accounts of the state generally tend to ignore this problem. Michel Foucault (1977) offers perhaps the most systematic exploration of the extension of the means of surveillance in the eighteenth and nineteenth centuries. During this period the state, dominated by instrumental forms of rationality, was increasingly drawn into the collection of information about and surveillance over subject populations. Foucault's writing argues forceably against a definition of surveillance that mainly concentrates upon the political Left. An historical explanation of the extension of surveillance techniques is necessary to an understanding of modern institutional settings from the work-place to the asylum. Foucault calls disciplinary power the particular forms of power and knowledge that characterise modern institutions. While this is a complex theoretical concern one could represent modern power relations as being based upon hierarchical observation and normalising judgement. In premodern societies, like the ancient regime, it was the sovereign who made himself visible, while the subject population, those upon whom power operates, remain unseen. There occurs a distinctive reversal of this situation in what Foucault describes as the modern carceral society. It is those subjects who are to be disciplined, observed and judged who the operation of power currently makes the most visible. Now it is power that seeks invisibility. Those who become its objects of control reappear through the reorganisation of institutional settings. For example, in the modern examination it is those who set and monitor the test that are 'absent', while the candidates make themselves 'present' by answering the questions and placing themselves at the appropriate desk. For Foucault, those like Thompson, who concern themselves with a discourse of rights have failed to understand the nature of the disciplinary society. Political theory must reform itself by theoretically cutting off the head of the monarch. Similar to Weber's account of the rationalisation process, the disciplinary society has emerged underneath traditional Marxist and liberal accounts of the state. For example, the exercise of power in the carceral society has often used a discourse of rights to disguise its operation. Hence, the introduction of social rights, in the form of the welfare state, was accompanied by an extension of the information to be processed and the widening of the normative gaze of the state.

Yet, I would like to argue, that while Foucault is correct to stress the historical generality of practices of surveillance, his treatment of democratic theory remains unacceptable. Thompson's writing on at least two counts can offer a corrective to Foucault's anarchistic leanings. Foucault by concentrating on the disciplinary techniques of modern society would not appear to be able to distinguish between democratic and totalitarian societies. Thompson through the tradition of the 'free-born Englishman' would surely argue that democratic societies should respect culturally independent traditions. These often act as a form of immanent critique both externally and internally to dominant institutional structures. That is to say, secondly, that implicit in Thompson's argument, is the view that while the modern state may seek to extend its areas of surveillance, there is no reason why a concern over 'rights' could not define areas of privacy and public autonomy. Trade unions have a right to expext that their telephones are not 'tapped', and that their activities are legally protected in relatively autonomous areas of civil society. Stalinism, as Thompson showed, by treating trade-unions as political organs of the state were necessarily authoritarian for failing to respect such autonomous development.

Norberto Bobbio (1987b), continuing on this theme, has argued in accordance with Foucault, that modern power aims to make itself invisible. However the concealed nature of power violates democratic notions of representation and decentralisation. The idea of democracy, according to Bobbio, is to make increasing areas of social life visible and present rather than invisible and abscent. The exercise of power may have been visible in premodern societies, however, what was invisible were the reasons as to why certain decisions were taken rather than others. The Enlightenment tradition, that Foucault is so mistrustful of, in Bobbio's terms seeks justification and the open public operation of power that had previously remained secret. Foucault, in his writing, tends to mistakenly equate visibility with subjection, rather than democratic forms accountability. In fact, one of the reasons that Thompson is alarmed at the appearance of an increasingly authoritarian state, is that it sought to undermine social visibility and democratic accountability. Thompson's writing, by focusing on the underhand operation of the state, is radical to the extent it makes visible that which was previously obscured from view. The act of making visible can either, depending upon the social context, be assimilated to the extension of the power surveillance or the practice of democratic accountability.

3. Bearing in mind that Thompson does not attempt to articulate a general theory of the state there remain areas of omission and errors of judgement in his writing that demand discussion. As has already been indicated, Thompson's writing, for someone in a Marxist tradition, pays very little attention to the modern state's role in the economy. The other perhaps more serious 'gap' is his lack of attention to what a future socialist state might look like. Here one is left with

the impression that such a state would be constantly kept in check by a morally informed public sphere. This begs many questions, for example, what, if any, are the limits of democracy? How could one avoid the problems of bureaucratic economic management encountered under 'actually existed socialism'? How would one make these organisations internally democratic, and capable of reflexivity? While Thompson combines a concern over liberty, with a Marxist interest in the internal policing of dissent, he also inherits some of the limitations of these perspectives.

4. There are further difficulties with Thompson's writing on the state when we come to look at the role played by civil society. The relative autonomy of civil society is dependent for its independence on the tradition of 'the free-born Englishman'.

> The freeborn Briton has been bred out of the strain, and the stillborn Britperson has been bred in. The people have been drugged into an awe of office, and into that diminished reality sense known as 'normality'. They can look at the nicely groomed expert on TV who is telling them about weapons of genocide, and they can suppose that this is 'authorised' by 'responsible persons' and in the normal course of things. An operation has been done on our culture and the guts have been taken out (Thompson,1980b, p. 255).

Once the tradition of moral independence has been extinguished civil society had become incorporated into the manufactured consensus of the mass media. Hence Thompson's reliance on a nineteenth century radical culture again lets him down. He ignores those institutional areas of civil society that cannot be directly equated with the living spirit of dead Englishmen. In opposition to Thompson, civil society should be thought of as a cluster of institutions such as churches, households, nurseries, literary associations, work-places and trade unions. While Thompson was correct to emphasise that civil society was always more than an ideological state apparatus he did not fully appreciate that its separation from the state was institutional as well as cultural. Current democratic socialist writers on the state, such as David Held (1987,1989) and John Keane (1988,1991), press the importance of civil society for socialist strategies of renewal. One should, according to Held and Keane, abandon the traditional socialist ploy of seeking to replace civil society with the state. A thriving civil society is a guarantee of areas of spontaneity and independence which a socialist state should seek to extend and democratise. The problem with liberal approaches to the state is that they traditionally fail to redress the relations of power that exist in civil society. These inequalities prevent equal participation in existing and future democratic structures. A reformulated theory of socialist transformation should look to reform the state and civil society as a 'double sided process'. This would entail a fundamental bill of rights that took seriously political, social and economic rights. These would place limits on the operation of public power and seek to maintain the independence of civil society. A written bill of rights would ensure an institutional separation of powers while democratising existing political and social practices.

If one were seeking to defend Thompson's writing, one could object that written rights are useless without the culturally felt necessity to defend and extend them. Thompson wrote in this vein:

> Written constitutions are for nations which are young (or reborn after imperial rule) or for regimes which are stiff jointed and insecure and need a suit of armour to hold them up. Unwritten constitutions nourish ambiguities; they mark out limits of the field, but the field remains in a state of play (Thompson,1980b, p. 238).

Rather than getting Thompson off the hook, this only produces further problems for his argument. Thompson pays little attention to the material inequalities that exist in civil society, that are not reducible to class. Arguably, in the case of ethnic minorities, women and the disabled such inequalities prevent citizens from taking up their rights. Further Thompson's adherence to masculine forms of independence obscures many of the reasons that disable women from equal forms of participation and representation in the public sphere. Held and Keane, in this context, justly criticise those who fail to link political and social rights together. Thompson's insistence that rights can be defined in 'lived' cultural terms explains his resistance to notions of citizenship that are embodied in a written bill of rights. But, in Thompson's own terms, this would appear contradictory; if the modern state had become increasingly authoritarian, then there would seem all the more reason to publicly instil the rights of the people into more concrete and codified forms. This would entail that access to rights is not dependent upon the rebirth of a masculinist nineteenth century cultural tradition. Instead such rights would have an institutional grounding that would make citizenship a more 'visible' phenomenon. This might also entail that they could not so easily be manipulated by anti-democratic forces.

The Culture of exterminism

Thompson's writing on liberty and the modern state took an international twist through his theorisation of global politics or Exterminism. His insistence that social theory should seek to capture social processes at a trans-national level, comes just at the time when other theorists, such as Lyotard (1989) and Foucault (1977), seem to deny any such possibility. Foucault extols the virtues of local knowledge and micro politics, while Lyotard argues that post-modern intellectuals should resist the 'terroristic' temptation to employ the use of grand narratives such as Marxism. On the other hand, Thompson's 'grand narrative' Exterminism, sought to explain the main dynamic of the Cold War in economic, ideological and cultural terms. Post-structuralist concerns for the local against the global are seriously misplaced while writers like E.P. Thompson continue to explore the connections between the local, the national and the global.

On the British Left, the two major critics of Exterminism have been Fred Halliday (1989) and Raymond Williams (1989c). Mary Kaldor (1990) has also made a significant contribution to this debate; although as we shall see, her position is similar to that of Thompson. Williams (1989c), in a largely supportive article, criticised Exterminism for being a form of technological determinism. This is connected to certain remarks in Thompson's original account of Exterminism that could be construed as arguing that just as the steam power gave us capitalism, so weapons of mass destruction deliver a society that is propelled towards genocide. Thompson (1982c), in a follow up discussion to his original article, accepts Williams's objection that he had phrased Exterminism in such a way that left him open to charges of technological determinism. In accepting Williams's criticism however he does not think that Exterminism as a concept needs to be radically rethought. Here he emphasises that the reciprocal logic of Exterminism was not so much the product of technological determinism, as of certain interests, in conjunction with a culturally deformed logic.

Williams's remarks on Exterminism have a double interest. They are both similar to those Thompson (1961) made in response to *The Long Revolution*, and reveal a shared theoretical orientation.Thompson initially objects that Williams's formulation of the cultural was an abstract process that needed to be reconnected to certain interests and power relations. These remarks of course stop some way short of accusations of technological determinism. Yet the reason why Williams's comments have such resonance for Thompson is that it brings to the fore their mutual concern that theoretical practice should not become reifying. For Williams to accuse Thompson of technological determinism is to suggest that Exterminism is an inflexible theoretical construct, that cannot take account of agency and historical process. If Thompson represented social relations as being determined by technology, this would, in his terms, represent a retreat away from 'lived experience' into theoretical abstraction. It would also reproduce some of the objectivist and overly reified assumption of post-structuralists such as Althusser. Williams's critique of Thompson's writing sought to remind him of their mutual commitment to a lived cultural complexity that criticised repressive forms of abstraction such as economism and technologism. I have argued elsewhere that while they were justified in their rejection of overly reductive theoretical arguments their mistrust of theory put an equally ideological emphasis on 'lived experience'.

Fred Halliday (1982, 1983), as less of a theoretical fellow traveller than Williams, has made out a more substantial case against Exterminism. In his recent writing, including intellectual exchanges with Thompson, he has offered an account of the Cold War that differs from that of Thompson (Halliday 1990). Exterminism as a theoretical attempt to understand the Cold War is misleading in two respects: 1) that while the ideological image of the 'other' is necessary for the policing of internal dissent, Thompson underestimated the extent to which each bloc is committed to overcoming the other; 2) at the same time, Thompson overstates the similarities between the social systems East and West. For Halliday these two competitive social systems were dominated by distinctive sets of material interests, namely the capitalist ruling class and the Communist party. What has happened with the end of the Cold War, according to Halliday, is that one social system has triumphed over the other.

Halliday's first point reveals the most marked differences between the two perspectives. Halliday's writing adopts what Kaldor (1990) has described as a revisionist approach to the Cold War. In opposition to initial Western academic responses to the Cold War, that sought to apportion blame to the Soviet Union, revisionist writers tend to place most of the responsibility at the feet of the United States. Revisionist approaches explain the Cold War as a series of diplomatic strategies that sought to ensure the continued military superiority of the United States. According to Halliday, the moral responsibility of the conflict between East and West surely rested with the side who were first to use and build nuclear weapons, and who had consistently refused demands, up until the early eighties, for a 'no first use' policy, despite such a commitment from the Soviets. One of the reasons Halliday gives for the breakdown of detente in the seventies, and the so called New Cold War in the early eighties, was the erosion of nuclear superiority of the United States. The Soviet Union leading up to this period had been spending more on nuclear weapons than it had previously, but not enough to challenge the superiority of NATO. On this reading, detente was abandoned as a strategy as the Soviet Union seemed unwilling to accept the military dominance of the United States. Thus Halliday represents the Cold War as a traditional conflict where one side is seeking to defeat the other. I shall argue that as a theoretical attempt to grasp the inner dynamic of the Cold War this view is only partially correct, with Thompson's writing on Exterminism is preferable on three counts;

1. To discuss the Cold War as possessing a reciprocal logic allows Thompson to explain the break down of detente at the end of the seventies. If one side, as Halliday admits the Soviets did, increases military spending on an armament programme, this leads to a sense of insecurity in the other. One of the problems with Halliday's account is that he seems to assume that the United States are able to rationally calculate in an objective manner what constitutes dominance. Firstly, one could argue, that any such assessment could only with difficulty be described as rational, given the shared conditions of mutually assured destruction. Moreover, in Halliday's argument, the calculation of what counts as military dominance, does not appear to be dependent on the cultural context of the Cold War. Such a context, in Thompson's writing, is depicted as informed not so much by rational assessment as it was by an atmosphere of paranoia and hostility. According to Mary Kaldor (1990), the Cold War was played out primarily on an imaginary symbolic level, where democracy was the main casualty. In a passage that reminds one of Thompson's description of the Cold War as culturally deformed, she wrote:

> Over and over again, in military exercises, in the scenarios of military planners, in the games and stories of espionage and counter-espionage, in the training of millions of men, in the hostile rhetoric of politicians and newspapers, we have fought an imaginary war between East and West. We have lived with the permanent anxiety of war, with many of the forms of organisation and control that are characteristic of war. Except for the fact that people are no longer actually killed (and that is, of

course a big difference) we have lived as if the Second World War had not really ended (Kaldor,1990,p.4).

For Halliday, the Cold War's symbolic dimension must be subordinate to the United States interest in domination over the Soviet Union. But, as Kaldor and Thompson suggest, the cultural dimension of the Cold War can not be seen as the legitimate expression of the intentional interests of either the Soviet Union or the United States. Instead the progress of the Cold War was determined by an outmoded culture, rather than expansionist or economic interests.

2. More recently other writers have sought to expand Thompson's argument that the two blocs were not so much trying to overcome one another, as reinforcing one another's hegemony. Gian Migone (1989) has described the Cold War as a 'conflictual alliance', and Mary Kaldor (1990), adopting a similar approach, has used the term 'imaginary war'. Both of these approaches are complementary to Thompson's writing on Exterminism. Migone (1989) argues that while there existed an antagonism between the two blocs, there were also considerable areas of mutual consensus. After Europe had been divided following the Second World War, there was never any real policy of 'roll back' adopted by the superpowers. Instead the Americans hegemonically sealed their dominance through the Marshall plan, while the Soviet Union depended more on force than consent for its authority over the nations of the Warsaw Pact. What tended to be sacrificed in the relationship between the two blocs was the interests of so called third parties. As the superpowers attempted to hold on to their respective spheres of influence, these interests were often prioritised over demands for democracy in, for example; Eastern Europe, Nicaragua and Chile. Similarly, Kaldor has argued, along with Migone and Thompson, that neither the Soviet Union nor the United States had interests in expanding their territories in the post-war period. The main consequence of the Cold War for Kaldor and Thompson was the limitation and infringement on the development of democracy. The ideology of the imaginary war helped legitimate decisions concerning 'national security', prevent debate on the rationality of the Cold War, and provide support for dictatorial regimes mostly in the Third World. What Kaldor,Migone and Thompson point to is that the Cold War cannot be satisfactorily represented as a conflict between absolutely opposed social systems. Instead the antagonism that existed between East and West contained substantial areas of consensus and mutual interest that should be recognised in any historical analysis.

165

3. Had the peace movement adopted Halliday's analysis of the Cold War this would meant that the main focus of their critique would have been American rather than Soviet foreign policy. Halliday's account of the Cold War, would as a consequence, have allowed the media some legitimacy in representing the peace movement as 'objectively' pro-Soviet. The argument that the West was principally involved in a conflict where it sought to dominate the other is not only partially false, but closed sown the symbolic space for the operation of the independent peace movement. The peace movement, according to Thompson, should avoid as far as possible being represented as aligned to either bloc. Failure to do that would be to participate in the ideological reproduction of Exterminism. Instead, through the articulation of a 'third space', the movement for peace sought to expose and dismantle the imaginary dimension of the Cold War. This could be done by making cultural connections from below. Through these mechanisms the peace movement sought to represent the common interests of peoples East and West in democracy, human rights and ecological survival.

The need for the peace movement to articulate a distinctive symbolic identity distinguishes it from older more traditional political formations. Alberto Melucci (1989) has shown that the new social movements are different from political parties not only in terms of their membership and degrees of commitment, but the extent to which they articulate alternative symbolic codes. According to Melucci, older forms of collective politics, such as the working-class movement, were viewed as having objective interests in a pre-defined destiny. The new social movements,while maintaining a link to ideas of citizenship, can be principally conceived as 'an experimentation with and direct practice of alternative frameworks of sense' (Melucci,1988, p. 248). The peace movement is difficult to understand as a new social movement unless one takes account of the symbolic challenge it poses to dominant codes of meaning. According to Melucci there are three main forms of symbolic challenge present in the cultural practice of the peace movement. These can also be related to Thompson's writing. They are what Melucci calls prophesy, paradox, and representation. Both Thompson and the women of Greenham Common claimed that there was more than one type of rationality. The belief that dominant forms of instrumental rationality are not the only ones available to human-kind is described by Melucci as symbolism based upon prophesy. Despite the differences between the cultural positions of Thompson and some of the women of Greenham Common, they commonly constructed a counter symbolic order that prioritised life and ecological well being over the logic of Exterminism. Unless, they argued, less destructive rationalities were allowed to short curcuit the systemic reproduction of the Cold War this could have devastating consequences. Thompson's writing is also a particularly good example of what Melucci describes as symbolism based upon paradox. This form of symbolic activity involves the exaggeration of those positions one is arguing against, in order to reveal their irrationality. Thompson's many polemical responses in newspapers and pamphlets on the Cold War often sought to utilise this very tact. Finally an exploration of the symbolic power of representation by the peace movement has led to the development of their own particular codes and symbolic forms. The peace movement not only made use of traditional forms of political communication, but also explored visible forms of symbolic protest such as photo montage and street theatre. One of the reasons this may have developed, that Melucci does not mention, but that Thompson certainly does, is that the peace movement were systematically denied the same access to the mass media enjoyed by more mainstream political organisations.

If we follow Melucci these three types of counter symbolic activity are attempts to make the exercise of power visible. This is taken as a reversal of administrative procedures that aim - as we have seen - to make the operation of power invisible. So far, I have argued, that Thompson's writing from the early sixties to his later ideas on Exterminism can be connected through notions of 'the free-born Englishman' and the prospects for democracy and socialism. To these, we can now add another region of continuity, that is his desire to make power visible. Just as Thompson opposed the hidden political manipulation of the secret state, so he aimed to make visible, in alliance with the peace movement, the drift towards Exterminism.

Is there some truth in Halliday's second argument; that Thompson assimilated the differences between the social systems that existed East and West? Again, it would seem not. By arguing that the Cold War had a reciprocal logic that sought to secure each blocs hegemonic hold over their subject population, Thompson was not arguing that East and West were becoming increasingly alike. It was true that the logic of Exterminism repressed possible differences by closing off more democratic options, but 'real differences' between members of the same bloc were also distorted by the assumed binary oppositions between 'freedom' and 'repression'. Thus Thompson was not arguing that East and West were becoming similar, but that the economic, political and cultural differences that existed between say Britain and Turkey, who were both members of NATO, were being ideologically obscured. Evidently Halliday is mistaken in his suggestion that Thompson's analysis created a 'homology' between East and West. Yet Halliday would have been closer to the truth had he focused his analysis upon certain areas that are missing from Thompson's formulation of Exterminism. Thompson's theory runs into trouble when it does not pay adequate attention to the restrictions placed on oppositional intellectuals in the East. Thompson throughout the eighties attempts to enter dialogue with dissident forces in the East. What is evident from these dialogues is that intellectuals in the East had a distinctively oppositional disposition towards socialism, and were ideologically and materially constrained in a way that was not 'mirrored' in the West. Despite all the limitations placed by the state and the media on those involved in the peace movement in the West, they enjoyed a 'freedom of speech' that was denied those in the East. Thompson,wanting to open up a common dialogue and cultural exchange, should have paid more attention to areas of difference For it was not clear at the time, nor is it currently apparent, that the collapsing of the divisions between East and West have brought us any closer to a democratic socialist Europe.

Political mobilisation and universal values

By melting the Cold War from below, Thompson hoped that this would bring about the possibility of more robust and independent forms of democratic socialism. Thompson's original brand of socialist humanism was less a commitment to certain identifiable values than it was to a specifically humanist disposition. Where Thompson was clear, in his early writing, he emphasised the values of human fellowship and understanding coupled with a moral independence from the state. Later, in his writing on the peace movement, he stresses the values of life and democracy over death and authoritarian state control. While there was undoubtedly a shift in focus over the specific values Thompson emphasises the informed disposition of socialist humanism was not incompatible with his writing on the peace movement. But, before I go on to ask whether Thompson was right to mobilise people for change around so called universal values, I want to look at whether or not the peace movement was being mobilised around the right or correct values.

In this context, Feher and Heller (1986) also stress the importance of universal 'value ideas' as opposed to narrowly defined class interests. Yet, despite this common perception, Feher and Heller disagree with people like Thompson. Feher and Heller opposed the peace movement as it threatened to privilege the value idea of life over that of freedom. This is neatly encapsulated for them in the slogan of the peace movement 'better red than dead'. The peace movement by counterpoising life to freedom were in danger of destroying freedom as a universal value idea. This accounts for the peace-movements anti-modern orientation that sought to mobilise people though a fear of death, rather than rational argument. For Heller and Feher the peace movement justified an ethic of passivity where literally nothing was worth dying for. In this case, they are doubtful that members of the modern peace movement would have violently resisted Nazism during the Second World War. Hence it is not nuclear weapons themselves that Heller and Feher find threatening, but the peace movements hostility towards an Enlightenment culture. It is worth noting that both Feher and Heller were East European intellectuals living in exile. They did not regard the 'Soviet threat' as a myth. This, as I argued above, counts as a further example of some of the problems Thompson encountered in constructing a dialogue with like minded intellectuals. That is despite their shared socialist humanism the real divisions that exists between these writers lies in their disposition towards state socialism. This of course connects with my wider point concerning Williams's and Thompson's failure to thoroughly consider the failures of these regimes.

It is impossible to judge the extent to which the peace movement attempted to privilege values of life over freedom. Feher and Heller themselves offer very little evidence in their writing other than a handful of slogans and evidence of religious symbolism. More definitely, if Thompson's writing is at all representative of the peace movement, Feher's and Heller's concerns would seem misplaced. Firstly, Thompson, like many members of the peace movement was not a pacifist and actively contributed to the defeat of Nazism in the Second World War. Also Thompson links the need for nuclear disarmament to a respect for human rights, and more accountable forms of government both East and West. Here, I would argue, what is more questionable than the so called reactive culture of the peace movement is the way that Heller and Feher themselves juxtapose the values of 'life' and 'freedom'. Thompson and others argue that the utilisation of resources for the creation of weapons is ethically unjustifiable in the face of world poverty. A more secure and less threatening world could not only enhance 'life', but improve the 'freedom' of those whose lives are dominated by scarcity. A concern for peace and security, as the discourse of the peace movement bears out, could easily lead one, if the political connections were made, to take a more global interest in politics. This, as Raymond Williams

(1980d) realised, had a definite radical potential in a world increasingly dominated by global forms of economic, political and cultural production.

Finally some post-structuralist writers might suggest that Thompson, by constructing a politics out of so called universal values, is repressing the free-play of post-modern cultural variety. What such arguments obscure is that if it is wrong to build and contemplate the use of nuclear weapons in the West; the same argument holds for the rest of the world. A politics of universal values has the advantage of not being collapsible into a discourse of hatred as there is no 'other' whom political strategy seeks to repress. The peace movement, I would argue, were able to mobilise people around appeals for understanding and tolerance of non-repressive forms of cultural difference. The universal commitment to democracy, human rights and peace are not of themselves repressive forms of cultural homogeneity, or indeed a matter of preferring life over freedom. The global realisation of such values, as Thompson's thought reminds us, would enable the production of more decent and democratic forms of life for everyone. This is as true today as it was during the Cold War period.

5   Culture, ideology and the future of socialism

There are three centrally related themes that I want to discuss in this concluding chapter. The first involves a theory of culture. The writing of the New Left expressed a concern with culture that marked an intellectual break with economistic forms of thinking evident within Marxism and Labourism. For Williams and Thompson, as we have seen, culture was as much the site of contestation and struggle as that of human community and ethical commitment. Here I want to suggest how their writing could be extended and improved in relation to theoretical developments in cultural theory. Secondly both Williams and Thompson sought to defend a conception of ideology in conjunction with cultural forms of domination or hegemony. They retained a tendency, however, to give hegemony a particularly culturalist interpretation, while sharing with others on the Left some of the problems this particular approach has encountered. My analysis, while guided by Williams and Thompson, will also, with reference to other writers, seek to point to ways in which their use of ideology could be reformed. After developing an outline of how we might theorise about ideology and culture, I shall consider whether or not their mutual commitment to socialism has any contemporary relevance. Both Williams and Thompson devoted a considerable amount of their writing to arguing in favour of socialism, whose status as a distinctive political philosophy and set of political practices now seems to be in crisis. The European revolutions of 1989 have raised questions deeply troubling to the Williams and Thompson generation of socialists. I shall aim to trace out whether or not there is an agenda for 'cultural' Marxism, and moreover, to

171

consider towards what possible theoretical direction, if any, their work could contribute.

A symbolic conception of culture

The early text's of Raymond Williams and E.P. Thompson articulate an anthropological conception of culture. An anthropological account tends to consider culture in terms of a specific social group that shares common practices, values and beliefs. Williams refers to this as culture that expresses a ' whole way of life '. Later however, Williams combines a symbolic and material approach to cultural practices within his theory of cultural materialism. Through a comparative analysis with Bourdieu, we saw that Williams offers a valuable corrective to idealist cultural theories that disregarde human culture's material aspects. Yet, while instructive, at this juncture, Williams displays a tendency to stress culture's material over its symbolic content. Williams did not adequately account for the radical instability of cultural meanings and processes in his overtly materialist analysis. This, it has been argued, was particularly evident in Williams's contribution on hegemony. Here he attempted to fix the meanings of cultural forms through an analysis of their institutional and social origins. Similarly E.P. Thompson, as I proposed in a critical discussion of his notion of hegemony, pays increasingly less attention to the cultural reception of meaning the more pessimistic he becomes politically. In his early historical writing Thompson pertained to show through a rich description of the 'life- worlds' of contextually located agents how the working-class 'made' their own radical culture in a way that was distinct from the politically conformist culture of the Cold War.

A symbolic account of culture, as opposed to an anthropological or materialist approach, involves the interpretation of meaning through the interaction of human subjects and symbolic forms. A definition of symbolic culture is offered by J.B. Thompson who writes:

> culture is the pattern of meanings embodied in symbolic forms, including actions, utterances and meaningful objects of various kinds, by virtue of which individuals communicate with one another and share their experiences, conceptions and beliefs (J.B.Thompson, 1990,p.132).

Symbolic cultures are radically open-ended in character. Distanciated symbolic forms are being continually interpreted and reinterpreted by socially and historically situated human subjects. Somewhat paradoxically, it is Thompson rather then Williams, who on reflection, has the greater understanding of the importance of social context to the production of meaning. This appreciation, as we saw, came through the significance that a notion of tradition has for Thompson's writing. In contrast to Althusser, Hindess and Hirst and Anderson, I argued that Thompson sought to create the moral and political space for other voices that had been written out of more traditional historical accounts.These 'other' perspectives were not simply resurrected from history, but had to be carefully brought out into the open by the tradition or the horizon's of the historian. Similarly his writing on the peace movement encouraged the beginnings of a dialogue from below across the boundaries of European nation states. The aim here was to heal ideological forms of fear that had been engendered by the Cold War. But, despite these insights, Thompson wanted to argue that historical writing, in the final analysis, was determined by a 'hard' factual dimension, rather than the interplay of perspectives both past and present. Thompson, like Williams, came to uphold a much greater appreciation than many of his contemporaries of the importance culture has for an interpretive dimension, without ever developing a more radically symbolic account of cultural processes.

Culture and social structure

Here I propose that one should take into consideration social structures and historical processes. This remains the case whether one is concerned to identify either how cultural forms are produced and reproduced in definite institutional relations, or how cultural forms are interpreted by social agents. Williams, as we saw, was concerned with a political economy of cultural forms that avoided the economic determinism of more traditional forms of Marxism. His writing on television, for example, demonstrates particularly clearly his conviction that to properly understand the evolution of cultural forms one should engage in a historically sensitive materialist analysis. Such an analysis should attend to the historically specific relations between the economic system, the state and related cultural institutions such as the BBC. But, as I have argued, Williams's and Thompson's cultural conservatism prevented them from adequately exploring how cultural forms are actually interpreted by social agents. Bourdieu's writing, on the other hand, despite many of the criticisms I make of his approach, has the particular strength of representing social agents reflexively interpreting modern cultural forms embedded in social fields structured by class relations. While I remain sceptical of many of Bourdieu's claims, particularly with reference to the habitus and symbolic violence, his analysis remains suggestive. Bourdieu's more sociological analysis, it has been argued, was despite its weakness, preferable to the 'scholastic internalism' offered by Williams.

E.P. Thompson repeatedly showed in his historical narratives, as we saw in the previous section, a much greater awareness of the problem of relating social relations to questions of cultural interpretation. Where Williams offered a political economy of culture, Thompson sought to explain how one's social location influenced the way in which social agents identified with competing and variable historical formations. This remains a valuable contribution against certain trends within social theory, that following Althusser, have sought to ignore comparable cultural processes. But, as the hitherto analysis revealed, this was much more in evidence in Thompson's early historiography than in his later work on Exterminism.

In Thompson's (1961) critical response to *The Long Revolution*, he insists that culture should be conceptualised as being articulated in relations of domination. But perhaps the more substantive point he makes at this particular juncture is that:

> Any theory of culture must include the concept of a dialectical interaction between culture and something which is not culture (Thompson,1961,p.32).

Here Thompson is reworking his earlier culturalist conception of class, initially conceived in *The Making of the English Working-Class* (1980a). In these revised terms, class is not the product of social consciousness, but the dialectical relation between social being and social consciousness. The structural position occupied by social agents in the class structure, therefore, is theoretically separable from an analysis of cultured hegemonic relations. The way in which Thompson expresses this relation is, however, not conceptually clear; and consequently resulted in the later rebuke by Perry Anderson (1980). But Thompson does appreciate the necessity of relating culture 'to something that is not culture'; that is, ones relationship to social structures. Social structures could be characterised, as we saw earlier, as rules and resources that are given a certain durability once they become institutionally grounded. This is a point that does not seem to be appreciated by much post-Marxist theory, where categories like class seem to have no empirical referent and exist only as discursive formations. Alternatively, other Marxist approaches, such as that which is offered by Althusser, tend to sever the relationship between agency and structure. Social structures remain, despite Althusser's claims to the contrary, dependent on the intersection between agency and structure. They are not the result of conscious agency, as Thompson's earlier work implies, or the site where the subjectivity of agents is mechanically manufactured. Thus an analysis of culture not only has to address questions of production, but also has to demonstrably illustrate how agents made 'sense' of cultural forms in contextualised social relations and structures.

Economic reason and questions of value

Leavisite literary theory tends to divide culture into distinct categories of high and low; where high culture is always constructed in opposition to a massified low or more popular culture. Despite Williams's and Thompson's critique of this particular binary opposition, both unintentionally reproduce similar cultural distinctions in their writing. For Williams and Thompson, a romantic literary tradition was being steadily eroded by more synthetic commercial forms of culture. Williams and Thompson, in this context, were both criticised for critical lapses and omissions concerning their writing on culture and aesthetics. While such criticism is surely accurate, I want to argue that their work remains a more dialectical phenomena than many of their critics seem aware. In this context, sociologists like Bourdieu may want to scientifically eliminate the distinction between culture in the aesthetic sense, and culture in the anthropological sense, but he consistently begs certain questions on notions of value. In Bourdieu's writing issues related to aesthetics are relativised. While Williams and Thompson remain tainted by their cultural conservatism, both were sceptical of instrumental forms of rationality that sought to submerge questions of cultural value. Notably, in this instance, Bourdieu has very little to say on the forms of economic domination that preoccupy writers in the Marxist tradition. For Bourdieu, writers like Williams and Thompson, who claim that cultural values are threatened by the operation of capital are merely involved in interested strategies accumulating cultural status. This remains an important insight, but, as Williams argues, Bourdieu cannot adequately explain the very real conflicts of interest that might be at stake. As is well known, there are those on the free market Right who would seek to introduce the market as a universal standard of assessment. Williams, like many of those on the Left, has defended values and forms of life connected to community, ecology and literature that cannot be adequately assessed by economic reason. A similar critique of instrumental forms of domination can be traced back through Marx, the Romantics and finally to the writing of Schiller. Hence Williams's and Thompson's cultural Marxism brings together a concern that the development of technical reason may come to stunt human capacity and potential, and a notion that the development of modern subjects are socially and institutionally dependent. As we shall see later in the social theory of Andre Gorz, this remains an essential feature of contemporary critical theory.

Williams and Thompson also insist, despite some of the problems they encounter, that the aesthetic of the text has a relative autonomy from its politics or ideology. Williams wrote perceptively about the 'feeling' of a text, while Thompson was concerned with the 'imaginative' critical dimension of Morris's Nowhere. A regard for aesthetics may, therefore, be thought of as related to but not reducible to the politics of representation. Arguably, the intellectual craft Williams brought to a critique of Dickens, has a different value to the particular interpretations that school children make of a television version of *Hard Times*. This remains true even if Williams interprets Dickens in such a way as to reinforce certain forms of cultural domination, while the school children's reading of television engaged in an ideology critique of Victorian values. The same could be said of certain forms of 'quality' journalism; as regardless of the ideological content of newspapers like the Guardian and the Independent, they operate, to some extent, through different rules to the popular press. The term 'quality journalism' could be applied to practices of patient investigation, not so evident in the tabloids. Hence the dominance of economic reason may culturally penetrate attempts to rationally 'inform' the public through the media of mass communication. This is again evident in Williams's political project for the democratic reform of the channels of communication which broke with both the control of capital and state paternalism. This is to uphold contextually located notions of quality, value and aesthetics that are preferable to cultural forms of analysis - and here I have in mind Bourdieu - that simply reduces such concerns to the effect of a field.

Self-identity, ethics and culture

The modern world can no longer be thought of as a hierarchically ordered ethical system. This poses a number of culturally complex questions. In this context, Williams's novels explore contextually dependent ethical issues; his characters are caught up within personal and political patterns related to commitment and belonging, where the crossing of cultural, social and geographical borders open up questions of self-identity. Thompson, rather differently, in his polemical attack on Althusser, alerts us to the durability of ethical dilemmas that cannot be 'scientifically' disposed of through sophisticated theoretical analysis. Both Thompson and Williams were concerned to elucidate how in a world without teleological guarantees, persons should respond to global inequalities, cultural misunderstanding and the threat of ecological destruction. Although this occasionally led them into a form of moralism, there was a real desire to represent the self in a state of metamorphosis and reflexivity. The reason, therefore, we are able to criticise Thompson's overly polemical reaction to Althusser is due to his commitment to these principles, and the dialectical quality of his writing. The self represented here is not the post-structuralist or post-modern self that celebrates difference and change for its own sake, without asking questions related to political value. Williams and Thompson shared a mutually earnest attempt to respond to the present openly and reflexively, without jettisoning their commitment to ethical socialism. Williams's open but critical response to post-structuralism, and Thompson's role in the rebirth of the peace movement are evident in this respect.

There are, however, many modern ethical dilemmas about which Williams and Thompson had very little of value to contribute. This is especially marked in relation to issues connected to gender and sexuality. It is as though, in both these writers, there is a repressed longing for a world where familial relationships are no longer a source of conflict and uncertainty. The family is represented as the site of biological connection and belonging. This is distinct from the conflict evident at the level of social class. Their theorisation of the self is also considerably weakened through their dismissal of unconscious processes. Williams, through his attachment to Timpanaro, and Thompson because of his connection to independent masculine forms of protest, fail to realise the theoretical insights a notion of the unconscious has for social theory. Thus the subject, for Williams and Thompson, remains a self-conscious rational subject that was able to form an ethical response to reified forms of cultural domination. While this analysis retains considerable critical insights, it is at least arguable, that their writing could have been strengthened had they developed a more sophisticated version of a gendered subject, that was radically de-centred through the operation of language and unconscious processes.

Globalisation

I want to argue, against Williams and Thompson, that the world is not becoming a more culturally homogeneous place. In fact, in line with my earlier remarks on questions of ideology, the opposite could just as easily be assumed to be true. Secondly, the way in which we should seek to ensure ourselves against globalising processes is not by radically reinvigorating local and national cultures. Instead, without wanting to deny the persistence of distinctively local and national cultures, I want to argue that global cultures are caught up in processes of integration and disintegration. The multiple, and often unintended, impact of a globalising cultures cannot be captured through an opposition to an imported synthetic American culture. Williams and Thompson sought to resurrect the barriers of an old radical national culture to prevent this particular tradition from being undercut by cheap imports. Hence nationalism may be an enduring cultural force in the modern world, but its persistence should not blind cultural theorists to the emergence and maintenance of more international networks. What I shall describe later as Williams's and Thompson's mutual investment in radical forms of cultural nationalism ignores, or at least displaces, the significance of the globalisation of cultural forms.

Paul Gilroy (1987), in this context, provides an interesting discussion of the formation of the culture of black Britons, a process which he describes as a diaspora. He argues that black culture cannot be understood in terms of a particular isolated community within the parameters of the British state. Through the historical analysis of a distinctive black musical culture, Gilroy is able to demonstrate how the culture and politics of black America, Caribbean and Africa have been intersected in various cultural practices. The production of a black diaspora is the result of the circulation of music and information concerning the marginalised status and racism that blacks have suffered in differing global and historical contexts. As Gilroy puts it:

A new structure of cultural exchange has been built up across the imperial networks which once played host to the triangular trade of sugar, slaves and capital. Instead of three nodal points there are now four - the Caribbean, the US, Europe and Africa. The cultural and political expressions of new world blacks have been transferred not just to Europe and Africa but between various parts of the new world itself (Gilroy,1987,p.157).

The emergence of what Williams might have called a global structure of feeling has been centred around the idea of Africa as a mythic homeland. The culture of British blacks, though shared cultural attachments and the circulation of a mostly music based culture, has retained a strong sense of international interconnection. One might also point to an Irish diaspora, that shares many similarities with what Gilroy described as being relevant to blacks. The experience of migration has been a common one amongst contemporary young Irish people, although there is often a shared sense of Ireland as being a point of connection. Through Irish literature, newspaper articles and the development of a distinctive Irish musical and pub culture a sense of cultural connection is maintained across time and space. The development of a distinctive Irish/Englishness and a black internationalism not only influences those more directly caught up within its formation, but also has an impact on British culture as a whole.

Other global cultural processes could be said to promote anything other than a more cosmopolitan culture. Thompson's writing on the Cold War brilliantly explores the ways in which the 'free' West were able to keep their hegemonic grip over an international alliance of nation-states. However, Williams's writing on the long revolution, that sought to create a radical national public sphere, now seems oddly isolated from international contexts. In his work on the long revolution, cultural institutions were criticised for failing to democratically include the social and cultural perspectives internal to the nation-state. Williams was surely correct to insist that the differing social and cultural groupings internal to nation-states should find their culture represented in institutional contexts. This could, as Bhikhu Parekh (1991) has argued, lead to a reassessment on the part of minorities and majorities concerning the value of other cultures. But Williams seems unaware of the extent to which conflicts related to cultural representation can be resolved within the borders of the nation-state. The news media, for example, through the deployment of new technology has become capable of a range of transmissions that easily exceeds national boundaries. Williams's writing in *Communications* (1962), and for the large part of *Towards 2000* (1985), conceives of a revised public-sphere along outmoded lines. In an international market where films and television programmes are traded across internal boundaries, one could argue that Williams's proposals, unless revised, could lead to a form of national isolationism (Featherstone, 1990).

Information overload

Modern societies, as many post-industrial thinkers such as Baudrillard (1989) and Melucci (1989) have recognised, cannot be characterised through a lack of information, but through what might be called information overload. The modern world market of late capitalism has through the financing of cable television, videos, books, popular magazines and newspapers filled the world with information. Such is the proliferation of modern culture that no one person would be ordinarily capable of digesting all the information offered in a single newspaper in a single day. Williams and Thompson would no doubt maintain that the market only offers the illusion of diversity by either actively repressing, or not promoting alternative radical cultural forms. But even if their arguments are accepted and one managed to create the kind of radical counter public-sphere outlined by Williams (1962) in *Communications*, this would only increase the amount of information modern societies made available for their citizens. While writers like Baudrillard have interpreted the growth of information in a politically conservative fashion, he does pose difficult questions for any attempt to reformulate the long revolution. Such is the overload of information that citizens encounter in the modern world through their television sets, morning newspapers, popular magazines, radio, they are no longer capable of the act of interpretation. In the post-modern world, described by Baudrillard, seemingly the most effective strategy of resistance is silence and passivity. Were Baudrillard correct concerning the implications of the expansion of information available in modern societies this would by necessity foreclose the possibility of a theory of ideology. But, while I have argued that Williams and Thompson do not take seriously enough the interpretive capacity of social agents; Baudrillard seems to completely ignore this dimension of social theory.

As I have already criticised culturally conservative tendencies within social theory that displace the accounts and forms of identification that are produced through the interpretation of cultural forms by lay actors, these arguments need not be rehearsed again here. Instead, as John Keane (1991) has suggested, one may disagree with the conclusions Baudrillard draws from 'information blizzards', while accepting that he raises some important issues. In this respect, Williams does not seem to appreciate that a more democratic media might consistently fail to produce greater understanding. This could be due to a multitude of reasons. Some of which are connected with the availability of information and the globalisation of culture. For example, citizens may be indifferent to the issues raised by the Gulf War, they may prefer to read about it in right-wing tabloids, they might glance over an article concerning the event on the way to the Sports page, or they may feel themselves to be too tired to absorb an hour long programme on the relevant issues. There will of course be those who do think the issues are important, but interpret them differently from the way that the authors intended. These considerations place limits on attempts such as Williams's to construct new national forms of solidarity and community through Britain's cultural institutions. But, while a sense of limits is important, this should not distract one from the substantive issues I have raised in connection with Williams's theory of democratic realism. Also, as John Keane (1991) reminds us, a concern over information blizzards should not be allowed to blur the distinction between democratic societies that allow for a plurality of expression, and totalitarian regimes that seek to repress discussion. That governments and private concerns often go to great lengths to control the flow of information should be criticism enough of Baudrillard's conservatism. A radical public-sphere could not ensure that citizens were more able to freely debate a wider range of concerns, but would make such practices more likely. Ultimately, however, one would have to accept that a more democratic media would increase the amount of information available, without necessitating a corresponding increase in the amount of time spent by citizens absorbing and interpreting the material.

A critical conception of ideology

Throughout the previous chapters I explained what Williams and Thompson meant when they used the term ideology, and discusssed whether or not their comments were particularly useful. Here I want to readdress the concept of ideology that has emerged from my critical engagement with Williams and Thompson. My writing at this point makes no particular claim to originality. Many of the themes that are dealt with here have been explored by the growing critical literature on the subject. I do, however, want to end by considering issues related to interests and domination, and critique and justification. I shall argue that the theorisation of ideology can only be successfully linked to patterns of domination through a discussion of interests. Also, as most sophisticated writers on the subject of ideology are aware, the concept raises issues that are of an epistemological character. Althusser, as we saw, through his famous science/ideology split was attempting to address difficult problems of justification and truth. But, as this case demonstrates particularly clearly, attempts to be suggestive in this area often conjure up more theoretical problems than they ultimately resolve.

The theorisation of ideology has been one of the major preoccupations of twentieth century critical social theory. In particular the Marxist tradition has made a positive contribution to our understanding in this area. Writers in this tradition have often resorted to the concept of ideology to explain the cultural cohesion of Western capitalism. We have already seen how a similar concern pervades the writing of E.P. Thompson and Raymond Williams. As a consequence, the concept of ideology is made to do ever more theoretical work, as the prospects for radical change seem to recede into the distant future.

My concern has been to develop a critical conception of ideology that explains how asymmetrical relations of power are reinforced through the discursive construction of meaning. While this interpretation of ideology can be traced back to Marx, there are two important differences between what he seemed to mean by the concept and what I take it to mean. Firstly, as Williams (1977) argues in his critique of mechanical materialism, ideology should not be taken to mean a symbolic inversion of the material social relations of production. Instead the study of ideology should be guided by an investigation into how linguistic meaning is mobilised by reflexive social agents contextually caught up within relations of domination. A second related point, and one often made by post-Marxists such as Earnesto Laclau (1977), is that the division between the real and the symbolic should be reformulated by modern social theory. For Laclau there is no essential outer reality that is not culturally coded and discursively constructed. Laclau however often takes this point too far. His writing could easily be interpreted as suggesting that social structures are no more durable than any other discursive construction. Instead we need to be able to distinguish culture from ideology, and the symbolic from social structures. Laclau's particular brand of post-Marxism does not seem to be able to successfully perform either of these two tasks. With this in mind, J. B. Thompson (1984, p. 126-147) argues that ideology operates in a critical fashion through processes of legitimation, dissimulation and reification. I shall now proceed to briefly illustrate how Williams and Thompson, despite some of the problems they encounter with the concept of ideology, offer examples of these processes.

According to Max Weber all systems of domination will attempt to legitimate their rule by appealing to their subjects on rational, traditional or charismatic grounds. Similarly, and more interestingly from my perspective, Gramsci argues that a ruling class or dominant groups can not maintain their position through force alone and have to win the consent of the people. It has surely become apparent since the European revolutions of 1989, that given some other structural conditions, regimes that fail to secure the consent of at least some of its people are more likely to crumble than those that do. In this context, E.P. Thompson's (1977) *Whigs and Hunters*, offers a complex account of the hegemonic struggles around the Black Act. Ultimately the Black Act could only be a short term measure as it violates the principle of equal treatment before the law. The idea of equal treatment not only operates as an attempt to legitimate domination, but also, as we saw, opens up the possibility of ideology critique. The Whigs, by undermining the concept of equality in order to punish the Blacks, were unintentionally stripping away their own ideological clothing. Not that, as Thompson skilfully argues, one should confuse the ideological battle for consent with a uniformly held and achieved consensus. The operation of hegemony, may be alternatively conceived, as the discursive legitimation of domination. To achieve this end, it may be more important to secure consent in what Gramsci referred to as the ruling bloc, than in society as a whole. The operation of hegemony, therefore, is better conceived as the battle for consent or legitimation, than the achievement of a fixed consensus.

Ideological process of dissimulation can be said to occur when relations of domination are symbolically obscured. Marx's writing on ideology often employs this particular definition. Here ideological phenomena misrepresent, ignore or distort the exploitative relations of domination that constitute the productive base of capitalism. Williams, perhaps unintentionally, adopts a similar definition of ideology in his discussion of pastoral poetry in *The Country and the City* (1973). The pastoral that once expressed both the pain and the misery of the rural labourer, and the aesthetic beauty of the natural, loses its critical function once it comes under the hegemony of the aristocracy. The pastoral, under the pedagogy of the aristocracy, becomes a celebration of rural life that obscures landed relations of domination.

Williams and Thompson make their most distinctive contribution towards a concept of ideology in a third way. To this end, both Williams and Thompson were specifically concerned to combat reificatory accounts of social processes. As radical social theorists, concerned with notions of historical process, both writers challenged ideological accounts that suggested that capitalism was somehow natural or in any way permanent. Williams's central concept the long revolution outlined the development of cultural institutions and suggested ways in which they might be further democratised. Thompson, on the other hand, preferred to rescue a radical culture from history, bringing it to bear on the present in the hope that it would raise good life questions. While I have argued that the way they both went about this is open to doubt-I hope I have produced sufficient evidence to suggest that their specific contributions deserve to be more influential then they are currently in contemporary debates.

Hegemony and ideology

Throughout my discussion of ideology, I have traced out Williams's and Thompson's writing concerning the effectiveness of the concept hegemony. In doing this I have been critical of the way in which the term hegemony became incorporated into British Left social theory through the so called Nairn/Anderson thesis. Although Williams and Thompson ultimately concurred with the theoretical practice of using the terms hegemony and consensus interchangeably; both writers exhibit alternative definitions of the concept. Williams and Thompson, at different periods in their analysis, suggest that the battle for consent was an ongoing historical process that was not to be confused with consensus. If this description of hegemony is accepted, as it should be, the ideological strategies of ruling groups could be said to be effective if they manage to produce disagreement and conflict, as well as consensus, amongst subordinate groups. We may want to argue that there is no empirical evidence to support a dominant ideology thesis, but this does not mean that the absence of a cultural consensus is not the result of hegemonic strategies. The history of the labour movement resounds with examples of strategies of division or divide and rule pursued by the representatives of the state and capital. This argument, on the other hand, should also not be interpreted as implying that divisions between social groups are

184

consequently always the result of hegemonic strategies. But if sociological studies are to capture the operation of ideology on the values, feelings and perspectives of social groupings, then social phenomenon need to be investigated over historical time. Unless sociology considers the development of social perspectives as a reflexive on-going process, continually intersected by hegemonic strategies and more critical cultural perspectives, then it would indeed be guilty of the kind of reifying abstractions Williams and Thompson often took to be characteristic of the discipline. Hence their mutual stress on the importance of historical process would seem appropriate to any investigation into the operation of hegemony.

The other point I want to make is that Williams and Thompson often ran together the related concepts of hegemony and ideology. In this respect, Williams and Thompson are both culpable of defining hegemony in culturalist terms. Instead hegemony should be conceived of as a broader category that includes ideological as well as political and economic practices. These considerations have consequences for both a theory of ideology and hegemony. Despite some of the claims of writers such as Stuart Hall (1988), Thatcherism did not ever effectively build an imaginary consensus around a Rightist agenda. More important in accounting for the political success of the Right during the Eighties are the divisions within the political opposition as well as the altering of the tax system that exaggerated long term trends in the labour market. That the New Right were able to hold onto power in the eighties might be better explained economically and politically, rather than ideologically.

This also points to limitations amongst those, like Williams and Thompson, who conceive of ideology as being solely connected to propositional belief claims or consciousness. More significant than whether workers accept rationalisations of forthcoming redundancies is the institutional separation between the economy and the state. The separation between these two spheres may mean, for example, that the workers conceive of their forthcoming unemployed status as economic rather than political in character. The material separation between the economic system and the state, if we follow Habermas (1976) and Offe (1984,1985),displaces the centrality of class conflict in modern industrial societies. The contradictory development of the welfare state has meant that has been asked to perform paradoxical functions of commodification and de-commodification. Hence the welfare state is dependent upon the successful operation of capital for revenue, while also being asked to compensate for the disruptive and disorganising consequences of capital. The intervention of the welfare state into the economy has meant that the old confrontational relationship between capital and labour has been superseded by the conflict between those in full-time work and those that are under employed. This does not imply that the relation between capital and labour does not remain a central one, but that through state intervention and the de-commodification of the labour process, old divisions have been replaced by new ones. A revised conception of hegemony that sought to express this relationship could only do so through a consideration of economic, political and ideological relations.

Ideology and interests

We have already seen that the Marxist tradition often wants to talk about objective interests; interests that are related to our position in the class structure. A number of objections to this thesis were considered including the idea that interests are constructed politically and historically, and are not fixed by the economic base. The main problem was that the Marxist notion of interests presupposes an authoritarian relation between the theorist or party and the people. This is one of the objections that both Williams and Thompson level against Althusser's Leninism. Yet there are contexts where social groups have interests of which they are not consciously aware. Steven Lukes (1974), reasonably argues, in accordance with this thesis, that persons have 'objective' interests in breathing clean air. I would, therefore, accept that while wants and interests are related, they are not the same.

For Marxists it makes sense to say that dominant hegemonic groups have interests in symbolically securing asymmetrical relations of domination. For example, as I would agree, it is in the interests of capital rather than labour to represent the relations of production as an equal contractual relationship. This is not intended to imply that ideology has any essential class 'belonging', but that a hegemonic strategy is always in the interests of some social groups rather than others. As Bob Jessop (1982) has argued, the class character of a particular hegemonic project is not determined by its genetic symbolic composition, but in terms of its long term aims. If the Labour Party decided to collectively commit themselves to a so called return to full male employment, this could be seen as ideological. Such a strategy could be said to be in the interests of male trade unionists but not in the interests of women looking for paid employment. Thus a notion of interests enables one to connect the operation of ideology and hegemony to the strategies and counter strategies of dominant and subordinate groups.

However, the broader question remains, how one can maintain the connection between ideology and interests without implying some form of authoritarian relationship. Firstly, both Williams and Thompson distinguish their version of socialist humanism by insisting on a dialectic between political means of representation and the people. Interests are then dialogically constructed and agreed on. Secondly, developing this theme, ideology critique should become part of everyday life. The long revolution was an attempt to promote and make commonly available new and more democratic cultural processes. Although differently formulated, Thompson points to the way in which subversive cultural traditions shape and give expression to notions of interest. For Williams and Thompson critical theory was not so much about the 'implanting' of revolutionary ideology, as the material reformation of the public sphere. A democratic revival of public institutions would seemingly allow the 'masses' to communicatively rethink their interests in light of 'other' considerations. Here interests are not immediately self-present to agents, or the privileged property of an elite group of revolutionaries, but can begin to emerge after full consideration in democratic settings.

Ideology critique and utopia

Both Williams and Thompson overestimate the role of an inherited radical culture in practices of critique, marginalising other cultural forms of sociological inquiry such as feminism. They also overstate the extent to which subjects are conscious of ideological practices. But, I would conclude, by maintaining the subjects capacity for reflexivity, their approach remains preferable to that of Althusser and others.To develop these arguments further I want to concentrate on the writing of E.P. Thompson, which displays an understanding of some of the theoretical problems that are related to ideology critique. Here I want to argue for both a historicist and a utopian conception of ideology critique. A historicist or contextualist critique is a form of immanent critique that allows agents to reflect upon certain social and cultural norms in such a way that is neither foundational nor transcendental. Thompson proposed an ideology critique that sought to develop those ethical principles that are embedded in certain forms of life and institutional practice. An immanent critique, in these terms, would engage with members of an oppressed social group

187

helping them to realise some of the implications of the epistemic principles that they already hold. We have already seen with Thompson's discussion of notions of equal value and the need to be ethically self-determining how this might be achieved. Thus Thompson opposed Stalinism as it violated the culturally dependent notion of human beings shared capacity to be relatively self-determining. To take the argument further, Steven Lukes (1977) has demonstrated that the ability to be self-determining is also related to notions of equality. The capacity to be relatively self-determining is dependent upon certain social conditions such as a free secure space, equality of respect and certain guaranteed material conditions. Racism, therefore, could be said to be ideological as it sustains relations of domination. We are able to engage in a critique of such practices as they violate the principle of self-determination. A person, it probably goes without saying, who is assumed to be culturally inferior due to his or her racial origin would be unlikely to enjoy an equality of respect from others. A society that accepted the principle of self-determination, through a process of immanent critique, would seek to reverse discriminatory social practices as far as possible. But, as I argued previously, what is presupposed here, is that the material conditions where a persons 'wants' can be reflexively examined are readily available. Evidently, in a society like ours, this is far from being the case. This makes Williams's reflections on the public sphere all the more important. Despite the limitations of his programme to democratically reform the mass media; he recognised that in a pluralist society the common conditions for the sharing of experience and the creation of a new structure of feeling have to be politically and materially realised.

The practice of ideology critique involves a utopian as well as a contextual component. E.P. Thompson, despite the valid representational claims of Jardine and Swindells, retains a certain endurance through his defence of the practice of utopian critique. Both Paul Ricoeur (1986) and E.P. Thompson have argued, in different contexts, that the utopian work or moment is always accompanied by the principle of self-reflection. The utopian writer and those involved in ideology critique are being asked to imagine a possible future where they are able to reassess their current needs and imagine new needs. Unless subjects, through their engagement with critical theory, are asked to place themselves in different social situations, they are unlikely to reconstitute their interests in ways that radically challenge their currently perceived set of needs. Unskilled persons, for example, who are only able to work six months a year may envisage a better future in terms of extended periods of employment rather more rewarding activity. The task of critical theory, therefore, would then be to suggest new and different interests to subordinate groups. If such persons were able to imagine themselves in a more economically secure society, than they currently inhabit, they may then come to realise different wants and interests (Geuss, 1981).

Thompson's own writing gives us an insight into how an immanent and utopian critique could work politically. Thompson has hitherto argued that the principle cause of the arms race was the division of Europe into two antagonistic blocs. Through the concept of Exterminism during the Eighties, we were being asked to collectively reimagine a Europe that was united, democratic and peaceful. During politically 'hot' periods of the Cold War such a future seemed politically unrealisable. Thompson's vision, I would argue, operated as a guiding principle of hope for at least some of those people actively engaged in the peace movement. Despite the political and ideological manoeuvrings both East and West, Thompson's contextual utopian vision acted as an inspiration for radical change, and just as importantly, as questioning of the ideology of deterrence. Deterrence theory as the staple ideology of the Cold War sought to legitimate anti-democratic processes, while assuming a divided militarised Europe to be historically inevitable. That the Cold War did not end as Thompson, or anyone else for that matter, expected does not invalidate the critique. The principle of validation remains, as Raymond Geuss (1981) says, an important one for a critical theory. If having experienced a united democratic Europe where human rights were respected people authentically demonstrated that they preferred the limited democracy of the Cold War, then Thompson's writing could be said to be disconfirmed. However, there is at the time of writing little evidence that this is the case, despite large scale unemployment and poverty in the East.

These arguments should not be taken to imply that society could be easily reorganised in terms of people's needs. An active process of immanent critique might result in people failing to be convinced by the arguments set before them, and moreover not all of societies institutions could be reorganised in terms of the principle of self-determination. Needs and desires would have to be renegotiated in terms of certain economic, cultural and political limits that attempted to maximise democratic principles. If alternatively an emancipatory theory proposed that such limits were only the product of a ruling-class ideology, such a theory would cease to deserve the title critical. Finally, I should add, that I have made no attempt to meet some of the possible objections to the way I have approached these issues.

Instead my aim was to offer some suggestions as to how the writing of E.P. Thompson and Raymond Williams could become more inducive to social theory and ideology critique. I have also proposed, somewhat unfashionably, that ideology needs to be reconnected to a notion of interests, and following E.P. Thompson, despite some of the claims made by those proclaiming an end of ideology, that a notion of critique can still operate through discursive, utopian and historicist modes.

The future of socialism

The commitment to a socialist tradition went to the heart of the writing of Williams and Thompson. Their contributions on culture and ideology, that I have discussed at length, can only be made sense of if it is contextualised in the discourse of the New Left. It is true, however, that Williams will be remembered primarily as a literary figure, and Thompson as a polemicist for peace and a historian. However a critical appreciation of their work should not be allowed to submerge their strongly felt affiliation with socialist humanism. This remains a connecting link across a broad range of concerns. The socialist humanist tradition, as conceptualised by both writers, provides the ethical basis for the critique of economic reason and 'actually existed socialism'. In this respect, the socialist tradition, through the writing of the New Left, always amounted to more than a formal commitment to socialised production. But, I would argue, that if the Left are to remain influential then it cannot restrict itself to questions concerning culture and ideology. Currently the Left is not a coherent or cohesive grouping, but primarily exists as a collection of splintered concerns ranging from women's, green and peace movements, to more 'disciplined' revolutionary sects. That these groups would probably accept that they belonged to a Left should not blind us to the extent to which they would accept that they had common interests. In this final section, I want to ask whether the future of the Left lies with a reformed socialist project? While Williams and Thompson were able to make a wider political contribution from the perspective of this tradition, I have already discussed many of the difficulties that their version of cultural Marxism encountered. Williams, as we saw, hoped that the labour movement would become invigorated by the cultural perspectives of the new social movements. But his belief that concerns related to feminism, peace and ecology could all be recentred around a working-class socialism, apart form being essentialistic, looks

190

increasingly unlikely to materialise. Similarly, Thompson's hope that the collapse of the Cold War would lead to a rebirth of socialism in Europe, at present seems misplaced. What then are the continuing cultural resources of the socialist tradition, and how might the Left be put back together as a progressive social movement? I want to introduce five theoretical projects that are both attempting to politically revive the British Left, and rethink its historic relation to socialism. This list is far from exhaustive, and I have deliberately chosen those perspectives that are seriously attempting to engage with the socialist tradition. Finally, I should also add, that I make no special claim to be able to offer the depth of discussion that these differing paradigms undoubtedly deserve.

Classical socialism

Williams's and Thompson's particular version of socialism is both a product of the Romantic and the Enlightenment tradition. This form of socialism has sought to subordinate potentially destructive forms of economic reason to ethical and cultural criteria, and remains an important intellectual source. But, while Williams and Thompson were critical of triumphalist and productivist versions of Marxism, fundamental to their conception of socialism remained issues related to the economy. There are, with reference to Marx, two distinct ways in which the political economy could be reformed (Bottomore 1990). The first version would argue that the means of production should be brought into social ownership subordinating the economy to the conscious control of the proletariat. This, through the romantic myth of the preindustrial craftsperson, is the form of socialist political economy that found expression in the writing of Williams and Thompson. Although Thompson was far more reluctant than Williams to commit himself to particular arguments concerning economic relations, he remains implicated in this tradition through the writing of William Morris. On the other hand, Marx through the progressive dominance of technology or machinofacture, also conceived of a possible future where work was no longer the dominant social activity. While I will return to these issues later, I want to argue at this stage, that despite their critique of Marxist theory, both Williams and Thompson can be roughly assimilated with the intellectual paradigm I shall call classical socialism.

Socialists who occupy this position, argue that capitalism remains an individualist competitive system that needs to be brought under the direct control of the community (Elson 1988, Blackburn 1991). A consciously controlled economy is preferred over a market economy, as investment decisions are often made in isolation from the impact they have on others. The long revolution aimed to provide a social community, reconnecting the economic system with peoples social needs. Williams felt that this could be done through a combination of centralised and decentralised planning. Where as the market produces atomised individuals and fragmented forms of community, socialised planning could collectively provide the basis for less atomised forms of life. This project would radically challenge the social authority of capital and bourgeois definitions of democracy, through locally and centrally planned self-management. The main problem that Williams and others encounter is that actual attempts to plan and control economies have proved to be far from successful. This difficulty in terms of Williams's specific contribution is exaggerated as he does not really consider the reasons for the economic failure of Eastern European socialism. Instead, like many of the writers on the Left, he is more concerned with the shortcomings of capitalism. But, in the wake of the European revolutions of 1989, one could more easily make out a case for market economies then one could for the old socialist regimes. While the classical socialists have some valuable points to make against the advocates of free markets, the idea that planned labour can replace disorganised capital has surely run its course. What the classical socialist's fail to appreciate is that the welfarist compromise between capital and labour, and the unpopularity of state administered socialism, provides the starting point for any Left analysis. The classical socialist dream of a wholly planned egalitarian society is finished.

Market socialism

Writers who are advocates of market socialism have been more attentive to the failures within Eastern European societies. Market socialists have tended to look to social democratic nations for progressive alternatives to liberal capitalism. This perspective stresses that social democracies like Sweden, Norway and Denmark have maintained high levels of employment, a commitment to democratic freedoms, and a strong welfare state. Market socialists argue that Marxism exhibits an obsession with means rather than ends. That is equality can not be guarenteed by public ownership and might best be achieved by a mixed economy. Thus there is nothing intrinsic in planning that guarantees equality. All advocates of market socialism aim to theoretically question the socialist critique of the ownership of private capital. In most versions of this theory, scope for independent entrepreneurial activity is defended, and the private ownership of the means of production only becomes objectionable when it is concentrated into monopolies and multinationals. The existence of smaller entrepreneurs both puts limits on the power of the state, and helps provide the efficient production of goods and services. However there remains large areas of disagreement amongst the advocates of market socialism as to precisely what mix between public and private agencies is desirable. If, for example, one compares the writing of two of the main advocates of market socialism, (Julian Le Grand (1989) and Alec Nove (1983)), they seem to agree on little other than the need for a mixed economy, and the relative efficiency of markets. While their writing and that of others remains suggestive, it is difficult to see what is distinctively socialist about these ideas. This theory, one could argue, does not seek to make clear some of the failures and contradictions of social democracy, and has often too little to say on how they intend to generate support for programmes of nationalisation. Market socialism also remains inadequately reconstructed in terms of ecological and feminist critiques. For instance, market socialists are often committed to restoring full employment, but in the past such a strategy has excluded women and other disadvantaged groups, and would probably require ecologically hazardous levels of economic growth. While market socialism remains preferable to classical socialism, in that it usually admits limits to the extent to which the economy can be self-managed, the theory remains underdeveloped by its advocates.

Radical nationalism

Most writers who have addressed the subject of nationalism seem to agree that it is a Janus-faced phenomenon. Nationalism, as Benedict Anderson (1983) has pointed out, is not inherently racist, instead it is more often an expression of a sense of belonging to a homeland that is maintained through shared cultural values and symbols. Nationalism, as Anderson puts it, is more usefully thought of as self-sacrificing love, than the active hatred of others. This, of course, is not to deny that nationalism does have another dark side; the symbolic cohesion of the nation, for example, may be maintained through variously invented traditions that serve to legitimate the interests of powerful social groups. For writers in the socialist tradition, Williams and Thompson being no exception, nationalism poses a peculiarly difficult set of problems. Nationalism can be either represented as a form of solidarity and collective belonging in a fragmentary and divisive world, or as inherently ideological. Such considerations have prompted some on the British Left to argue that a radical cultural nationalism could provide the cultural basis for an emancipatory politics. This particular theoretical move can be traced back to Gramsci, where the construction of the national-popular movements are not judged ethically, but in terms of their ability to bind together class alliances. Ideology in this view is described as 'effective' the extent to which it can cement a union between diverse groups. Here I want to argue that a radicalised nationalism could not adequately address some of the problems progressive social movements would inevitably encounter. However, this argument need not entail that the Left should vacate this space altogether. As Williams recognised to give the need for belonging a symbolic content is often satisfied in this way. Hence, if the Left are unable to articulate certain signs of belonging this position will be occupied by the Right.

Both Williams and Thompson maintain a certain ambivalence in connection to culture and nationhood. Williams's Welshness - similarly with his preoccupation with Marxism - comes to play an increasingly important role in his later writing. His posthumously published novel *The People of the Blackmountains* (1989b) sought to trace through the historically shifting patterns of life in a Welsh rural community. Williams's Welsh national identity, like other nationalisms, could be said to be culturally and historically rooted in a mythological sense of community. While Williams (1989) is critical of essentialistic definitions of Welshness and Englishness he often commits similar mistakes himself. Cultural nationalism can have ideological consequences. Francis Mulhern (1989), in an article devoted to *Towards 2000*, argues that Williams makes a distinction between so called natural communities and the artificial culture of the nation-state. As both Mulhern and Paul Gilroy (1989) comment, this leads Williams into a theoretically uncomfortable position when confronted with concerns around cultural racism. Here Williams dismisses what he refers to as the liberal claim that black immigrants who came from Commonwealth nations are as British as anyone else. This is because, for Williams, one's social identity is the product of social and cultural definitions, not the abstract legal constructions of the nation-state. Gilroy rightly objects, contrary to Williams, that citizenship should not be dependent upon notions of cultural identity. The new forms of racism that have emerged on the political Right, have to some degree been reproduced by the Left. It is ideological to construct nationhood in terms of a common culture,

194

instead, one could say, that all modern nation-states attempt to institutionalise a collective culture amongst its citizens. Thus nation-states, despite some of the claims made by certain national movements, are not the result of a shared ethnicity. It is more acurate to point to the ways nation states impose and construct cultural boundaries and symbols. Williams by juxtaposing an authentic sense of belonging against the pseudo cultural strains of the modern nation-state, seemingly misses this point.

E.P. Thompson also retains a certain degree of uncertainty on issues related to culture and the nation. As we have seen, Thompson's historical writing and his work on the peace movement utilised the 'free-born Englishman' as a cultural touchstone. I have already argued with respect to feminist theory, and debates over issues related to citizenship, that Thompson's cultural Englishness has certain ideological implications. A further dimension to this debate has been added by Rapheal Samuel (1990), who as a fellow historian, has argued that Englishness is currently felt by a wide political spectrum to be under attack. There has historically been an erosion of English patriotism that was much more in evidence between the wars. Sections of the political Left and Right, as a reaction against American hegemony and the fashionable politics of life-style, are now united around the need for national rejuvenation. Commercially capitalism, has according to Samuel, through theme parks and the growth of the heritage industry sought to cash in on the sense that our national culture is being steadily eroded. While Samuel mistakenly ignores cultural and political processes external to the nation-state, he sheds theoretical light on some of the limitations of Thompson's nostalgic cultural nationalism. As Eric Hobsbawn (1990) has also shown, the time when a radical politics could be based on national grounds is over. The older nationalisms of the nineteenth century were both unificatory and emancipatory, in sharp contrast to the nationalisms of the late twentieth century, that are largely, although not in every instance, defensive reactions against the globalising tendencies of the modern world. In the context of the growth of trans-national organisations and the globalisation of capital, Thompson's radical Englishness has a reactive character. This is especially marked when one considers Thompson's own international vision of a unified socialist Europe.

Another writer on the British Left in favour of a radical national solution is Tom Nairn (1988). Nairn is an advocate of what he calls 'quiet republicanism'. Unlike Williams, however, he does not juxtapose an authentic cultural community against a synthetically constructed national one. Readdressing the themes of the Nairn-

Anderson thesis he maintains the argument that the dominant culture of Britain's ruling-class is in need of reform and renewal. A specifically Southern hegemonic ruling bloc has, according to his account, been cemented together primarily through the cultural dominance of the Royal Family. The symbolic superiority of the 'enchanted glass' has fostered a backward anti-industrialism amongst Britain's ruling class. The solution to this peculiarly British disease is a form of republican national redemption. The dominant national culture needs to be revived to carry through the unfinished business of a rational enlightenment culture. This can only be achieved through a specifically Northern industrial civil rights based culture. Contrary to Thompson, therefore, Nairn argues that Englishness is part of the problem rather than the solution.

But the difficulty remains as to whether or not a radical politics could be based on a form of Left nationalism. Paul Gilroy (1989), for example, argues that a reinvigorated Left nationalism, even in Nairn's more cautious terms, remains politically suspect. Firstly, despite Nairn's relative sophistication when compared to Williams and Thompson, the difficulty persists that the language of British nationalism is historically connected to the memory of imperial greatness. Instead, as Nairn in part suggests, the Left should reconstruct itself around a less culturally loaded language of rights and obligations. If a sense of belonging is to be fostered amongst persons within the boundaries of a nation-state, or wider political communities, it would seem politically responsible to do this through a discourse connected to citizenship. This takes us to Gilroy's second point; that political mobilisation based upon a radical nationalism diverts attention away from the ways in which the boundaries of the nation state are being continually transcended. There is a need for a re-emerged Left to develop the means of organisation and information exchange that is local, national and international in character. I would conclude, along with Gilroy and Hobsbawn, that in a British national context, the Left should adopt a wholly different approach from that of the cultural nationalists. This revised approach should not only embrace the language of a rights based citizenship, but should also seek to form alliances in more global contexts. Yet, as I indicated, I do not think that the Left can simply ignore symbolic questions of national belonging. Gilroy's argument comes close to the assertion that nationalism equals racism. This may be currently true in a British context, but diverts the necessary energy away from the task of forging more multicultural aspects of belonging. Thus the challenge here is to allow for the development of inclusive, plural indentities in different social spheres.

196

Post-Marxism

Post-Marxism is the attempt made by certain post-structuralists to rethink and mostly abandon Marxist theory. It is the influential writing of Laclau and Mouffe (1985), who have drawn upon discourse theory in order to reveal the essentialising nature of Marxist critiques, to whom I want to pay most attention. According to their approach the classical Marxists posit the material economic base as a 'constitutive outside' that is inherent in any antagonistic relationship. The relation between capital and labour only becomes contradictory when it has been discursively constructed as such. The relations of production, therefore, are not essentially conflict ridden, but can only be represented as such through a theory of subjectivity. Thus this becomes based on conflict once workers realise themselves as citizens with certain historically and socially defined needs. In other words, the base/superstructure model attempts to formulate the economic base as a transcendental outside that constitutes the inside or social identities of citizens. Social identities are alternatively defined, by Laclau and Mouffe, as being the product of a multiplicity of antagonisms in a field that is discursively constructed. Hence the social identity of the worker has no essential fixity as it is articulated through political, economic and culturally discursive fields. The worker as a revolutionary figure, on this reading, is not the essential identity of the worker, but one of the many historically possible identities that are open to him or her.

One of the more impressive features of traditional or classical Marxist social theory was the analysis of social structures and institutions. The absence of such a dimension in the writing of the post-Marxists has led other writers, such as Norman Geras (1987) and Gregor McLennan (1989), to reaffirm the dominance of the economic base. As Laclau and Mouffe continually oppose the plurality and radical contingency of modern identities to the hard determining shell of the material base, they tend to evade rather than engage with their theoretical opponents. But as I have already theoretically dealt with the shortcomings of the base/superstructure model- I will not try to reassert it here. Instead, I would like to take up some of the suggestions made by Williams (1975) in *Television, Technology and Cultural Form*, where the economy, state, and the family act as structuring devices for the production of cultural forms. In the development of television the economy and the state could be said to act as steering mechanisms. To put the point crudely, the economy and the state by continually reshaping class structure, cultural institutions and the material space of society become a focal point for social theory in the way that fragmented cultural identities are not. While cultural identities have important implications for social theory, they should not be allowed to replace a concern with institutional structures. Williams's concern to link cultural processes to institutional structures, and admittedly less often reception contexts, is preferable to Laclau's and Mouffe's radical subjectivism (Mouzelis, 1990).

This leads me to a second point: that while Laclau and Mouffe provide an interesting discussion of the class essentialism of classical teleological Marxism, their analysis remains theoretically suspect. I accepted earlier, in line with some of Laclau and Mouffe's remarks, that Williams maintains an essentially reductive approach to problems associated with political mobilisation. Following Laclau and Mouffe, I argued, that it was the task of a reformed Left to give these multiple antagonisms a symbolic unity that they do not possess in essence. In *Hegemony and Socialist Strategy* (1985), Laclau and Mouffe argue that a counter- hegemonic strategy could be founded on the deepening and widening of democracy. For the present, I want to leave open the question as to whether or not democracy should be the guiding principle of the Left. But, in the context of Laclau's and Mouffe's discussion, they are not able to argue very convincingly for a more democratic society, as they favour democratic pluralism soley because it gives expression to the diversity of antagonisms and identities that exist in civil society. This is not a very strong argument. Their lack of attention to an institutional dimension does not admit that becoming a more equal society takes a certain precedence over whether or not the Conservative party becomes more internally democratic. To suggest, against an economist Marxism, that there are a plurality of political struggles involving peace, feminism and green politics that cannot be reduced to a single essential conflict is surely correct. Yet Laclau and Mouffe often go further than this by celebrating diversity and pluralism as ends in themselves. Further, Laclau and Mouffe provide little discussion of the radical possibilities and limitations that any theory of democracy would have to address. If they are in favour of representative as opposed to direct democracy, as I assume they are, this should have led them to analyse how the rules of democracy could be grounded institutionally. Inevitably this would bring them into an analysis of the economy and the state beyond the endless 'play' of identity. Finally, I would argue, democracy is not only a set of procedural rules but has normative implications. Earlier I tried to suggest that democracy could be distinguished from totalitarianism through the concept of self-determination. But, we have already seen, through my discussion of the decline of the nation-state and the limits of self-management, that democracy in the modern world can only find expression within certain boundaries. Democracy, I would contend, is less about the celebration of culturally diverse identities than it is concerned with the reflexive rule from below and the de-concentration of power. If democracy were simply the political expression of plural identities, it is unlikely that revolutions and political movements would ever have become so attached to the idea.

My intention here is not to suggest that there are theoretically 'hard' issues of political economy and state formation, that have a primacy over 'soft' issued such as ecology or feminism. This would be to fail, as Williams often said, to make the necessary connections. Ecologists and feminists should be as concerned as Marxists to maintain institutional critiques. Unless a reformed Left is able to answer questions connected to the future of dominant institutions, that are global, national and local in character, then it will probably only exist as a collection of plural and marginalised identities. My suggestion is that the way in which we conceptualise the subject and institutional processes should be brought together. The theoretical path suggested here steers a clear route between the subjectivism of Laclau and Mouffe, and the structural determinacy of Althusser. Williams wrote perceptively on this subject:

> To see a change of heart and change of institutions as alternatives is already to ratify an alienated society, for neither can be separated, or ever is, from the other; simply one or the other can be ignored (Williams,1984,pp.49-50)

Post-industrial socialism

Recently it has become fashionable to argue that Britain and other European nations are entering into a new stage of development called post-industrialism. The term is usually taken to signify, amongst other things, a decline in employment in Western manufacturing industries, and the expansion of the so called service sector. But, rather than the service sector 'soaking up' displaced workers, the decline in Britain's manufacturing industry has resulted in a corresponding rise in unemployment. Conservative and orthodox Keynesian writers have interpreted this phenomenon as either an argument for cutting welfare expenditure or a case for publicly reinvesting in the economy. Both approaches would accept that the aim of this strategy would be to increase profits, free capital for investment and thereby reduce unemployment. There are however growing doubts across the political spectrum concerning the feasibility of such a strategy. Such policies, some have argued, exhibit a misplaced nostalgia for social conditions that are unrepeatable in the present. According to Phal (1984) and Kumar (1988) the boom period for male employment during the 1950s and 1960s is not a norm against which the present should be measured. Even if, as unlikely as this might seem, we found a way back to a period of full male employment, further employment would have to be created for others traditionally marginalised in the labour market. The economic growth levels necessary to sustain 'truc' full employment are not only unrealistic, but would probably have negative ecological and social consequences. The long term restructing of the labour market has consequences for socialist and democratic theory. The historic compromise between organised labour, capital and the state needs to be reassessed in view of these changes. If an alternative political strategy cannot guarantee full-employment this removes the central plank of post-war British and European citizenship, and undermines the context within which the welfare state itself was formed.

Earlier I suggested that Marx could be read as providing two distinct models of possible socialist futures. The first of these, which I called classical socialism, held out the promise of a self-managed rationally controlled society. This project with the collapse of Eastern European socialism is at an end. The other possible future, that Marx had admittedly little to say about, was where workers were free from necessity to develop their own intellectual and emotional resources. It is the aim of Andre Gorz's utopian socialism to stress the importance of the latter; replacing the idea of freedom within work, with freedom from work.

In *Farewell to the Working Class* (1982), Gorz wants to defend the central themes of the liberation of time and the abolition of waged labour. The sphere of paid employment, that is to be minimised, is governed by what he calls heteronomous activities. The functional requirements that dominate waged labour are not freely chosen by those subjects performing the tasks, but are technical imperatives pre-programmed by the dominant organisational structure. Alternatively, for Gorz, social practices that take place outside of the work-place should be self-determined activities. An activity is self-determined, if that activity is freely chosen, subject to ethical rather than performance related criteria and seen as an end in itself. These two distinct spheres of activity operate as ideal-types in Gorz's writing. Otherwise, one could easily object, that many social practices that take place outside of paid employment such as housework, hardly fulfil the criteria demanded by autonomous forms of agency. Instead, Gorz is attempting to redefine freedom, as freedom from necessity and freedom to engage in activities that are not dominated by economic reason. Through this definition he arguably offers a more substantive and materialist account of freedom than negative conceptions of liberty that seem to be solely concerned with placing limits on state power. The shared resource of free-time, given the necessary institutional contexts, would provide the backcloth for the development of new creative activities.

That economic rationality should be subordinate to social and cultural goals is one of the defining features of Williams's and Thompson's cultural Marxism. Yet, while Williams and Thompson connect the myth of the romantic craftsperson to arguments for economic management and the democratisation of cultural practices, self-fulfilment for Gorz can only be achieved outside of the workplace. The complex division of labour inherent in modern productive and administrative systems, means that each worker can only master a fraction of the knowledge that is utilised within modern bureaucratic settings. Hence the modern labour process has become rationalised and standardised, while becoming increasingly detached from the will of the worker. Here Gorz has been strongly influenced by the so called deskilling thesis. Bravermann's seminal work *Labour and Monopoly Capital* (1974) describes the historical degradation of the labour process under capitalism, which has progressively stripped workers of their individual autonomy through the centralisation of control. This has meant that paid work has become increasingly fragmented, with the shop floor losing sight of the plan of production, while capital has tightend its grip over the control of work.

Gorz argues that the dominance of economic rationality has historically prevented the working-class from conceiving of an alternative rationality to that of capitalism. The working-class are unable, therefore, to act as the agency for change to a new society based on free time. The consciousness of the working-class has become the mirror image of capitalism, as they are only capable of conceiving of their salvation in terms of waged labour. At this early stage in his writing, Gorz suggests that a possible agency for change could be those workers whose identity has not been formed through a life long commitment to full-time work. On the basis of this interpretation, the unemployed, the disabled and women working part-time are more likely, he suggests, to be attracted to a possible future that separates the right to an income from formal paid employment. This is usually called a social income.

A politics of free-time would also aim at achieving a genuinely democratic civil society freed from heteronomous activities. This could be brought about through the development of an autonomous sphere that was not subordinable to the nation-state or capital. Gorz is vague concerning the social composition of this sphere, but it would seem to consist of a cluster of localised self-governing institutions. While Gorz does not envisage the state withering away, he does insist that the means of production are centralised and brought into common ownership. The state is then in position to centrally plan the production of goods and services satisfying the basic material needs of most citizens. The autonomous sphere would become the site of individual freedom, where non-essential goods and services could be produced and bartered. It would become the responsibility of a rational politics in this new society to constantly renegotiate the relationship between heteronomy and autonomy.

A later work *Paths to Paradise* (Gorz,1985) concentrates on developments in new technology. These are the main cause of the growing unemployment suffered in Western societies. In this context, Gorz offers a radical argument to redeploy technology in order to reskill everyday life. Gorz argues that micro-technology can be used as both labour saving devices and as a means of learning new skills. It is probably in this work that Gorz is at his most utopian, and I would argue that *Paths to Paradise* (1985) should be read, as Thompson suggests we read William Morris, as a work of the utopian imagination. What is troubling, however, in the context of earlier discussions, are the possible implications of the centralisation of the means of production. Earlier we saw how the market socialists thought that such demands were economically regressive and politically authoritarian due to the failure of European socialism. This is a matter for concern, as in Gorz's terms the sphere of autonomy would be entirely free from the dominance of economic reason, leaving needs that could not be satisfied through centralised production to be met locally. It remains a mystery as to how Gorz's centralised system of production avoids the information overloaded, inefficient bureaucratic nightmare of actually existed socialism. Why, one might ask, should we believe Gorz when he suggests that decentralised localised production would make up for the inefficiencies of state managed production? This would seem particularly evident if the activities of civil society are to be solely governed through the principle of autonomy. Even Alec Nove (1983), who envisages more state control than many of the market socialists, would not want to argue that the satisfaction of peoples needs could, or should, be satisfied locally by non-profit making local enterprises or centrally by the state. Instead, as Nove suggests, entrepreneurial activity, as long as it does not become organised into monopolies, should be re-evaluated by socialists as putting limits on state power and providing necessary goods and services.

Notably there is a significant change in tone in Gorz's (1989) next book *Critique of Economic Reason*. Here Gorz is evidently attempting to appease some of his critics by intellectually bridging the gap between the present and a possible future society based upon free time. Before I go on to discuss the main body of this text, I want to point to some of the revisions and reversals his argument undertakes when set in the context of his earlier writing. Firstly, Gorz makes clear that he is not opposed to the humanisation of work, but that it should not be the main aim of radical movements for social change. Next, and more importantly, Gorz argues emancipatory social theory no longer has a specific target group. While we can expect certain marginalised groups to have a greater interest in a politics of free time than others, the generally negative psychological impact of under-employment, and the relative powerlessness of such groups means that they do not constitute a new universal class. Thirdly, the Left in mobilising people in favour of free-time should attempt to construct alliances across class fractions. Gorz usefully goes against the prevailing Gramscian trend by arguing that the social cement that holds the alliance together should have a strong ethical component. Unless full-time workers are prepared to lower their consumption levels, become attracted to having more free time, and are concerned with the quality of life of those outside of full-time employment, then the future would seem a bleak one. Finally, Gorz is to be commended for his recommendation that the Left, if it is to survive at all, must become a European Left. In stark contrast to the other perspectives I have reviewed so far, Gorz realises that the power of international capital and trans-national organisations has restructured economic and political boundaries. Unless the Left can secure a common European framework that will lead to the progressive expansion of free time - the alternative would seem to be a nationally atomised social regression.

Gorz locates the pitfalls of post-modernity somewhat differently from other more fashionable writers. Gorz writes:

> The unequal distribution of work in the economic sphere, coupled with the unequal distribution of free time created by technical innovations thus leads to a situation in which one section of the population is able to buy extra spare

time from the other and the latter is reduced to serving the former (Gorz 1989, p. 6).

This situation is the result of two distinctive economic trends within late capitalism. The first, and in my view most important trend, is the structural division between the core and the periphery sectors of the labour market. Gorz suggests, along with others, that the traditional division between capital and labour has been increasingly overlain by the antagonism between core workers and peripheral, part-time or unemployed workers. In this respect the core workers do not represent a new universal subject, or a return of the repressed craft worker, but the displacement of heteronomy. According to Gorz, it is the task of a reformed Left, to persuade the core workers that they have long term interests in the promotion of free time and more equal economic distribution. The other economic trend Gorz draws attention to is the expansion of the service economy, or what he occasionally calls the housewifization of the economy. The economy has become increasingly domesticated subjecting the work that used to be done by housewives to economic forms of rationality. This has led to the absurd situation where one section of the population (core workers and professionals) are over employed and have no free-time for domestic labour, while the others are forced to take on the domestic labour of the former as well as their own. As an alternative to this situation, Gorz suggests, as before, the guiding principle for the introduction of new technology should be the saving of public labour time. Gorz, however, ignores the possibility that the so called housewifization of the economy has liberating consequences for some women workers. It provides them with paid employment, and access to services they would otherwise have to provide for free in the private sphere. That Gorz consistently leaves himself open to attack on these issues by feminist writers, will be the subject of a later discussion.

The central theme of Gorz's writing remains the dominance of economic rationality. He agrees with Habermas (1976) that instrumental reason has been allowed to dominate and colonise the life-world, whose relational fabric forms the basis for social integration. Gorz, however, constructs the relationship between heteronomy and autonomy somewhat differently from Habermas. Gorz defines economic rationalisation as human activity that is subject to counting and calculation. So long as agents are not subjected to economic rationality they can be said to be, 'at one with the time, movement and rhythm of life' (Gorz,1989,p.109). The problem, therefore, with the feminist demand that housework should be a paid activity is that it expands the scope of economic rationality. This would mean that productive activities such as baking a cake for a friends birthday, making love, or taking a telephone message for someone could all potentially come to have an exchange value. For Gorz the other problem with economic rationality is that it does not admit to the principle of self-limitation, that is external boundaries have to be placed upon its development. Capitalism, according to Gorz, has severed the connection between work and human need by continually expanding the needs and desires of consumers. The subjects of capitalism are locked into a vicious consumption cycle where they are working longer and longer hours, to satisfy ever expanding wants and needs. Here Gorz illustrates his argument through an empirical study of workers in a shoe factory. He demonstrates that once labour time was reduced subjects were able to develop a more reflexive relation towards their needs and desires. The reduction of labour time, according to Gorz, automatically leads subjects to reconsider issues related to the quality of their life.

The limits of the critique of economic reason

Here I want to restrict the discussion to the way that Gorz handles the critique of economic reason. This will serve as a prelude to the final, concluding section.The importance of the dominance of economic reason intellectually connects Gorz with the tradition I referred to as a classical socialism. Capitalism as a social system is blind, as Marx fully realised, to use values or needs and limitations that are external to its own purposes. Unless the economic system can become socialised to the extent where, to paraphrase Gorz, more is not always better, then we run the risk of the ecological system collapsing, continued global inequalities and the disintegration of communal life. If socialism is to have a future in a world where complex heteronomous systems make self-managed socialism look conspicuously out-dated, then it must be able to set limits on the development of economic reason. The problem being that Gorz's writing on this subject is far from convincing. Instead of providing a general explanation of the dominance of economic rationality, his argument remains, despite his constant attempts to update it, a form of economic determinism.

This should become more evident through a feminist critique. In the final section of *Critique of Economic Reason* (1989) Gorz argues that agents should be able to form relationships in an autonomous sphere as sovereign persons without interference from outside agencies.

Although he maintains that the private sphere should be reformed along democratic lines, he maintains that the root of all domination can be found in the economic base. Such a perspective, that makes a fetish out of a critique of economic rationality, is unable to adequately account for other forms of domination. One gets the impression with Gorz, along with other writers in the Marxist tradition, that once human activities are freed from reifying forms of abstract calculation they can be considered autonomous. Elsewhere Nancy Fraser (1987), writing on Habermas's analysis, argues that it is a mistake to neglect private frameworks of power.

> actions coordinated by a normatively secured consensus
> in the male-headed, nuclear family are actions regulated
> by power. It seems to me a grave mistake to restrict the
> term 'power' to bureaucratic contexts (Fraser,1987,p.38).

This is precisely, following Fraser, what both Habermas and Gorz do in their writing. That Gorz ignores issues related to masculinity, for example, means that he overstates the part played by economic reason in closing down alternatives to a work based society. The felt need for full-time employment in capitalist societies is not only an expression of economic rationality, as Gorz suggests, but is bound up with the masculine identity of the male breadwinner. There is, therefore, a relationship between being a man and provider that partly explains the psychological trauma of unemployment. If a theory of cultural domination is to remain non-essentialising in its analysis then male domination over women must be treated as separate problem to the need to set limits on economic reason. Anne Phillips (1983) has also suggested that feminists have interests in the re-distribution of paid employment and the extension of free-time. Instead of collectivising housework or arguing that domestic labour should be a paid activity, feminists should be encouraging men to take a more equal role in child rearing and in the home generally. If men and women worked for an equal number of hours, in work of roughly equal status, they would perhaps be more likely to share some of the burden in the home. But, if such a strategy were not to lapse into a false totalisation of the economic base, it would, I suggest, be prudent to couple the restructuring of the economy with complementary attempts to re-value 'women's activities' generally.

While Gorz usefully criticises subject centred arguments for self-management, he makes a similar mistake to Althusser, by reducing subjective processes to the supports of social structures. What is absent in Gorz's writing is the subjective side of labour, or what

Williams and Thompson might have referred to as living labour. Such an appreciation would have led Gorz to recognise, as he does in part in his discussion of core workers, that it is technically impossible and counter-productive for capital to over specify the performance of labour. Gorz unrealistically characterises workers in a Marcusian fashion as having a social consciousness that is completely modelled from the clay of economic forms of rationality. While Williams and Thompson were not able to offer a theoretical path through issues related to agency and structure, neither sought to crudely homogenise the mediating cultural characteristics of complex forms of consciousness. I am arguing that Gorz's writing is not dialectical enough. The distinction between heteronomy and autonomy should not be theorised as a binary opposition between, what I shall call a democratised everyday life, and the 'cold, codified, legalistic and mechanical' relations of the public sphere (Gorz,1985,p.72). This opposition not only represents an inadequate account of agency and structure, but also prevents Gorz from addressing fundamental issues related to how the economic system and the state might be further democratised. The distinction between heteronomous and autonomous practices is a matter of degree. Although, I would accept, if a future society is to enlarge the scope of autonomous activity there would seem some sense in making a distinction between working on a car assembly line and making a decision to enter into therapy to deepen self-understanding. While Gorz is correct to associate civil society with the practice of autonomous activities, in a future society based on the social market, there will be important limitations placed on the operation of this principle.

Socialism: democracy and community

Francis Fukayama (1989) has proposed we are now at the end of history. By this he means that the Marxist alternative has failed, and that the end of the century is marked by the triumph of economic and political liberalism. The problem with Fukayama's political vision is not so much the prematurely predicted death of Marxism, but his ideological blindness to the failings of liberal capitalism. Fukayama makes the mistake that the global history of the twentieth century can be conceptualised through the opposition of capitalism and socialism. That the history of post-war Europe could not be adequately expressed in these terms was a repeated theme of my earlier analysis of the Cold War. Instead, I would agree with Mary Kaldor (1990) and E.P. Thompson, that it is the task of the Left, in the so called 'new world order', to reimagine a common European home. A secure de-militarised Europe, that would include the old Warsaw pact countries, could only be based upon a common framework that ensured the democratic accountability of trans-national, national and local institutional structures. The shared European context would not only seek to integrate differing nationalities into a broader framework of collective agreements, but would also act as a democratic counter-force in a world that has only one remaining superpower. Displacing the opposition between free market capitalism and state directed socialism, the 'new European order' would be based on a different set of principles. I agree with Kaldor when she writes:

> on the one hand, the establishment of certain common values or standards and a framework for implementing those values and, at the same time, maximum autonomy and diversity in order to ensure the democratic accountability and the preservation of Europe's rich and very varied cultural heritage (Kaldor,1990,p.45).

This would not amount to the end of history, but the end of the cynical and democratically asphyxiating politics of the Cold War. Yet while Kaldor is illuminating more flesh needs to be put on the intellectual bones of her proposals. I want to suggest that the guiding principles for the achievement of these ends are neither self-managed socialism nor old style social democracy, and neither scientific socialism nor liberal capitalism. Instead I would propose that a more integrated and autonomous Europe is dependent upon the values of democratic socialism. My particular version of this tradition would seemingly have much in common with others, but the points of emphasis remain my own. These propositions are not intended to contribute to a so called 'third way', in that they remain dependent on the relative historical success of social democracy. The following propositions are intended to both offer a vision of a better world, without lapsing into a form of bad utopianism that neglects to analyse the present conditions of late capitalism.

The particular version of democratic socialism that is being imposed here stresses the importance of democracy over socialism. By this I mean that the need for a common framework of European democratic norms and values has priority over arguments for socialised production. To this end I want to reverse the relationship between socialism and democracy that is evident in Williams and Thompson.

A reformed Left would have to mobilise support for a more genuinely pluralistic democracy in a specifically European and international context. This should, by this point, be obvious from my earlier discussion of radical nationalism. Secondly, and most importantly, such a movement would be concerned to extend publicly debated decision making processes. These would have to be widened to cover trans-national organisations, and ensure the decentralisation of power to more local democratic units. Thirdly and finally, such proposals could only be effective if new forms of economic, political and cultural community could be developed. I have already stressed some of the difficulties that such attempts might encounter in my earlier discussion of the possibilities for the realisation of a reformed public sphere. It is however in the debate concerning new forms of social community that the writing of Williams and Thompson have a particular contribution to make. Here, in the final two sections, I want to briefly outline the importance of democracy and community to the future of political theory. Many of the arguments restated below have been the subject of lengthier and more extended discussion elsewhere in the thesis. This being the case I want to briefly re-state four basic themes of the argument in connection with democracy.

1. Much recent writing has sought to criticise both liberal and Marxist theories of the state through a more democratic conception of civil society. As we saw, while Williams and Thompson fail to provide an adequate theoretical appraisal of the social processes connected with the state, they were both dissatisfied with the available Marxist and liberal accounts. I would in turn suggest that in the past socialists, through the socialisation of the means of production, have sought to replace civil society with the state. Liberals, on the other hand, have been more concerned to safeguard the pluralistic relations of civil society. As many commentators have pointed out, liberals have often failed to address the inequalities of power, such as those maintained by white males and capital, that systematically distort democratic processes. An alternative approach would suggest that civil society should become, as far as possible, the site of relatively autonomous activities that are neither dependent on large scale capital, nor centrally controlled by the state. Civil society, on this reading, would become the focus of an elaborate network of rights protecting spheres of autonomy while addressing inequalities of power and influence. Citizens would be both enabled and constrained by social and political rights and obligations. Citizenship would become a permanent thorn in the side of agencies that sought to undermine democratic procedures, and enable wider forms of participation. This

view of civil society would radically depart from the traditional conception of this domain held by liberals and Marxists.

One such proposal that sought to democratise civil society was the Swedish Meidner Plan of 1975 (Keane, 1988). Although the details of the plan are complex, the intention behind its conception was the creation of democratically controlled investment funds that place social controls over capital investment. However it also recognised the importance of private property as a means of placing limits on state power. The Meidner Plan would therefore seem to come under the rubric of market socialism. But, unfortunately like much market socialism, the Meidner Plan under modern conditions seems to both overestimate the power of individual nation-states and underestimate the liquidity of capital. Instead, I would argue, that the underlying democratic intentions of such a plan could only be secured in a wider European and international context.

2.Following the writing of Andre Gorz a European democratic socialism should have the goal of maximising free-time. While Gorz's predictions concerning the future of the labour market are suspect the possibility of modern European societies being based upon full time work would seem remote (McIlroy 1988). A more convivial society would seek, as far as possible, to reduce the number of hours spent at work, re-distribute employment and guarantee a minimum social income. Such an enabling framework would not follow Gorz's ideas in socialising and centralising production. Such proposals, it seems at present, run the risk of repeating many of the failures of state socialism. The democratisation of everyday life would be dependent upon democratic consultation between state structures, capital and labour. While such proposals remain necessarily vague, in this context, a politics of free-time would seek to make the day to day activities of persons the site of self-determination.

3.Democracy, as we have seen, is related to the concept of self-determination. This implies that modern selves and modern societies are not pre-given or predetermined. They share the capacity to realise themselves through a reflexive ethical dimension. Other social systems, such as Stalinism, that sought to repress human-beings shared cultural capacity to be relatively self-determining, could be described, following Thompson, as evil. According to Zygmunt Bauman (1989) those societies that have historically sought to repress and manipulate the moral feelings of others on a mass scale, may also be called evil. In this respect his investigation of the ethical consequences of Nazism bears some resemblance to Thompson's writing on Stalinism. Thompson, we may recall, theoretically connected the Gulag to the belief in the scientific leading role of the party, where the state always already had a monopoly on the truth. Similarly, Bauman argues, that sociology, through its discussion of socialisation, has been slow to articulate a discourse of moral responsibility. Unless, as Thompson also proposes, persons are conceptualised as being capable of moral reasoning, then one could not effectively judge those involved in barbarous crimes. However Thompson does not really investigate the roots of a humanist sensibility and respect for others. On the other hand, Bauman proposes that our feelings for others are 'pre-societal' and come through the experience of 'being with others'. Both Bauman and Thompson, despite their differences, agree that societies should be morally assessed the extent to which they allow the free expression of ethical critiques by their citizens. In this respect, I would accept the words of Vaclav Havel (1978) when he suggests, that the minimal requirement for 'living within the truth' is to live with democracy.

4. The preceding discussions of democracy were not only guided by an attempt to stress the qualities of democracy, but by a sense of the concepts limitations. We have already seen that democratic procedures cannot guarantee a community of persons respect 'otherness' and treat one another with equal respect and consideration. In addition, I would add to my far from exhaustive list of limitations, that democratic rule from below can no longer be achieved within the borders of the nations-state. The problem with the guiding principle of 'self-determination', as David Held points out, is that it is difficult to know whether the relevant institutional agency for democratic decision making is local, regional, national or international. According to Held (1991) the parameters for democratic representation are considerably widened in the modern world. Political, economic and social activity are becoming increasingly global in scope, while the borders of nation-states are being continually permeated by the operation of international agencies. There has also been a corresponding intensification of the connections between states and international contexts. This can be seen through a variety of global issues such as migration patterns, communication networks and ecological questions. The processes cogently described by Held necessitates that democracy be rethought in terms of European and international contexts.

A commitment to democracy cannot on its own prevent the further atomisation of social life. Indeed, if anything, a democracy that is working properly would provide hateful and divisive social movements with the oxygen of publicity. Here I aim to argue that a more secure, peaceful and co-operative society could only be achieved through the value of community. Williams radically

211

overestimated the extent to which cultural institutions could promote modern forms of community. However he wisely reminds us that the notion of community is crucial in mediating some of the negative effects of capitalism. The Left, I would argue, could only mobilise support for its programmes by insisting that the most marginal of human groupings are worthy of respect and play a part in a wider shared community.

The value of the ethic of community is shared by a number of perspectives in social theory. For example, it is the idea of community that provides the link between some branches of psychoanalysis and socialist humanism. In Jessica Benjamin's (1990) *The Bonds of Love*, she stresses a view of the self that is dependent upon processes of mutual recognition. She aims to correct the view of the self, propagated by ego psychology, that the individual is assumed to 'grow out of' the dialectic between self and other. Instead Benjamin's more inter-subjective account stresses the way that:

> the individual grows in and through the relationship with other subjects. Most important, this perspective observes that the other whom the self meets is also a self, a subject in his or her own right. It assumes that we are able and need to recognise that other subject as different and yet alike, as an other who is capable of sharing similar mental experience (Benjamin 1990,p.20).

The idea of community, therefore, is not so much a matter of simply being with others, but is governed by the quality of human relationships. Socialist humanism places a similar emphasis on the need for community; only through social relationships can men and women become relatively self-determining, while remaining connected to others, nature and the past. Both Williams and Thompson strongly felt that our relations with others were being ideologically poisoned by the Cold War and continued class domination. In such a reificatory culture men and women are routinely portrayed as 'others' who are always something less than fellow human-beings. Instrumental forms of domination according to Williams produce:

> the culture of distance, the latent culture of alienation, within which men and women are reduced to models, figures and the quick cry in the throat (Williams, 1989b,p.43).

Yet attempts to produce cultural understanding could have consequences not intended by participants within cross-cultural dialogues. However these unintended consequences could be significantly mediated by relations of mutual respect that helped produce trust between social groups. What should be added is that relations of trust are unlikely to be secured unless there is a corresponding recognition of the way that power operates to distort communicative relations. This would not only demand an equality of respect, but also a certain cultural openness, and the recognition following Bourdieu (1984), that symbolically certain cultural styles are arbitrarily socially privileged over others. As Williams often stressed, if persons are to gain a greater understanding of others this will not come primarily through face to face discussions, or a literary culture, but modern cultural institutions and processes. This aside, I would maintain that stronger communal relations even in global contexts are not solely cultural problems, but are also economically and politically dependent.

The quality of community relations depends upon how persons relate to one another in differing social spheres. One such context, that socialists have traditionally attempted to integrate into a more socialised framework is the economy. Raymond Williams, writing in *Culture and Society* (1961), argues that the creation of modern social communities are dependent upon economic forms of co-operation. He perceptively criticises those like T.S. Eliot who sought to promote forms of life based upon the principle of community, without addressing the atomising effect of the capitalist economy. Liberal communitarians have also argued that a commitment to formal rights will only promote a sense of solidarity amongst its citizens if they are connected to a social market. Socialists, they argue, though are misleading when they propose that political rights are in some way less substantial than social rights. Marx, the communitarians suggest, was wrong to resist the idea of rights. For Marx 'rights' were an expression of the egotism of the bourgeoisie, and were both fragmentary and ideological in practice. For liberals and communitarians political and social rights can forms the basis of new forms of human community. Claude Lefort (1988) offers a typical version of this argument; the creation of a network of rights, that are not owned or controlled by any one subject, can become, contrary to Marx's expectations, a form of social cement binding people together. If the rights of a citizen are violated, then this harms the corresponding network of rights that are simultaneously the property of no-one and everyone. If this is the case, the failure to treat British

Muslims with equal respect, not only violates their specific rights, but the quality of British and European citizenship.

Communitarians that advocate both social and political rights expose the theoretical limitations of economistic Marxism and free-market liberalism. David Marquand (1990) and Jonathan Boswell (1990) reject traditional socialist solutions connected to the socialisation of the means of production, and suggest that relations of trust are promoted through new institutional structures bringing together the state, capital and labour. While I share their commitment to an ethic of community and to a mixed economy; the communitarians still have something to learn from the socialists. Boswell and Marquand erroneously assume that the institutional agencies of state, capital and labour have shared economic interests, and similar positions within the labour market. Instead socialist writers, Williams and Thompson included, would argue that the relations between state, capital and labour, from this perspective, could only be effective if differing sets of interests and inequalities are fully appreciated. For example, labour would be unlikely to accept limitations placed upon wage demands if this was only to lead to increased profits for capital. Capital and labour cannot be assumed to be equal partners. This is because of unequal balence of power evident between capital and labour. Further, as both Williams and Thompson realise, more fully than the communitarians, economic forms of rationality has corrosive effects upon human communities. We cannot be certain, in other words, that talks between capital and labour would produce the necessary consensus to move towards an ecologically secure economy, that minimises inequalities and secures a high quality of life for their respective citizens. The communitarians do not seem to appreciate that economic co-operation can only be realised at the expense of the liquidity of capital. Capital, as socialist humanists have long been aware, serves the interests of profit rather those of the people. A change in the way we relate to one another can only be effective if it is accompanied by 'socialised' institutional structures. One of the future tasks of European democratic socialism would be to undermine the rationality of capital through arguments related to the social and psychological needs of persons. To this end, the writing of Raymond Williams and E.P. Thompson remains an important resource in our journey of hope.

Bibliography

Abercrombie, N. etal (1980), *The Dominant Ideology Thesis,,* London, Allen and Unwin.

Abrams, P. (1982) *Historical Sociology,* Shepton Mallett, Open Books.

Adorno, T. andHorkheimer, M. (1979)*Dialectic of Enlightenment,* London, Verso.

Alexander, S. (1984) 'Women, Class and Sexual Differences in the 1830s and 1840s', *History Workshop* 17.

Althusser, L. (1977) *For Marx,* London, Verso.

Althusser, L. (1984) Ideology and Ideological State Apparatuses, *Essays on Ideology,* Verso, London.

Anderson, B. (1983) *Imagined Communities,* London, Verso.

Anderson, P. (1964) *Origins of the Present Crisis,* New Left Review 23.

Anderson, P. (1980) *Arguments within English Marxism,* Verso, London.

Ascherson, N. (1991) 'In defence of the New Nationalism', *New Statesman,* 20 & 27 December.

Barnett, A. (1976) Raymond Williams and Marxism: A Rejoinder to Terry Eagleton, *New Left Review*, no 99.

Barrett, M. (1980) *Women's Oppression Today*, London, Verso.

Barrett, M.andMcIntosh, M. (1991)*The Anti-Social Family*, London, Verso.

Barthes, R. (1974) *S/Z*, London, Jonathan Cape.

Baudrillard, J. (1988) *Selected Writings*, Cambridge, Polity Press.

Bauman, Z. (1989) *Modernity and the Holocaust*, Cambridge, Polity Press.

Bauman, Z. (1990) 'Make it Personal', *Times Literary Supplement*, July 6-12.

Benjamin, J. (1990) *The Bonds of Love*, London, Virago.

Benjamin, W. (1977)' Authoras Producer', *Understanding Brecht*, London, New Left Books.

Bennett, T. (1986) 'The Politics of the 'popular' and popular culture', ed.Bennett, T., *Popular culture and Social Relations*, Milton Keynes, Open University Press.

Benton, T. (1984)*The Rise and Fall of Structural Marxism*, London, MacMillan.

Blackburn, R. (1991) *Socialism after the Crash*, New Left Review 185.

Bobbio, N. (1987a) 'Democracy and Invisible Power', *The Future of Democracy*, Cambridge, Polity Press.

Bobbio, N. (1987b) *Which Socialism ?*, Cambridge, Polity Press.

Bologh, R. (1990) *Love or Greatness: Max Weber and masculine thinking - A feminist inquiry*, London, Unwin/Hyman.

Boswell, J. (1990) *Community and the Economy*, London, Routledge.

Bottomore, T. (1990) *The Socialist Economy Theory and Practice,* Harvester and Wheatsheaf, London.

Bourdieu, P. (1984) *Distinction,* London, Routledge and Kegan.

Bourdieu, P. (1987) *What Makes a Social Class?* Berkeley Journal of Sociology 22.

Bourdieu, P. (1988) *Homo Academicus,* Cambridge, Polity Press.

Bourdieu, P. (1990)*In Other Words; Essays towards a reflexive sociology,* Cambridge, Polity Press.

Bourdieu, P. and Passeron, J.-C. (1977) *Reproduction in Education, Society and Culture,* London, Sage.

Bravermann, H. (1974) *Labour and Monopoly Capital,* Monthly View Press, New York.

Callinicos, A. (1983) *Marxism and Philosophy,* Oxford, Clarendon.

Callinicos, A. (1987) *Making History,* Cambridge Polity Press.

Castoriadis, C. (1987)*The Imaginary Institution of Society,* Cambridge, Polity Press.

Chodorow, N. (1978) *The Reproduction of Mothering,* California Press.

Chodorow, N. (1989)*Feminism and Psychoanalytic Theory,* Cambridge, Polity Press.

de Lauretis, T. (1987) *Technologies of Gender,* MacMillan, London.

Dews, P. (1987) *Logics of Disintegration,* London, Verso.

Dunn, J. (1984) *The Politics of Socialism,* Cambridge, Cambridge University Press.

Eagleton, T. (1976) 'Criticism and Politics; The Work of Raymond Williams', *New Left Review* 95

Eagleton, T. (1979) 'E.P.Thompson's Poverty of Theory: A Symposium', *Literature and History,* Vol15:2

Eagleton, T. (1984) *The Function of Criticism*, London, Verso.

Eagleton, T. (1989) 'Base and superstructure in Raymond Williams', ed Eagleton, T.*Raymond Williams: Critical Perspectives*, London, Verso.

Eagleton, T. (1990) *The Ideology of the Aesthetic*, Oxford, Basil Blackwell.

Eagleton, T. (1991) *Ideology; an introduction*, London, Verso.

Elliott, A. (1992) *Social theory and Psychoanalysis, Self and Society from Freud to Kristeva*, Oxford, Basil Blackwell.

Elliott, G. (1987) *Althusser: The Detour of Theory*, London, Verso.

Elson, D. (1988) 'Market Socialism of Socialisation of the Market', *New Left Review* 185

Featherstone, M. (ed.) (1990) *Global Culture: Nationalism, Globalisation and Modernity*, London, Sage.

Feher, F.andHeller, A. (1986)*Doomsday or Deterence?* London, M.E.Sharpe Inc.

Feher, F.and Heller, A. (1988) *The Postmodern Political Condition*, Cambridge, Polity Press.

Feher, F.and Heller, A. (1989) 'Freedom as a Value Idea and the Interpretation of Human Rights', *Eastern Left, Western Left*, Cambridge, Polity Press.

Forgacs, D. (July/Aug 1989) 'Gramsci and the British Left', *New Left Review*, 176.

Foster, J. (1985) 'The Declassing of Language', *New Left Review*150.

Foucault, M. (1976)'Neitzsche, Freud, Marx'.*The Foucault Reader*, ed.Paul Rabinow, Harmondsworth, Penguin.

Foucault, M. (1977) *Discipline and Punish*, Harmondsworth, Penguin.

Foucault, M. (1986)Disciplinary Power and Subjection, ed.Lukes, S.*Power*, Oxford, Basil Blackwell.

Fraser, N. (1987) 'What's Critical abour Critical Theory?' ed.Seyla Benhabib, *Feminism as Critique*, Cambridge, Polity Press.

Frisby, D. (1981) *Sociological Impressionism*, London, Heinemann.

Fukayama, F. (1989)'The End of History', *National Interest*, Summer.

Fuller, P. (1988) *Art and Psychoanalysis*, London, Hogarth.

Gadamer, H.G. (1975) *Truth and Method*, , Sheed and Ward, London.

Geras, N. (1987)'Critique of Laclau and Mouffe', *New Left Review*, 163.

Geuss, R. (1981) *The Idea of a Critical Theory*, Cambridge, Cambridge University Press.

Giddens, A. (1973) *The Class Structure of Advanced Societies*, New York, Harper and Row.

Giddens, A. (1981) *A Contemporary Critique of Historical Materialism*, Polity Press, Cambridge.

Giddens, A. (1985)*The Nation State and Violence*, Polity Press, Cambridge.

Giddens, A. (1987a) Out of the Orrey: E.P.Thompson on consciousness and history, *Social theory and Modern Society*, Polity Press.

Giddens, A. (1987b)'Nation States and Violence', *Social Theory and Modern Society*, Cambridge, Polity Press.

Gilroy, P. (1987)*There Ain't No Black In The Union Jack*, London, Hutchinson.

Giroux H.A.and Simon R (1988) ' Critical pedagogy and the politics of popular culture ' , *Cultural Studies* no3.

Gorz, A. (1982) *Farewell to the Working-Class; An essay in Post-Industrial Socialism*, London, Pluto Press.

Gorz, A. (1985)*Paths to Paradise; On the liberation from work*, London, Pluto Press.

219

Gorz, A. (1989) *Critique of Economic Reason*, London, Verso.

Gramsci, A. (1982) *Selections from the Prison Notebooks*, Lawrence and Wishart, London.

Habermas, J. (1976) *Legitimation Crisis*, Heinemann, London.

Hall, C. (1990) 'The Tale of Samuel and Jamima: Gender and Working-class Culture in the Nineteenth Century England', ed.Kaye, H.J.and McClelland, K., *E.P.Thompson Critical Perspectives*, Cambridge, Polity Press.

Hall, S. (1981) 'In Defence of Theory", ed.Samuel, R., *Peoples Hisory and Socialist Theory*, London, Routledge and Kegan.

Hall, S. (1988) *The Hard Road to Renewal*, London, Verso.

Hall, S. (1989) 'Politics and Letters' ed T.Eagleton, *Raymond Williams: Critical Perspectives*, Cambridge, Polity Press.

Hall, S., Williams, R.andThompson, E.P, (1968)eds, *MayDay Manifesto*, Penguin, London.

Halliday, F. (1982) 'The Sources of the New Cold War', *Exterminism and the Cold War*, ed.New Left Review, Verso.

Halliday, F. (1983) *The Making of the Second Cold War*, London, Verso.

Halliday, F. (1990) 'A Reply to Edward Thompson', *New Left Review* 182.

Havel, V. (1978) 'The Power of the Powerless', ed.Vladislav, J.*Vaclav Havel or Living in Truth*, London, Faber.

Hebdige, D. (1979) *Subculture; the meaning of style*, London, Metheun.

Held, D. (1987) *Models of Democracy*, Cambridge, Polity Press.

Held, D. (1989) *Political Theory and the Modern State, Essays on State, Power and Democracy*, Cambridge, Polity Press.

Held, D. (1991) 'Democracy, the nation-state and the global system', *Economy and Society*, Vol.20, no.2.

Held, D.and Thompson, J. (1989) *Social theory of modern societies: Anthony Giddens and his critics,* Cambridge, Cambridge University Press.

Heller, A. (1979) *A Theory of Feelings,* Assen, Van Gorcum.

Heller, A. (1990a) 'The Death of the Subject', *Can Modernity Survive ?,* Cambridge, Polity Press.

Heller, A. (1990b) 'Are we living in a world of emotional impoverishment?', *Can Modernity Survive?,* Cambridge, Polity Press.

Higgins, J. (1982-3) 'Raymond Williams and the Problem of Ideology', *Boundary* 211.

Hindess, B. and Hirst, P. (1977) *Mode of Production and Social Formation: An Auto-Critique of 'Pre-Capitalist Modes of Production',* London, MacMillan.

Hirst, P. (1985) 'The Necessity of Theory', *Marxism and Historical Writing,* Routledge and Kegan, London.

Hobsbawn, E. (1964)*Labouring men;studies in the history of labour,* Weidenfield and Nicholson, London.

Hobsbawn, E. (1990)*Nations and Nationalism since 1780,* Cambridge, Cambridge University Press.

Jardine, L. and Swindells, J. (1989)'Homage to Orwell', ed.Eagleton, T. *Raymond Williams: Critical Perspectives,* Cambridge, Polity Press.

Jardine, L. and Swindells, J. (1990) *What's Left?* London, Routledge.

Jessop, B. (1982)*The Capitalist State, Marxist Theories and Methods,* Oxford, Robertson.

Jessop, B. (1985) *Nicos Poulantzas Marxist Theory and Political Strategy,* London, MacMillan.

Johnson, L. (1979) *The Cultural Critics: from Mathew Arnold to Raymond Williams,* London, Routledge and Kegan.

Johnson, R. (1979) 'Three problematics: elements of a theory of workingclassculture', ed.Clarke, J.etal, *WorkingclassCulture*, London, Hutchinson.

Kaldor, M. (1990) *The Imaginary War;Understanding the East West Conflict)*Oxford, Basil Blackwell.

Kaye, H.J. (1984) *The British Marxist Hisorians*, Polity Press, Cambridge.

Keane, J. (1987)" More theses in the philosophy of history ", J.Tully and Q.Skinner, Meaning and Context, op.cit.

Keane, J. (1988) *Democracy and Civil Society*, London, Verso.

Keane, J. (1991) *The Media and Domocracy*, Cambridge, Polity Press.

Kiernon, V.G. (1959) *Culture and Society*, New Reasoner, 9.

Kumar, K. (1988) *The Rise of Modern Society*, Oxford, Basil Blackwell.

Laclau, E. (1977)*Politics and Ideology in Marxist Theory*, London, Verso.

Laclau, E. (1990) *New Reflections on the Revolution of Our Time*, London, Verso.

Laclau, E.and Mouffe, C. (1985)*Hegemony and Socialist Strategy*, London, Verso.

Larrain, J. (1979) *The Concept of Ideology*, London, Hutchinson.

Le Grand, J. et al (1989) *Market Socialism*, Oxford, Oxford University Press.

Lefort, C. (1988) 'Human Rights and the Welfare State', *Democracy and Political Theory*, Cambridge, Polity Press.

Lenin (1964) *What is to be Done?* Moscow, Progress Publishers.

Levitas, R. (1980) 'Competition and Compliance: The Utopias of the New Right', *The Ideology of the New Right*, Cambridge, Polity Press.

Lukacs, G. (1971) *History and Class Consciousness*, Merlin Press, London.

Lukes, S. (1974) *Power; a radical view*, London, MacMillan.

Lukes, S. (1977)'Socialism and Equality', *Essays in Social Theory*, London, MacMillan.

Lukes, S. (1985) *Marxism and Morality*, Oxford University Press.

Mann, M. (1988) *States, War and Capitalism*, Oxford, Basil Blackwell.

Mann, M. (1970) 'The social cohesion of liberal democracy', *American Sociological Review*, 35 p423-439.

Marcuse, H. (1972) 'The Affirmative Character of Culture', *Negations*, Harmondsworth, Penguin.

Marcuse, H. (1977) *The Aesthetic Dimension : Towards a Critique of Marxist Aesthetics*, London, MacMillan

Marquand, D. (1990)'Citizens', *LondonReviewofBooks* Vol.12, no.24, December.

Marx, K. (1961) *Economic and Philosophical Manuscipts of 1844*, Moscow.

Marx, K. (1963) *The German Ideology*, London.

Marx, K. (1973) *Grundrisse*, London.

McIlroy, J. (1988) *Trade Unions in Britain Today*, Manchester, Manchester University Press.

McLennan, G. (1989) *Marxism, Pluralism and Beyond*, Cambridge, Polity Press.

McRobbie, A. (1991) *Feminism and Youth Culture: From Jackie to Just Seventeen*, MacMillan, Basingstoke.

Melucci, A. (1988) 'Social Movements and the Democratisation of Everyday Life' , Keane, J.*Civil Society and the State*, London, Verso.

Melucci, A. (1989) *Nomads of the Present*, Hutchinson Radius, London.

Merrill, M. (1978-9) 'Raymond Williams and the Theory of English Marxism', *Radical History Review*, 19.

Migone, G.G. (1989) 'The decline of the biopopular system, or a second look at the history of the Cold War', ed.Kaldor, M.*The New Detente*, London, Verso.

Morris, W. (1970) *News from Nowhere or an epoch of rest*, London, Routledge and Kegan.

Mouzelis, N. (1990) *Post-Marxist Alternatives*, London, MacMillan.

Mulhern, F. (1989)'Towards 2000, or News from You Know Where', ed.Eagleton, T.*RaymondWilliams:CriticalPerspectives*, Cambridge, Polity Press.

Nairn, T. (1964) 'The English Working Class', New Left Review 24.

Nairn, T. (1988) *The Enchanted Glass; Britain and its Monarchy*, London, Radius.

Nove, A. (1983) *Economics of Feasible Socialism*, London.

O'Connor, A. (1989) *Raymond Williams*, Oxford, Basil Blackwell.

Offe, C. (1984) *Contradictions of the Welfare State*, Hutchinson, London.

Offe, C. (1985) *Disorganised Capitalism*, Cambridge, Polity Press.

Parekh, B. (1989) *Ghandi's Political Philosophy* , MacMillan, London

Parekh, B. (1991)'BritishCitizenshipandCultural Difference', ed. Andrews, G.*Citizenship*, London, Lawrence and Wishart.

Pateman, C. (1982)'Critique of the Public/Private Dichotomy', ed.Phillips, A.*Feminism and Equality*, Oxford, Basil Blackwell.

Phal, R.E. (1984) *Divisions of Labour*, Oxford, Basil Blackwell.

Phillips, A. (1983) *Hidden Hands*, Pluto Press, London.

Phillips, A. (1991) *Engendering Democracy*, Cambridge, Polity Press.

Polan, A.J. (1984) *Lenin and the End of Politics*, London, Methuen.

Poulantzas, N. (1983) *Political Power and Social Classes*, London, Verso.

Ricoeur, P. (1973) *Hermeneutics and the Human Sciences*, Cambridge, Cambridge University Press.

Ricoeur, P. (1986) *Lectures on Ideology and Utopia*, New York, Columbia University Press.

Rose, G. (1978) The Melancholy Science, London, MacMillan.

Rose, G. (1978) *The Melancholy Science*, London, MacMillan.

Rustin, M. (1985) *For a Pluralist Socialism,* , London, Verso.

Rustin, M. (1991) *The Good Society and the Inner World*, London, Verso.

Said, E. (1978) *Orientalism*, London, Routledge and Kegan.

Said, E. (1983) *The World, the Text, and the Critic*, Cambridge, Harvard University Press.

Said, E. (1992) " Culture and the Vultures ", *Times Higher Education Supplement*, 24.1.92.

Samuel, R. (1990) 'Exciting to be English', *The Making and Unmaking of British National Identity*, Vol One, London, Routledge.

Searle, J. (1969) *Speech Acts*, Cambridge, Cambridge University Press.

Skinner, Q.and Tully, J. (1988) *Meaning and Context; Quentin Skinner and his critics*, Cambridge, Polity Press.

Smith, D. (1989) 'Relating to Wales', ed.Terry Eagleton, *Raymond Williams: Critical Perspectives,* Polity Press, Cambridge.

Soper, K. (1979)'Marxism, Materialism and Biology', ed.Mepham, J. *Issues in Marxist Philosophy;Materialism*, Brighton, Harvester.

Soper, K. (1981) *On Human Needs*, Brighton, Harvester.

Soper, K. (1990a) *Troubled Pleasures*, London, Verso.

Soper, K. (1990b)'SocialistHumanism', ed.Kaye, H.J.and McCelland, K. *E.P.Thompson: Critical Perspectives*, Cambridge, Polity Press.

Sope, K. (1991) 'Postmodernism, Subjectivity, Value', *New Left Review* 186.

Stedman Jones, G. (1983) *Languages of Class.Studies in English working class history 1832-1982*, Cambridge University Press.

Taylor, C. (1985a) 'What is Human Agency?', *Philosophy and the Human Sciences, Philosophical Papers 1*, Cambridge Press.

Taylor, C. (1985b) 'Foucault on freedom and truth', *Philosophy and the Human Sciences, Philosophical Papers 2*, Cambridge, Cambridge University Press.

Taylor, C. (1985c) 'Understanding and Ethnocentricity', *Philosophy and the Human Sciences, Philosophical Papers 2*, Cambridge University Press.

Taylor, C. (1985d) 'Atomism', *Philosophy and the Human Sciences, Philosophical Papers 2*, Cambridge, Cambridge University Press.

Taylor, C. (1989)'Marxism and Socialist Humanism', ed Oxford University Socialist Discussion Group, *Out of Apathy*, London, Verso.

Thompson, E.P. (1955) *William Morris: Romantic to Revolutionary*, London, Lawrence and Wishart.

Thompson, E.P. (1957) ' Socialist Humanism ', *The New Reasoner*, 1.

Thompson, E.P. (1960) 'Revolution Again, Or shut your ears and run', *New Left Review* 6.

Thompson, E.P. (1961) *The Long Revolution*, New Left Review no.9 and no.10 (May/June and July/August)

Thompson, E.P. (1976) 'Romanticism, Moralism and Utopianism: the case of William Morris', *New Left Review* 99.

Thompson, E.P. (1977) *Whigs and Hunters: The Origins of the Black Act*, Harmondsworth, Penguin.

Thompson, E.P. (1978a) 'The Poverty of Theory: or an Orrey of Errors' *The Poverty of Theory and Other Essays*, London, Merlin Press.

Thompson, E.P. (1978b) 'An Open Letter to Leszek Kolakowski', *The Poverty of Theory and Other Essays*, London, Merlin Press.

Thompson, E.P. (1978c) 'The Pecularities of the English', *The Poverty of Theory and Other Essays*, London, Merlin

Thompson, E.P. (1978d) 'Outside the Whale', *The Poverty of Theory and Other Essays*, London, Merlin

Thompson, E.P. (1980a) *The Making of the English Working Class*, Penguin, Harmondsworth.

Thompson, E.P. (1980b) *The State and Civil Liberties*, Writing by Candlelight, Merlin, London.

Thompson, E.P. (1982a) 'Time, Work, Discipline, and Industrial Capitalism', ed.Giddens, A.and Held, D., *Classes, Power, and Conflict*, London, MacMillan.

Thompson, E.P. (1982b) 'Deterrence and Addiction', *Zero Option*, London, Merlin Press.

Thompson, E.P. (1982c) 'Notes on Exterminism, the last stages of civilisation', *Zero Option*, London, Merlin Press

Thompson, E.P. (1982d) 'War in Thatchers Face', *Zero Option*, London, Merlin Press.

Thompson, E.P. (1985)*The Heavy Dancers*, London, Merlin.

Thompson, E.P. (1988) *The Sykaos Papers*, London, Bloomsbury.

Thompson, E.P. (1990a)*The Ends of the Cold War*, New Left Review 182,

Thompson, E.P. (1990b) Untitled, *The Nation*, 29 January.

Thompson, J.B. (1984) *Studies in the Theory of Ideology*, Cambridge, Polity Press.

Thompson, J.B. (1990) *Ideology and Modern Culture*, Cambridge, Polity Press.

Timpanaro, S. (1976) *On Materialism*, London, Verso.

Trotsky, L. (1973) *The Revolution Betrayed*, London.

WallachScott, J. (1988)'TheProblemofInvisibility', ed.Klienberg, S.J., *Retrieving Womens History*, Berg Ltd.

Warnke, G. (1987)*Gadamer*, Polity Press, Cambridge.

Williams, R. (1952) Drama from Ibsen to Eliot, London, Chatto and Windus.

Williams, R. (1958) 'Culture is Ordinary', reprinted in Williams, R. (1988) *Resources of Hope*, Verso, London.

Williams, R. (1960) *Border Country*, London, Chatto and Windus.

Williams, R. (1961) *Culture and Society*, Harmondsworth, Penguin.

Williams, R. (1962) *Communications*, Penguin, Harmondsworth.

Williams, R. (1964) *Second Generation*, London, Chatto and Windus.

Williams, R. (1965) *The Long Revolution*, Harmondsworth, Pelican.

Williams, R. (1966) *Modern Tragedy*, London, Chatto and Windus, p.60.

Williams, R. (1968) *Drama from Ibsen to Brecht*, London, Chatto and Windus.

Williams, R. (1973)*The Country and the City*, Chatto and Windus, London.

Williams, R. (1974)*Television:TechnologyandCultural Form*, Fontana/ Collins, London.

Williams, R. (1985) 'You're a Marxist, Are'nt You?', reprinted
Williams, R. (1989) *Resources of Hope*, London, Verso.

Williams, R. (1976) *Keywords: A Vocabulary of Culture and Society*,
Glasgow, Fontana.

Williams, R. (1977)*Marxism and Literature*, Oxford University Press,
London.

Williams, R. (1979a)*Politics and Letters: Interviews with New Left Review*,
London, New Left Books.

Williams, R. (1979b)*The Fight for Manod*, London, Chatto and Windus.

Williams, R. (1980a) " Beyond Actually Existing Socialism ", *Problems
in Materialism and Culture*, London, Verso, 1980.

Williams, R. (1980b) 'Problems of Materialism' *Problems in Materialism
and Culture*, London, Verso.

Williams, R. (1980c) 'Base and Superstructure in Marxist Cultural
Theory', *Problems in Materialism and Culture*, London, Verso.

Williams, R. (1980d) 'The Politics of Nuclear Disarmament', *New Left
Review* 124.

Williams, R. (1980e) 'The Bloomsbury fraction', *Problems in
Materialism and Culture.*, London, Verso.

Williams, R. (1981) *Culture*, Fontana, London.

Williams, R. (1983) *Towards 2000*, London, Chatto and Windus.

Williams, R. (1984a), 'The Ragged Arsed Philanthropists', *Writing and
Society*, London, Verso.

Williams, R. (1984b) 'The Reader in Hard Times', *Writing in Society*,
London, Verso.

Williams, R. (1984c) *Orwell*, Fontana, London.

Williams, R. (1985a) *The English Novel from Dickens to Lawrence*,
London, Hogarth Press.

Williams, R. (1985b) *Loyalties*, London, Chatto and Windus.

Williams, R. (1988a) 'Towards Many Socialisms', *Resources of Hope*, London, Verso.

Williams, R. (1988b)'Art: Freedom as Duty', *Resources of Hope*, London, Verso.

Williams, R. (1989a)'A Defence of Realism', *What I Came to Say*, London, Hutchinson.

Williams, R. (1989b) 'Distance'.*What I Came to Say*, Hutchinson, London.

Williams, R. (1989c) *The Politics of Modernism*, London, Verso.

Williams, R. (1989d) *The People of the B;lack Mountains: 1 The Beginning*, London, Pelican.

Williams, R.and Orrom, M. (1954) *Preface to Film*, London, Film Drama.

Williams, R.and Garnham, N. (1986) 'Pierre Bourdieu and the sociology of culture: an introduction to an economy of symbolic goods', ed.Collins, R.etal, *Media, Culture and Society; a critical reader*, London, Sage.

Willis, P. (1980) *Learning to Labour*, Westmead, Saxon House.

Willis, P. (1990) *Common Culture*, Buckingham, Open University Press.

Wolff, J. (1983) *Aesthetics and the Sociology of Art*, London, Allen and Unwin.

Wolff, J. (1990) *The Feminine Sentence*, Cambridge, Polity Press.